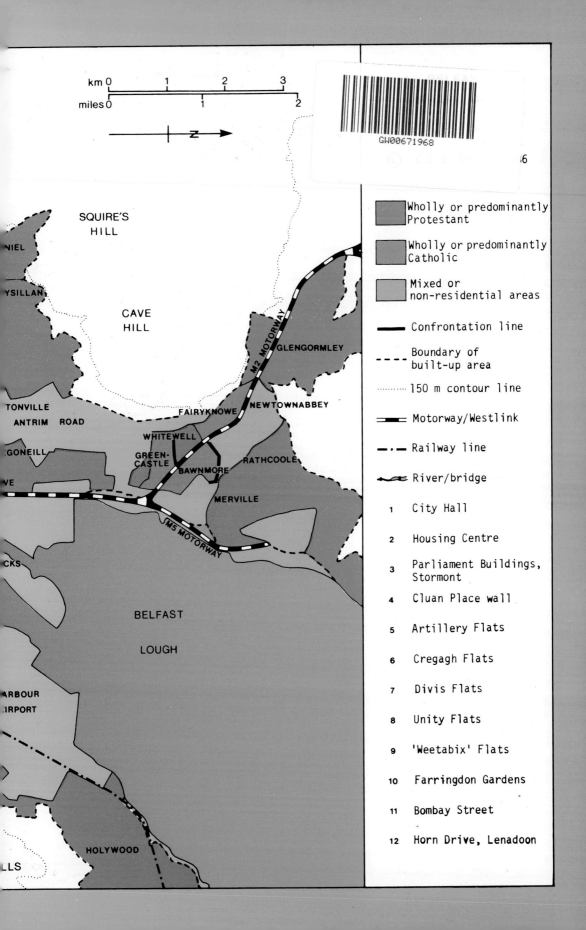

km 0     1     2     3

miles 0       1       2

N

SQUIRE'S HILL

CAVE HILL

GLENGORMLEY

M2 MOTORWAY

NIEL

YSILLAN

TONVILLE

ANTRIM ROAD

FAIRYKNOWE

NEWTOWNABBEY

WHITEWELL

GONEILL

GREEN-CASTLE

BAWNMORE

RATHCOOLE

VE

MERVILLE

M5 MOTORWAY

CKS

BELFAST

LOUGH

ARBOUR

IRPORT

HOLYWOOD

LLS

**Legend**

- Wholly or predominantly Protestant
- Wholly or predominantly Catholic
- Mixed or non-residential areas
- Confrontation line
- Boundary of built-up area
- 150 m contour line
- Motorway/Westlink
- Railway line
- River/bridge

1   City Hall

2   Housing Centre

3   Parliament Buildings, Stormont

4   Cluan Place wall

5   Artillery Flats

6   Cregagh Flats

7   Divis Flats

8   Unity Flats

9   'Weetabix' Flats

10   Farringdon Gardens

11   Bombay Street

12   Horn Drive, Lenadoon

# HOUSING
# A DIVIDED
# COMMUNITY

**Plate 1**

*David,*

*They will never "photo-copy" your like again.'*

*Vuti*
*10/10/89*

# HOUSING
# A DIVIDED
# COMMUNITY

## C.E.B. BRETT

Institute of Public Administration, Dublin
in association with the
Institute of Irish Studies, Queen's University of Belfast

First published 1986
by the Institute of Public Administration
57-61 Lansdowne Road, Dublin, Ireland

in association with
The Institute of Irish Studies
Queen's University of Belfast

Designed by Della Varilly

Cover photograph: Northern Ireland Housing Executive.

ISBN 0 906980 49 6

Typeset by Wellset Limited, Dublin
Printed by W. & G. Baird Limited, Antrim

# Contents

List of Illustrations                                        vi

Map                                                          ix

Introduction                                                 1

The Origins of the Housing Executive                         7

The Historical Background, 1885-1971                         16

The Housing Executive                                        38

House or Home: Need or Desire?                               55

Sectarianism, Violence and Housing                           62

Allocations, Sitings and Discrimination                      81

The Physical Fabric of Housing                               89

Tenants: their Rights and Wrongs                             108

The Executive and the Private Sector                         121

Clients, Customers, Critics and Colleagues                   132

Postscript                                                   146

Principal Sources and Select Bibliography                    152

Appendix: Strategy for New Building                          154

Index                                                        163

# List of Illustrations

**Plate 1:** The author with toy houses made by him for his children twenty years earlier, 1979. *(Belfast Telegraph)*.

**Plate 2:** Peace Wall, Cluan Place, Belfast

**Plate 3:** Hamill Street, Belfast 1912 *(Ulster Museum)*

**Plate 4:** Crozier's Row, Belfast 1912 *(Ulster Museum)*

**Plate 5:** Beatty's Entry, Belfast 1912 *(Ulster Museum)*

**Plate 6:** Plate from 'Labourers' Cottages for Ireland' *(Linenhall Library)*

**Plate 7:** No 590, Antrim Road, Glengormley

**Plate 8:** Plan and elevation from 'Labourers' Cottages for Ireland' *(Linenhall Library)*

**Plate 9:** Porch, No 590, Antrim Road, Glengormley

**Plate 10:** Sir Daniel Dixon, from 'Belfast Labour Chronicle' *(copy in author's collection)*

**Plate 11:** Donegall Road, Belfast, taken from City Hospital tower

**Plate 12:** J. C. Bretland, from 'Nomads Weekly', 1902 *(Linenhall Library)*

**Plate 13:** Nos 56 and 58, Great Patrick Street, Belfast *(Patrick Rossmore)*

**Plate 14:** Gable painting, Little Ship Street, Belfast *(Belfast Public Library)*

**Plate 15:** Gable paintings, South Belfast

**Plate 16:** 12th July decoration, Glenalpin Street, Belfast

**Plate 17:** Republican graffito

**Plate 18:** Republican gable painting, Andersonstown, Belfast *(Kieran MacGowan)*

**Plate 19:** Republican gable painting, Beechmount Avenue, Belfast *(Kieran MacGowan)*

**Plate 20:** Bombay Street, Belfast August 1969 *(Bombay Street Housing Association)*

**Plate 21:** Bombay Street, August 1969 *(Bombay Street Housing Association)*

**Plate 22:** Glenard Estate, Belfast 1938 *(Ulster Museum)*

**Plate 23:** Farringdon Gardens, Belfast 9th August 1971 *(Pacemaker Press)*

**Plate 24:** Farringdon Gardens, 10th August 1971 *(Belfast Telegraph)*

**Plate 25:** Aughton Terrace, Donegall Pass, Belfast after bomb-damage *(Irish Times)*

**Plate 26:** Harry Simpson, Desmond Lorimer, the author

**Plate 27:** Bob Spence, James O'Hara, Don Concannon

**Plate 28:** The first Housing Executive Board in session *(Project)*

*Illustrations are reproduced by courtesy of the Northern Ireland Housing Executive save where otherwise stated.*

**Plate 29:** Bomb at Housing Executive offices, 1972 *(Belfast Telegraph)*
**Plate 30:** Turf Lodge flats, Belfast
**Plate 31:** Derelict housing, McClure Street, Belfast
**Plate 32:** Demolition of Shankill Road flats, Belfast
**Plate 33:** Rehabilitation, Essex Street, Belfast
**Plate 34:** Unimproved back entry
**Plate 35:** Bathroom extensions
**Plate 36:** 'Welcome to the home of your dreams', Craigavon
**Plate 37:** No 81, Lord Street, Belfast
**Plate 38:** Aerial view, Lough Lea, Short Strand, Belfast
**Plate 39:** Aerial view, York Street, Belfast
**Plate 40:** Rossville flats, Derry
**Plate 41:** New housing, Divis, Belfast
**Plate 42:** Barrack Street, Derry
**Plate 43:** Gortnamonagh estate, West Belfast
**Plate 44:** Vernon Street, South Belfast
**Plate 45:** Poleglass estate, Co. Antrim
**Plate 46:** Glenarm, Co. Antrim
**Plate 47:** Killyleagh, Co. Down
**Plate 48:** Tandragee, Co. Armagh
**Plate 49:** Joy Street, Belfast
**Plate 50:** Handing over the keys of the Executive's 50,000th house

*Outline map of Northern Ireland, showing the principal places mentioned in the text; also the boundaries of the six counties before the local government reorganisation of 1972.*

## Acknowledgements

For permission to make use of quotations I am indebted to the following: the lines from *Four Quartets* by T. S. Eliot are reprinted by permission of Faber & Faber Limited, as are the quotations from A.T.Q. Stewart's *The Narrow Ground*, 1977, and Richard Rose's *Governing Without Consensus*, 1971; that from an article by Thomas Pakenham in the Sunday Times of 18th January, 1981, by his leave and by permission of Times Newspapers Ltd; from Kenneth Clark's *Civilisation*, 1969, by permission of the British Broadcasting Corporation and John Murray (Publishers) Limited; for quotations from J. M. Mogey's *Rural Life in Northern Ireland*, 1947, and R. J. Lawrence's *The Government of Northern Ireland*, I am grateful for the permission of the Oxford University Press; to Professor Birrell for permission to quote from the University Working Paper on *Housing in Northern Ireland* published in 1971 by the Centre for Environmental Studies, London; to Mr. James Callaghan, and Collins Publishers, for leave to quote from his *A House Divided*, 1973; for quotations from Jonathan Bardon's *Belfast: An Illustrated History*, 1982, and from Richard Deutsch and Vivien Magowan's *Northern Ireland 1968-1973; a Chronology of Events*, both published by Blackstaff Press, Belfast; for the quotation from Hywel Griffiths' article in *Violence and the Social Services in Northern Ireland*, 1978, the permission of Gower Publishing; finally, the quotations from David Donnison and Clare Ungerson, *Housing Policy*, 1982, are reprinted by permission of Penguin Books Ltd.

                        In succession
    Houses rise and fall, crumble, are extended,
    Are removed, destroyed, restored, or in their place
    Is an open field, or a factory, or a by-pass.
    Old stone to new building, old timber to new fires,
    Old fires to new ashes, and ashes to the earth
    Which is already flesh, fur and faeces,
    Bone of man and beast, cornstalk and leaf.
    Houses live and die: there is a time for building.

                    T. S. Eliot, *Four Quartets:* East Coker


Next indeed to the homes of Heaven, there are not perhaps many things more
desirable than a well-ordered dwelling, beautiful within and seemly without,
with garden if it may be, a dwelling exempt alike from stagnant air and
grovelling impurity, in fine a dwelling occupied by self-respecting intelligent
people ... Let the architect, then, for it devolves on him in a large measure to do
so, cover the surface in town and country with erections, at once pleasant to look
upon, and delightful to occupy.

        Henry MacCormac, M.D., address to the Belfast Architectural
        Association, 19th January 1874, on 'The Arrangement of Houses,
        considered in reference to Sanitary and Artistic Requirements'


The ancient Irish quarrel is ... a conflict of tribal minorities — who are also,
confusingly, majorities. Perhaps you could represent this historical puzzle as a
set of ill-fitting Chinese boxes. The outside box is the British Isles, where, as we
all know, English Protestants have dominated since the Reformation. Trapped
inside is Ireland, a box full of Catholics, the majority of the island since the time
of St Patrick. Trapped inside that is Ulster, a box of northern Protestants, the
majority in the north east since they were settled there in the 17th century. And
at the heart of the puzzle are the northern Catholics, outnumbered two to one in
Northern Ireland, yet part of the island's overall Catholic majority.
    Remove or rearrange one of the boxes and you just might resolve the puzzle.
But that is forbidden by the rules set by historical geography. The boxes must fit
as they are. In other words, we must somehow learn to live with our neighbours.

            Thomas Pakenham, *Sunday Times,* 18 January 1981


What is civilisation? I don't know. I can't define it in abstract terms — yet. But I
think I can recognise it when I see it ... If I had to say which was telling the
truth about society, a speech by a Minister of Housing or the actual buildings
put up in his time, I should believe the buildings.

        Kenneth Clark, *Civilisation: a personal view,* London 1969.

                            xi

# Introduction

The purpose of this book is to discuss the extraordinary problems of providing a vital public service in a community so deeply divided into two factions that the recourse to violence by both sides has been, in recent years, a recurrent fact of life. They include the problems of framing an allocation system fair not only as between members of the majority and minority communities, but also as between the competing categories of claimant; of the siting of new developments; of the equitable administration of a housing stock partly modern and in good order, partly modern but deplorable, partly worn-out and substandard; of maintaining firm control over housing management in the face of concerted efforts by armed paramilitary groups to usurp it; of assessing and (despite a large-scale rent strike) collecting rents, and administering housing benefits, as fairly as possible; of achieving a social and geographical balance, yet not unrelated to comparative needs, in the distribution of funds for renewal, repair, and renovation; of responding to genuine needs, while resisting the pressures of the more vociferous but less deserving; of outlawing favouritism, nepotism, corruption, the old pals' act, and bigotry from the service: all this in an atmosphere of suspicion where every decision may be greeted with cries of 'blatant discrimination!' from one faction or the other: or even both.

It is not, and cannot be, the dispassionate, objective, analytical book of a detached observer, academic or otherwise: since I was far too deeply involved as an active participant in many of the decisions and events recounted. Rather, it is a consciously subjective and at times frankly autobiographical book: though I have tried to be as fair and impartial in my judgements as I possibly could.

My qualification for writing it rests on my involvement in the work of the Northern Ireland Housing Executive: first as a board member, from its inception in 1971, then, for over five years until I relinquished office at the end of March, 1984, its chairman. At the outset, we had no staff, no housing stock, no experience. At the end of my time, we had around 5,250 employees; a housing stock of over 185,000 even after sales of around 20,000; we had completed nearly 60,000 new dwellings; and we had an annual capital and revenue budget of around £450 million.

There has never, to the best of my knowledge, been any comparable regional all-purpose comprehensive housing authority, either in the British Isles or elsewhere. Although it was a once-only expedient conceived to meet the extraordinary circumstances of the time and place, the general concept had been in the air for some time amongst English housing administrators, frustrated by the shortcomings and limitations of local government. So the novel experiment was watched with much interest, and some jealousy, by many housing managers — and still is. But it now seems unlikely to be emulated elsewhere, so long as both publicly-provided housing for rental, and large organisations, remain out of political favour.

It is unique in another, unenviable, respect. From its very inception, the Executive has had to carry out its functions amidst bombings, shootings, riots, squatting, intimidation, enforced population movements, and murders — often in an atmosphere of tension, passion, and bodily fear. Indeed, it owed its birth to the conflicts within the divided communities of Northern Ireland; divisions which grew more, not less, polarised over the years between 1971 and 1984. It has been the Executive's challenging task to try to administer, humanely and with impartiality, the very branch of the public service whose previous maladministration, in the view of some independent observers, lay at the roots of the civil rights movement which preceded our latest Troubles.

My qualification for membership of the Executive's Board, and later its chairmanship, are not so easily stated; but they are not irrelevant, and the reader is entitled to know something of my background, if only to enable him to weigh up my opinions, judgements, and prejudices. My family has lived in Belfast and County Down for upwards of three centuries; I am a solicitor, sixth generation in a family firm in central Belfast. Politically, the family tradition has been radical or liberal, rather than unionist or conventional; though I never stood for election to any public office, I myself was for almost twenty years active in the Northern Ireland Labour Party until I quit in despair in 1969. Indeed, I was the principal draftsman of a policy paper for the party entitled 'Rents and Houses', published in 1956.

In matters of religion, I was brought up in the Church of Ireland, from which by degrees I have detached myself: I now describe myself either as an agnostic, or as an inter-denominational anti-clerical. In my spare time, I am a conservationist and an architectural historian; I spent ten years compiling a book on the buildings of Belfast; and for another book, I visited systematically every town and village in the nine counties of Ulster; so that my knowledge of the physical fabric of Northern Ireland, and especially its capital, is fairly extensive. And I can claim some knowledge of its thrawn but estimable people, their needs, wishes, and modes of thought, from the experience of canvassing voters on their own doorsteps — and from a busy legal practice too.

Some aspects of this background I found invaluable when I took on the chairmanship of the Executive. I by no means felt myself to be a square peg in a round hole, however challenging and arduous was such a task at such a time. My freedom from past associations with either the Orange-Protestant-Unionist faction, or the Nationalist-Catholic-Republican one, might elsewhere have seemed merely negative; but to me it has proved a very positive asset. The task of chairing a controversial quango in Northern Ireland calls for a curious combination of physical characteristics: a warm heart, a cool brain, a firm hand, a smooth tongue, and a thick skin. I do not claim to have been endowed with all of these desirable qualities. I have not been spared the outspoken hostility of extremists and bigots on both sides. Many of my friends and colleagues commiserated with me on occupying so thankless and thorny a chair, but in fact I found it endlessly absorbing and rewarding. But then there can be few if any other positions in public life where the end-results of success are so tangible and visible. For the rest of my days, wherever I go in Northern Ireland, I shall see on the ground some of the 60,000 odd houses built during my time: and if they continue to satisfy their occupants, they will continue to give satisfaction to me too — especially if they are found acceptable by those who care about the quality of architectural design, layout, townscape, and villagescape.

I started on my chairmanship with three very specific objectives. First, to provide a service both absolutely fair and impartial, and seen to be so. Second, to improve the quality of the new houses of the province. Third, to step up the quantity of new houses provided. I believe that, in my time, the Executive was not unsuccessful in achieving the first two objectives; if we failed to meet the third, the reasons are set out later in this book: and not least of them was the change in Government which took place in the spring of 1979, just five months after I had started my term of office.

It was an advantage that from the outset I knew what I wanted to do, and did not have to waste precious months in learning my job. Especially in a long-lead field such as house-building any major change in policy or practice is slow to come to fruition; it seldom takes less than three years, often far more, from the beginning of the site acquisition procedures to the handover of keys to the first tenant. Tedious as these procedures are, any attempt to short-circuit them may lead to unacceptable encroachments on the liberties of individuals, so they just have to be lived with. The hierarchies of quangos, ministers, their accounting departments, and treasury, are as ponderous to turn from their pre-selected courses as a fully-laden supertanker. What is not begun in the first six months of a three-year term of office is all too likely to remain unachieved at its end.

As I have said, this does not claim to be an academic work, though I hope it may be of some interest to practitioners of several disciplines. I have not burdened it with the *apparatus criticus* of footnotes, sources, and references; nor with statistical tables and graphs. For the years since 1971, all the main facts and figures are already available in the published Annual Reports of the Executive. I have made no attempt to provide an exhaustive bibliography: in recent years there have been very many surveys, reports, books and learned papers on housing-related subjects, especially if planning is included. I have simply noted, under the heading *Sources*, those publications (and a few unpublished theses) which I found most useful.

I have taken as my general closing date 31st March, 1984, when my own chairmanship of the Executive came to an end; having once withdrawn, of my own accord, from the housing scene, it would not be fitting that I should return to plague my successors with a carping running commentary on their actions and decisions. In the concluding chapter, I have allowed myself some observations on the way in which matters have developed since then: perhaps some such remarks of a general kind, and even perhaps a little crystal-ball-gazing, may not be wholly out of place.

I half-considered providing a glossary not only to the vivid colloquialisms applied to housing in Ulster, but also to the jargon used by those who work in the housing field. Indeed, *housing* itself is a markedly less agreeable word than *house* or *houses*. But it does convey a larger meaning, and its use is inescapable if unacceptable periphrasis is to be avoided. Equally, the unlovely word *dwelling* serves a purpose, since its meaning embraces not only family houses, but also flats, old persons' bungalows, and maisonettes. I can only humbly beg the tolerance of the reader for my use of various other convenient shorthand words which have made their way into the technical vocabulary of housing manager and administrator.

As to local usage, I had supposed that the distinction between a kitchen house and a parlour house was universally understood, until

Harry Simpson told me that this is not so. A *kitchen house* is, in Ulster, a terrace house of the very smallest kind, in which the front door opens directly into, and the steep staircase runs directly up from, the single ground-floor living room, with only a narrow kitchen-cum-scullery in the return at the rear. A *parlour house,* though still very small, is one degree superior: the ground-floor is divided into a narrow hall-passageway, a tiny front parlour, and a small back living-room or kitchen, still with the scullery in the return. A *jawbox* is an old-fashioned but capacious sink, of brown earthenware or (more commonly today) thick white porcelain, in which the dishes, the pans, the clothes, and the householders themselves, must be washed in houses otherwise lacking running water and modern amenities — and there are too many such still in use. *Slob* and *sleech* are expressive local words for the smelly estuarine mud on which most of the inner city of Belfast is built.

If, as I have earlier remarked, I found my term of office as chairman of the Executive satisfying, it was largely because I enjoyed working closely with so many committed, intelligent and enthusiastic colleagues who shared my own detestation of bigotry, sectarianism, and the recourse to violence. They shared also my own aspirations towards fairness, justice, and humanity; in short, a social conscience; an article I already owned, and did not have to acquire after my appointment. The building and running of the Executive were very much team efforts, involving the corporate and non-sectarian commitment of a large number of people. Many of them have helped me in the preparation of this book; but I must make it plain that the opinions (or prejudices) here expressed are mine and mine alone. I formed certain views about housing matters some thirty years ago. In some instances I have changed my mind in the years since then, in others not. It is not for me to say whether I have demonstrated laudable pertinacity, or obstinate pig-headedness; or a mixture of the two.

It remains to acknowledge, with gratitude, the help I have received in writing this book from the following: my two predecessors as chairman of the Executive, both good friends, Sir Desmond Lorimer and James O'Hara; Herbert Bryson, former chairman of the Housing Trust; Kathleen Robinson and Norman Capper, who served both Trust and Executive; Harry Simpson; David Donnison; John Lazenbatt; Ken Mercer, Robin Harrison, and Trevor McCartney of the Executive's corporate planning department; Geraldine McGuigan; Brian Henderson, Reg Perry, Alex McRitchie, and other members of the staff in the information services department and library; Victor Blease, Don Crawley, Arthur Halligan, Billy McGivern, and Margaret McEneaney. The text has also been read by my successor, Norman Ferguson, and by John Gorman, both of whom made helpful suggestions though I should not wish to saddle either with the slightest degree of responsibility for anything I have to say. I am also grateful to Ken Darwin; to Fred Heatley of the North Belfast Historical Society: Brian Boyd, Michael McGuigan and Robert Jennings of Dublin; Trevor Carleton; John Hendry; Anthony Malcolmson of the Public Record Office of Northern Ireland; John Gray, John Killen, Gerry Healey, and other members of the staff of the ever-admirable Linenhall Library, Belfast; the Belfast City Library, and the former Parliamentary Library at Stormont; above all, to Patricia Body, Patricia Crossan, Sally Lowry, and Elizabeth Cavanagh, who at different stages typed successive drafts of this work: as well as to many others who cannot be named individually here. I am grateful to Miss Maura Pringle for the preparation of the maps in the endpapers and on page viii. It is fair to add, however, that she bears no responsibility for the accuracy of the information as to the religious complexions of different districts of Belfast, and the confrontation lines between them. So far as I know, no map quite like this has ever before been made public. Although very appreciative of the help accorded to me by various officers of the Northern Ireland Housing Executive, I must, and do, accept personal responsibility for this.

I must also record my grateful appreciation to the Northern Ireland Housing Executive for providing many of the illustrations (individually acknowledged) and for making possible the inclusion of so many photographs in this book.

C.E.B.B.
November 1985

# The Origins of the Northern Ireland Housing Executive

The episode known as the 'Squatting at Caledon', in June 1968, brought housing to the very forefront of the political dissensions in Northern Ireland. Indeed, a number of commentators have identified it as the starting-point of the Troubles which were to follow.

The facts are confused and confusing. The Unionist-controlled Dungannon Rural District Council allocated a new house at No 11, Kinnaird Park to a Mr Brady, a local Catholic, and No 13, Kinnaird Park next door to a Miss Emily Beattie, a single girl of 19, and a Protestant, who was secretary to an influential local figure. A Mrs Gildernew, a Catholic with three small children aged under four, squatted in No 11; from which she was evicted in a glare of publicity on 18th June. The television cameras showed horrified viewers the bailiffs breaking down the front door; the family being dragged out, Mrs Gildernew clutching her infant child; and her mother receiving cuts from broken glass.

Austin Currie, a young and articulate Nationalist MP, raised the matter the next day at Stormont with such vehemence that he was ordered out of the House. Unionist ministers, predictably, refused to interfere either with the discretion of the local council or with the enforcement of the law. At this stage, the allegation was mainly that the Council made no attempt to allocate new houses on a basis of need; since No 11, the house first squatted in by Mrs Gildernew, had been allocated to another Catholic, the charge of sectarian discrimination was weak. Nonetheless, the moderate-Unionist Belfast Telegraph gave expression to public uneasiness in a leader on 20th June, advocating a thorough inquiry into housing allocations in the province: adding, 'As things stand, a local councillor for a district effectively decides who gets houses and who does not ... The natural tendency of a councillor to preserve the status quo that won him his seat must create tension.'

Next day, Austin Currie, accompanied by Mrs Gildernew's brother Patsy, and a local farmer, very publicly and deliberately squatted in the next-door house which had been allocated to Miss Beattie; after three hours, they were removed by policemen, one of whom happened to be Miss Beattie's brother. Short and symbolic as Austin Currie's squat was, it effectively drew attention to the disparity between the claims of Catholic Mrs Gildernew and her three small children, and those of the Protestant Miss Beattie. And so public interest was sharply focused on the burning question whether or not Unionist councils in Northern Ireland discriminated unfairly on sectarian or political grounds against Catholics in matters of housing. Austin Currie's lead was followed by the Campaign for Social Justice and the Civil Rights Association which organised a protest march in August in Coalisland; which in its turn led to the Civil Rights march in Derry of October, and the rioting which then first followed: and so to the Burntollet march and the Bogside episodes of January 1969: and the appointment of the Cameron Commission of Inquiry into 'Disturbances in Northern Ireland'.

The Report of the Cameron Commission, published in September, was clear and unambiguous: one of the prime causes of the disturbances, it found, was

> a rising sense of continuing injustice and grievance among large sections of the Catholic population in Northern Ireland, in particular in Londonderry and Dungannon, in respect of (i) inadequacy of housing provision by certain local authorities (ii) unfair methods of allocation of houses built and let by such authorities, in particular, refusal and omissions to adopt a 'points' system in determining priorities and making allocations (iii) misuse in certain cases of discretionary powers of allocation of houses in order to perpetuate Unionist control of the local authority.

This conclusion has, ever since, been accepted as incontrovertible by most Catholic politicians and commentators, and indeed by many others. Yet it must be said that it is still equally vehemently denied by Unionist apologists; who do have some telling arguments on their side.

In the first place, the Cameron Report itself was to some extent superficial and subjective; it cannot be said that the Commission carried out any very thorough research or analysis, nor that it produced any very convincing evidence or statistics in support of its findings. Moreover (and writers such as John Morrison and Hugh Shearman have made much of this) Professor Richard Rose's study *Governing without Consensus*, published in 1971, reached the conclusion that 'in aggregate, Catholics are more likely than Protestants to be living in council houses.' But he added: 'Aggregate figures do not necessarily evidence the absence of any discrimination'. And

> To acquit the Unionist regime of blanket charges of discrimination in public housing is not to assert the absence of any religious discrimination ... The copious files of civil rights organisations indicate that blatant cases of discrimination can and do occur ... From a civil rights point of view, each *individual case* of discrimination is matter for protest.

In fact, it is clear that protagonists of the Unionist case make far too much of Professor Rose's negative findings, as well as misrepresenting their implications: they occupy only four pages in a 500-page book; and neither his evidence nor his conclusions are put forward as definitive.

There are, however, various pleas in mitigation that can be raised: first, that Protestants and Catholics have traditionally, over several centuries, tended to live in segregated areas in many of the cities, towns and villages of Ulster, a fact which has been studied in some depth, and established as historically well-founded, by a number of social geographers. Second, it is argued that the electoral consequences of new housing can never be ignored, and that the siting of new estates to maintain the status quo went no further than in some closely-contested English, Welsh or Scottish constituencies. Third, that since Catholic families tend to be larger than Protestant ones, any allocation scheme based on family size must result in discrimination against Protestants.

There is some truth in each of these arguments. But against them must be weighed the number of well-documented cases brought to public notice by the Campaign for Social Justice; and some of the damningly candid admissions made by indiscreet Unionist politicians. And if many Catholics in many areas did get houses, there were certainly some Catholics in some areas who had no hope of ever doing so. It is my view that the majority of councils did not consciously or deliberately engage in this kind of discrimination; but a minority did so, and thereby discredited the whole. It is to the discredit also of the Stormont government that it never made any attempt to intervene, or to temper the excesses of some of its followers. Certain it is, that this was a deeply emotive and divisive issue during the 1960s and early 1970s; and that, even though fifteen years have now passed since housing functions were transferred to the Executive, it is a subject still capable of raising passionate feelings of grievance and indignation on both sides.

So long ago as 1956, the Northern Ireland Labour Party included in its electoral manifestoes proposals for a single unified points scheme to govern allocations throughout the province. These proposals were rejected with contempt until, under the pressure of events, in November 1968, in the aftermath of the squatting at Caledon, a package of reforms was introduced: the appointment of an ombudsman; the appointment of the new Londonderry Development Commission in place of the former city and rural councils; and the mandatory requirement that every council adopt an allocation points scheme. One or two councils, including Belfast, had already done so; but their schemes were of a crude and unsophisticated character; and the new schemes, unwillingly framed by the councils and submitted to an unenthusiastic Stormont for approval, were no better.

In 1964, the Northern Ireland Labour Party had included in its elec-toral manifestoes proposals for a single all-purpose housing authority for the province, based on an expansion of the functions of the old Housing Trust, but with a more representative Board. These proposals were rejected with even greater contempt until, in August 1969 — in the aftermath of riots in Belfast which resulted in an appeal from Chichester-Clark to Harold Wilson to send in British troops, acceded to on 16th August — the Home Secretary, James Callaghan, visited Northern Ireland. On 27th August he met the Stormont Cabinet and has recorded:

> Amongst the flurry of suggestions that I put to them that afternoon the one that caused the greatest consternation was my proposal that there should be a single authority for the allocation and building of houses. They regarded the idea with near horror on political and administrative grounds for, of course, it went to the heart of political patronage.

Nevertheless, at his insistence, a working party of officials was set up to explore the idea. James Callaghan again:

> I had already received a study by the Ministry of Housing com-menting very favourably on the work of the Northern Ireland Housing Trust, whose policies and standards were far superior to those of the local authorities . . .. The standard of local authority housing management was in general abysmal.

Six weeks later, the Home Secretary returned to Belfast. In the interim, the Report of the Cameron Commission had been published and the working parties of civil servants had made their recom-mendations. On 10th October, James Callaghan announced that it had been agreed between the two Governments that a new central housing authority should be set up. There were strong and immediate protests from numerous councils, and from the chairmen of the Fermanagh and Belfast housing committees.

The communique was couched in terms which were, perhaps, designed to save (so far as possible) the face of the Stormont Government. The advantages stated were:

> a common public authority rent structure throughout Northern Ireland; improved mobility, which is the key to regional development; an end to allegations about discrimination in housing allocations; the attraction of more high-quality professional and administrative staff to housing work and the opportunity to use modern efficient management techniques; economies of scale; the organisation of contracts to ensure a steady demand on housing contractors and thus more efficient building; the elimination of unnecessary variety coupled with greater opportunities for research and experiment; the introduction of advanced estate management throughout the country, which will be in the hands of qualified housing managers; but above all a new opportunity to solve Northern Ireland's housing problems in the foreseeable future.

Brian Faulkner, Minister of Development, stuck firmly and defensively to this line (since unkindly described by one researcher as 'romancing of the real issue') in speeches in October and November 1969. Somewhat disingenuously, he argued:

> This question of having a central authority for building houses is something that has been under consideration in my Department for many years. It is something which has been considered in authoritative circles (surely he was not referring to the Northern Ireland Labour Party?) for many years but something which we never had an opportunity to go into until we had discussions with the British Government three or four weeks ago and had for the first time the opportunity of support for a really streamlined housing drive.

The opposition from the Unionist back-benchers, and especially from the Unionist councillors, was considerable; but the Housing Executive Bill was nonetheless presented to Parliament in July 1970. Brian Faulkner had, in the meanwhile, come up with a curious compromise, which on the whole pleased nobody much. The new Central Housing Authority — as it had hitherto been referred to — was to have two tiers: an advisory but non-executive Housing Council, consisting of the mayor or chairman of each local authority (or an alternate); and a nine-person Housing Executive, enjoined to consult both with the individual

local authorities and with the Housing Council. The structure of the
Board itself was, obviously, closely modelled on that provided for by the
English New Towns Act of 1965, which specified a Board of not more
than nine ministerial appointees for each Development Corporation,
the minister being enjoined to 'have regard to the desirability of
securing the services of one or more persons resident in or having special
knowledge of the locality.' The sop to democracy (from a Unionist point
of view) or the fly in the ointment (from an opposition point of view) was,
that the Housing Council was to have the right to elect three of its own
members to the Board of the Executive: thus providing a link between
the two, very disparate, bodies. It was Brian Faulkner's intention that
the Chairman, Vice-Chairman, and four other Board members
appointed by him should be chosen 'for their personal qualities and
suitability for the job, and I shall not be nominating anyone to represent
any particular interest.' No consideration appears to have been given at
the drafting stage to the question whether the Housing Council would
be likely to select its three nominees on a representative basis, or all from
the majority party; throughout the debates at Stormont, it was assumed,
it now appears wrongly, that the minister would have a veto over the
nominations of the Council.

The Bill had its second reading and committee stage in October and
November 1970; it was debated by the Senate in January 1971; and
finally received the royal assent at the end of February. It had by no
means a smooth passage. Republican and Labour MPs bitterly
opposed the concept of a Housing Council as proposed, and equally its
power to appoint three members to the Board: they foresaw constant
conflict between the two tiers, and deliberate obstructiveness on the part
of the old and discredited guard of discriminatory councillors. They
argued forcefully for a quite different kind of housing council, made up
primarily of tenants' representatives, trade unionists, and spokesmen for
the consumer.

Not surprisingly, the Paisleyite party and the rump of dissident right-
wing Unionists led by William Craig and Harry West went to the
opposite extreme; they objected violently to the 'undemocratic' and
'unaccountable' character of the new Board, with its majority of six
ministerial nominees; they would have preferred a directly elected
Board, perpetuating the Protestant and Unionist majority control and
patronage over all housing matters, but would have been prepared to
settle for a Board under reverse control: Chairman, Vice-Chairman,
and one other member nominated by the Minister; six elected members.
Indeed, Dr Paisley made a valiant attempt to talk the Bill out — in the
process placing on the Parliamentary record the following gem of
reporting:

**Rev. Dr. Paisley:** We are being asked to accept a scheme with which, to say the least, many hon. Members are not happy. Many Members have voiced strong objections outside the House, but it seems that when they come here they change their minds. By no stretch of the imagination could this body be called democratic. If that is what hon. Members want no doubt they will vote for it. However, I, for one, will not vote for the establishment of a housing authority in the form which is at present suggested. The housing of the homeless is a serious matter.

**Mr. Hume:** Half a minute left.

**Rev. Dr. Paisley:** Tens of thousands of houses are unfit for human habitation and should have been ...

**Mr. Fitt:** Thirty seconds.

**Rev. Dr. Paisley:** renovated long ago.

**Mr. Hume:** Twenty-five seconds.

**Rev. Dr. Paisley:** These houses should have been made fit ...

**Mr. Hume:** Twenty seconds.

**Rev. Dr. Paisley:** for the citizens of this country.

**Mr. Hume:** Fifteen seconds.

**Rev. Dr. Paisley:** I made a promise to the House ...

**Mr. Hume:** Ten, nine ...

**Rev. Dr. Paisley:** that I would talk this out ...

**Mr. Hume:** eight ...

**Rev. Dr. Paisley:** and I intend to keep my word.

**Hon. Members:** Seven, six ...

**Rev. Dr. Paisley:** I just want to say ...

**Hon. Members:** five, four ...

**Rev. Dr. Paisley:** that without the numerics ...

**Hon. Members:** three, two ...

**Rev. Dr. Paisley:** coming from the members opposite ...

**Hon. Members:** one, zero.

**Rev. Dr. Paisley:** I will wait until you rise from your seat, Mr. Speaker. I do not need any assistance from members of the newly constituted party opposite.

*It being Six o'clock the debate stood adjourned. Debate to be resumed on Tuesday next.*

**Rev. Dr. Paisley:** And I have the Floor for Tuesday.

In the Senate, a recently appointed Unionist member, Mrs Edith Taggart, who had served on the Board of the Housing Trust, was successful in having accepted an amendment requiring that at least one member of the Executive's Board should always be a woman.

The greater number of the back-bench Unionists glumly, and

without much enthusiasm, followed Brian Faulkner's lead; the Bill eventually got through with a comfortable majority; to the last, Faulkner presented it as all his own and his Government's idea; to the last, both Republicans and Unionist malcontents preferred to disbelieve him: as may posterity.

On 4th March 1971, Brian Faulkner announced that the first chairman of the new body would be a distinguished and quite non-political local chartered accountant, and member of the Macrory Review Committee, Desmond (later Sir Desmond) Lorimer: an announcement received with no great generosity by the members of the Republican opposition, who felt that they should have been consulted. On 5th April 1971, the Housing Council held its first meeting, 59 members being present; there were 13 nominations for the three seats on the Board; after a discreet adjournment of 15 minutes, to allow for some tactical manoeuvring, the three members elected were Eddie Elliott of Fermanagh County Council (an old-fashioned Unionist); Mrs Mildred Jones of Ballymena (a very moderate Unionist); and Pat McArdle of Crossmaglen (a well-liked Nationalist of the old school). The elected were to hold office for three years; and the pattern of their affiliations followed the hopes expressed by Bertie McConnell MP, the blind and moderate member for North Down, that 'two of the elected members would represent . . . the majority and one would represent the minority, therefore reflecting the two-thirds-one-third ratio throughout the country.' I am informed by some of those present at that meeting that this happy and conciliatory result came about more by accident than design; the Unionist councillors spread their votes over too wide a list of candidates, and were taken by surprise when the co-ordinated voting of the opposition councillors resulted in the election of a Nationalist in third place. On 6th May 1971, Roy Bradford, who had succeeded Brian Faulkner as Minister of Development when the latter became Prime Minister, announced the names of the vice-chairman — James O'Hara, a leading Catholic solicitor who had been appointed in 1968 to the Board of the Housing Trust; — and the other four first Board members: Hugh Brown, James Donnelly, Frank Kinghan, and the author. The resultant Board accordingly comprised, on a sectarian analysis, five Protestants, three Roman Catholics, and one agnostic: but it must be said that, from the outset, its members worked well together with little regard to sectarian distinctions. Once again, the opposition members of parliament complained that they had not been consulted about any of these names; it afterwards transpired that, to his justifiable annoyance, Desmond Lorimer (the new chairman) had not been consulted either.

\*　\*　\*　\*　\*

The new organisation which came to birth after so difficult a gestation was of an entirely novel kind: a single-purpose but all-embracing housing authority on a regionwide basis: an authority designed to take over the allocation and management of a public-sector stock of nearly 200,000 dwellings; to undertake a public-sector new-build programme on a scale large enough to cure the deficiencies of the past; to undertake an extensive programme of modernisation, renewal and rehabilitation both in the private and the public sectors; and to administer grants, and provide mortgages, home loans and other essential housing services for the private sector.

The experiment was watched, and continued to be watched, with considerable interest from England and farther afield. Though it is something of an over-simplification, it may be postulated that fashions in the theory of public administration are governed by the swing of two separate pendulums, oscillating at different speeds. The first pendulum covers the arc between two extremes of opinion: at one end the view that 'small is beautiful', and that the most responsible and effective service is to be obtained from a multiplicity of small organisations close to their roots and their customers: at the other end, the view that a large, specialised, unitary organisation, though more cumbersome and less responsive, can be vastly more efficient. The second pendulum covers the arc between the view that each specialist service should be provided independently — housing, planning, communications, water and sewerage, employment, education, community centres (and many others) — each to be the function of an entity with special expertise in its own field; and the contrary view that such a system leads to a lack of co-ordination, and that as many functions as possible should be provided by all-embracing multi-purpose organisations, such as the New Town Development Commissions. It is not without significance that, at the instant in time when the Housing Executive came into existence, the first pendulum had reached the latter end of its traverse; the second pendulum stood, on the contrary, poised at the opposite end of its swing.

In assessing the development and success of the Executive in fulfilling its formidable task it is well to bear in mind the preconceptions under-lying its initial structure, and the inevitable changes in fashion which have taken place in the intervening years. But first, it is necessary to des-cribe the historical process which led to a situation which was to earn for the Executive the unhappy title of 'the largest slum landlord in Europe'.

# The Historical Background, 1885-1971

It is astonishing and paradoxical, but true, that a century ago, housing conditions in Belfast and Londonderry were amongst the best, and perhaps indeed actually the best, anywhere in the British Isles. In May 1885, the Royal Commission on the Housing of the Working Classes took evidence in Dublin. It had already published its influential Reports on conditions in England, and in Scotland; now it was concluding its work with a survey of urban housing conditions in Ireland — rural housing was excluded, as it had recently been investigated by a Select Committee on agricultural labourers.

The Royal Commission was a star-spangled body, whose chairman was Sir Charles Dilke, and whose members included Cardinal Manning, the Prince of Wales, Lord Salisbury, and a cross-section of social reformers and members of all parties (including the Irish Party) in and out of Parliament. Its findings in relation to Dublin, Cork, Limerick, Waterford, Galway, New Ross and Kingstown were uniformly critical. But:

> In Londonderry a far more satisfying state of things is found . . . the death rate is low and decreasing . . . There has been a vast improvement in the dwellings of the working classes there during the past ten years . . . 1,137 new houses have been built during that period, and . . . tenement houses which at one time prevailed largely, and in very bad condition, have almost ceased to exist. The sanitary arrangements in the town, except in the case of a few old houses, are good . . . Most of the artisans own their own houses and the number who do so is increasing, and savings are largely invested in building property.

And:

> The condition of Belfast seems to be on the whole satisfactory. The borough is the most prosperous in Ireland ... Its death-rate is not low, but it appears to be decreasing ... The dwelling accommodation seems to have kept pace with the population, the number of new buildings erected each year being over 1,000 ... the tenement house is scarcely found at all. The rule is that houses are usually built for only one family. The cost of building in Belfast is remarkably low. The borough surveyor stated ... 'I believe that a working man can get a self-contained house cheaper in Belfast than in any other manufacturing town in the three kingdoms.'

The witnesses who gave the evidence upon which these findings were based were, Josiah Bretland, the borough surveyor of Belfast, an architect and engineer originally from Nottingham, author of the town's drainage system, and himself a landlord and developer in a small way; Alexander Bowman, secretary of the Belfast Trades Council and one of the earliest Irish socialists, a flax-dresser who was ultimately to be one of the first Labour men to be elected to the Belfast Corporation; and Robert McVicker, the Mayor of Londonderry, a garrulous witness with a great enthusiasm for his new water supply. Despite (or perhaps because of) their very different backgrounds, I think their evidence was reliable and to be believed.

Naturally enough, Bowman took a less sanguine view than Bretland; the former referred to 'districts in the town that are year by year getting worse. I do not know by what means they can be got rid of'. Interestingly, he added: 'We do not want the State to spend money upon improving the condition of our dwellings; but we do think that some of the surplus value created by the community should be devoted to the amelioration of the condition of the community.'

Bretland was asked to explain how the people of Belfast became anxious to live in better houses than other people had been content with elsewhere: his response was illuminating.

> I know that the people very much prefer those houses, and I notice that year by year they will select and choose and prefer houses that are built and finished in a rather better style, and there is a great deal of competition going on in the town amongst those who speculate in buildings to finish the houses better in order to get a better class of tenants in. As an instance of that, although it is a little thing, I may mention that I happen to own a few houses myself, and I remember I put in venetian blinds, and such like little fittings, and some ornamental brickwork, and the people would prefer those houses ... and latterly I am very glad to say that the

builders are voluntarily putting areas in front of these single houses, and in some cases they are even going so far as to put two houses together in a semi-detached way, each with its little garden; but still they are let at a very reasonable rent.

Of course, it would be wrong to paint too rosy a picture: there were certainly appalling slums, over-crowded and insanitary alleyways, rack-rented mill-workers' hovels, byres and stables used for human habitation. But, *by the standards of that time,* Belfast was an uncommonly well-housed city. There were few if any tenements comparable to those of Dublin; there was nothing to compare with the rookeries described by Charles Dickens and Henry Mayhew; above all, there were no back-to-back houses such as were to be found in most northern English cities, and indeed never had been any. This was in part due to the provisions of a series of Belfast Local Acts of which the most important were those of 1847, 1864, and 1878. The 1847 Act, by laying down minimum standards of space and layout, put an end to the building of insanitary alleyways sharing a single privy and dungpit. The 1864 Act, unique to Belfast as the Royal Commission noted, laid it down that the landlord, not the tenant, must accept responsibility both for the rates and for the repair of every house with a poor law valuation under £8 (in effect, all working-class houses). This very useful provision served both to protect the poorest tenants, and to provide builders with a real incentive to build to a standard which would keep down the future burden of maintenance. The Act of 1878 greatly increased the minimum standards to which houses must be built and, significantly, provided for the first time that each house must have a rear as well as a front means of access. For if there were no back-to-backs as such, there were a century ago many streets and alleys where the back-yards abutted directly on each other without any intermediate passage. (In this connection, the terminology is important: the term 'back-to-back' means that terraces of small houses, facing in opposite directions, were divided by a spine wall, without any back yard or rear-facing openings of any kind; some authors have used the expression, loosely and incorrectly, to refer to terraces of small houses where rear windows and doors face each other).

The comparatively satisfactory state of Belfast's housing in the late 19th century was not due only to the framework of local laws and bye-laws. There were other favourable factors. First, there was plenty of virgin building land; and there were plenty of landowners and developers eager to profit from it. A telling jingle of 1875 is quoted by P. G. Cleary:

The richest crop for any field
Is a crop of bricks for it to yield.

> The richest crop that it can grow
> Is a crop of houses in a row.

And indeed, many of the new houses of Belfast were built from the earth of the very fields upon which they stood: and in parts of the city, unexpected changes of level, humps and hollows, still mark the sites of old brickfields.

Other materials, and labour, were likewise readily available. Lime for mortar is plentiful in Ulster; slates from North Wales, timber from America and the Baltic, could be brought cheaply and easily to the city once the deep-water harbour had been dredged out of the shallow estuary. Bricklayers, joiners, plasterers and slaters were a-plenty; there was small need of the more sophisticated skills of plumber and gasfitter, none at all for those of the electrician. Until well into the 20th century, most households still cooked on an open fire, and their homes were lit by candle and oil lamp. Only after the introduction of coin meters in 1903 did gas jets and rings become widespread: a gas cooker with an oven was still a luxury. Until around the same date, plumbing consisted solely of a cold tap to the kitchen jawbox: the outside privy in the back-yard was normally a dry closet.

Indeed, by the turn of the century Belfast was unique in retaining the old dry system: water-closets were still few and far between: in 1896, the special committee established by the Corporation to consider the death-rate heard evidence that there were still 20,000 houses without back passages, only a common privy and ashpit, which had to be cleared four times a year — by bringing the accumulated excreta through the houses. It heard too that many of the sewers were only elongated cesspools with little or no fall: that the high death rate was directly attributable to privies and middens without proper access, and to the keeping of horses, cattle and pigs within the city: in that year there were 834 dairies in Belfast! The water supply was inadequate and polluted until the arrival of water from the Mourne mountains in 1901. Outbreaks of typhoid remained endemic for some years more. A network of main and dis-tributor sewers was laid out by the same J. C. Bretland who had given evidence to the Royal Commission on Housing; it was his pride and joy; but he stood discredited when, in September 1902, the system failed to cope with a sudden rain-storm coinciding with high tide: and the whole centre of the city was flooded with a mixture of rain-water, sea-water, and sewage.

The local capitalists who financed house-building were none too scrupulous about their sites. Under pressure, James Munce, Assistant Town Surveyor, admitted to the special committee that ground upon which houses were being erected was 'an enormous dunghill' ... 'horse

manure, cow manure, human excrement; everything of the most
abominable character' ... 'you would have to go on stilts' ... 'No lan-
guage is too strong to describe it'.

Yet these local capitalists and developers performed an essential
service: if they and their like had not chosen to invest in building,
the houses would not have been built at all. The mill-owners no
longer found it profitable to build tied houses for their workers; the
banks seem to have played little or no part. To some extent the early
building societies channelled small savings to the builders and
developers — they were then, in truth 'building' societies, not as of
recent years, householders' pawnbrokers — but it was the influential
private developers who played the main part.

There were large fortunes to be made. The most prominent, but not
the least criticised, of these entrepreneurs was Dan Dixon, a timber
importer and builders' supplier who amassed a fortune of half-a-million
pounds — was seven times Lord Mayor; knighted in 1892, made a
baronet in 1903; Unionist MP for North Belfast for the last two years of
his life. He and his company bought up great tracts of slobland: filled it
with any material they could lay their hands on (as the special committee heard): laid it out in plots to the highest possible density: then
leased these out to small builders, reserving for themselves the largest
obtainable ground rents — and no doubt a profit on the builders'
materials. Out of a tract of 75 acres of mud near the Connswater river,
they created ground rents totalling nearly £3,000 a year, and all without
the bother of individual rent collections, evictions, or the burden of
repairs; but this was only one of many such ventures. Smaller men pros-
pered too; for example, James Rea and his brother, who developed the
area now known from its biblical street-names as the Holy Land. They
worked in partnership with Robert McConnell, an exceptionally shrewd
estate agent who followed in Dan Dixon's footsteps by becoming Lord
Mayor, a baronet, and an extremely rich man.

But, in Belfast, the turn of the century was a watershed. On the
assumption that the growth of the city would be never-ending, new
houses had been built regardless of demand: and more importantly,
regardless of the ability of the tenants to pay the economic rents. In 1899,
the *Irish Builder* reported that 10,000 new houses were lying empty; and
the census of 1901 showed that this was an under-estimate. The period of
Belfast's greatest expansion was over; the economic climate was highly
unsettled; the growing conflict over home rule added to the general
insecurity. Small wonder, perhaps, that, given such gross over-
production, the city fathers were slow to embark upon municipal
housing schemes. Although by 1910 most major cities — including
London, Liverpool, Glasgow and Dublin — had completed many such

**Plate 2**

The three-and-a-half metre high Peace Wall at Cluan Place, East Belfast: housing occupied by Roman Catholics to the left, Protestants to the right. Before this redevelopment area was vested, there were 38 condemned houses occupied by Protestants on part of the site, the rest of which was a 'neutral' former bus depot. 69 new houses were built on the 'neutral' site between 1980 and 1982, and used to house the overspill of families from the Catholic Short Strand enclave nearby. Local Protestant leaders insisted on a high wall between these and the 23 houses completed in 1985 now forming a new salient in the boundary of Protestant Ballymacarrett. Additional net fencing had to be added on top of the wall to deflect missiles during the summer of 1985; followed by demands that the wall be permanently further heightened.

**Plate 5**

Alleyways scheduled for clearance under the Belfast Improvement Order of 1910: photographed in April 1912 by A. R. Hogg (from the Ulster Museum collection). *Above*, a lantern slide of the children of Crozier's Row, Boundary Street; *below left*, Beatty's Entry, off Hamill Street; *above left*, old and new houses in Hamill Street.

Interior View of Labourer's Kitchen as it should be, looking towards the hearth.

Plate

Plate

Plate 8

In 1907, the romantic Belfast antiquarian Francis Joseph Bigger published an idealistic pamphlet on the design of rural cottages to be built under the Labourers (Ireland) Acts; the two illustrations *above*, are from this source. He practised what he preached, and actually built a group of such cottages at Glengormley, near Belfast – No. 590 Antrim Road, *below left*, with porch detail, *below right*. No doubt the Celtic interlace ornament of the porch amply compensated the tenants for the total absence of bath, lavatory, wash basin, gas, electricity, cooking range, or even kitchen sink.

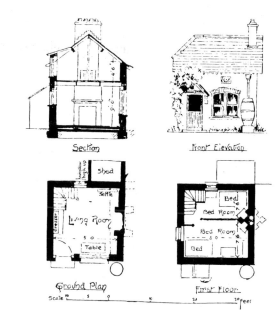

Section    Front Elevation

Ground Plan    First Floor

### Three-Roomed Cottage.

The upstairs can be made as one room. Cheap plan for small house, well adapted for building in pairs.

SLOBLAND

Plate

Plate

MR. J. C. PECKSNIFF BRETLAND, M.I.C.E.

WONDERFUL MAIN DRAINAGE!

**Plate 12**

*Above left:* caricature of Sir Daniel Dixon, the Lord Mayor of, and an MP for, Belfast, from the *Belfast Labour Chronicle*, 9 December 1905. The Labour councillor, William Walker, wrote: 'Too long have the electors allowed themselves to be hoodwinked and cajoled into returning to representative positions rack renters, land speculators, jerry-builders, usurers, etc., all of whom have set themselves to the (to them) congenial task of acquiring swamps and then using their positions on the corporation so that the swamps are filled up at the corporation expense by ashpit refuse, road scrapings, etc.; after which, street upon street of doggery houses are erected thereon, irrespective of the grave and imminent danger to the public health'.

*Below left:* the kind of crowded building development in which Sir Dan Dixon and his contemporaries specialised.

*Above:* caricature of J.C. Bretland from *Nomad's Weekly*, 20th September 1902. Town Surveyor of Belfast, and witness before the Royal Commission on Housing of 1885, he was also the author of the town's main drainage system: which failed conspicuously to perform its function, on 3rd September 1902, when heavy thunderstorms coincided with high tide, and the entire town centre was flooded.

**Plate 13**

Contrary to appearances, this photograph was taken as recently as 1966, by Patrick Rossmore, to illustrate *Buildings of Belfast*. These tiny houses at 56 and 58 Great Patrick Street dated from about 1770. The lintel of the front door was only five feet above the pavement; fortunately Mrs. Annie McGrattan, seen here peaceably smoking her pipe, was even smaller. These houses were demolished to make way for the Dunbar Street link road.

schemes, it was only in that year that the Corporation embarked upon its first Improvement Scheme involving some 700 houses in the most crowded area of courtyards and alleyways; in fact, largely due to opposition from nationalist councillors who saw their vote threatened, the first new house was not completed until 1917. The suggestion by Budge and O'Leary that

> by 1910 the Corporation should have been building municipal houses. This, however, was strongly opposed by the great builders and property owners on the Corporation, Sir Daniel Dixon and Sir R. J. McConnell, to whom the idea of municipal competition was most unwelcome

hardly stands up. Sir Dan Dixon was then three years dead; and the stock of houses (though, of course, not of good houses) was still in surplus, not in deficit. But they are right in identifying the beginning of a period of apathy and stagnation in housing matters within the city, which was to last for half a century, and to lead to many of the Troubles of the recent past.

The Great War, the troubles and rioting which accompanied partition, the side-effects of the Civil War in the Free State, perhaps above all the heavy losses of the best young men at the Somme and elsewhere: all these factors acted as brakes. The call to build 'Homes for Heroes', and the new legislation which made this possible in Great Britain, did not extend to Northern Ireland. The Belfast Corporation did indeed establish a Housing Committee and Housing Department in 1919; but by 1925, both were in deep trouble, with allegations of corruption which the Megaw Commission concluded were not unfounded. The city solicitor and surveyor resigned. The Corporation decided not to proceed with 870 new dwellings already approved. In consequence, only 2,562 new houses were built by the Corporation in the inter-war years, none of them after 1930; and even that figure included 375 houses at Seaview built not for rental but for sale. Such building as there was was almost entirely promoted by estate agent-developers such as the McKees, the McConnells and the McKibbins. The latter, in particular, embarked in 1935 on an ambitious scheme to build some 2,500 new houses for sale at £200 each on the steep and windy hillsides above Ardoyne and the Crumlin Road. Unhappily, the still uncompleted houses in the Glenard estate were squatted in by refugees from the riots of 1935-6 in the Docks area of Belfast; the squatting was followed by a long and acrimonious rent strike; and the estate became so notorious that in 1937 it was thought expedient to change all the street names: a stratagem which was seen to have failed when, in later Troubles, Farringdon, Velsheda and Cranbrook once again hit the headlines.

There was no city in England, Wales or Scotland whose house-building record in the inter-war years, whether in the public or private sector or taking the two together, was worse than that of Belfast. Whereas in England, since the Wheatley Act of 1924, the provision of adequate housing as a social service, whether by central or local government, had been accepted; and a steady stream of new houses and flats designed to gradually higher standards was accordingly provided, the position was very different in Northern Ireland. Perhaps the government of the day at Stormont should not be too harshly judged: the city's housing stock was still better than most; the idea of parity as between different parts of the United Kingdom had not yet been conceived; and it was hard enough to find finance to keep the administration going, let alone to mitigate the miseries of recession and mass unemployment. Nevertheless, the failure to keep on foot a consistent rolling programme of renewal was to have disastrous consequences.

\*  \*  \*  \*  \*

Outside Belfast, the state of the province's housing was variable, but on average little better. On balance it was probably better in the countryside than in the small towns and villages. The Famine, and the subsequent emigration, had not only overturned the entire rural economy: it had also pricked the Victorian social conscience. In 1861, there were still nearly 600,000 occupied mud cabins in Ireland, as well as countless others, roofless and decaying. Philanthropic persons began to propound the need for landlords to provide new and better cottages for their tenants. In 1883, a Parnellite introduced as a private member's bill the first of the Labourers (Ireland) Acts, and the principle was established that public authorities had a part to play.

The scheme was unsophisticated and open to abuse: any three ratepayers or labourers could make a representation to the Poor Law Guardians that a need existed in a specified locality; and the Guardians were then bound, using money advanced by the Local Government Board, to prepare and carry out a scheme. The original idea was that each cottage should have an acre of land; but to this the farmers objected violently, both to the loss of so many acres, and to the fact that the labourers were inclined to spend more time on their own land than in ill-paid service; so the plot was reduced from an acre to a mere rood.

Between 1883 and the major revision of the Acts in 1906, some 21,000 such cottages were built in Ireland; but mostly in Munster and Leinster, only a few in the northern counties, and those mostly in Antrim and Down. Most of these cost a mere £150 to build, and had only the scantiest amenities. A rather superior example near Downpatrick cost

£210 to build on a one-acre site for which £25 compensation was paid; first let in 1904 at a weekly rent of 1/3d, increased to 2/- only when the original tenant died in 1941; during that entire period, according to the Labourers' Act ledger, the expenditure on repairs was only £1.12.9 in 1914, and £2.2.5 in 1918. The 1906 Act introduced a direct contribution from taxpayers' funds, and thereafter more cottages were built in Ulster, though some councils still objected to any payment from the rates. The matter thus became one of public debate. In a highly romantic essay, the Belfast antiquarian Francis Joseph Bigger outlined his own slightly eccentric views. The cottage should be whitewashed inside as well as out ('wall paper should be avoided'); 'a few Irish pictures and Gaelic mottoes go far to make the home bright and attractive'; there should be in all cases a half-door; 'the washing-up is usually done in a bucket or basin on a large stool or low table, and the contents thrown out so soon as the work is done. This is cleanly, and never so unwholesome as a sink.' He practised what he preached, and built three pairs of model cottages by the roadside near Glengormley, of which one survives almost unchanged. Instead of wasting money on bathroom, lavatory, cooker, or kitchen sink, he lovingly installed a panel of Celtic interlace ornament in the porch, together with door furnishings hand-made by local craftsmen.

Between 1919 and 1939, 4,300 labourers' cottages were completed in the six northern counties; but their distribution was uneven; not a single one was built in Co. Fermanagh, where the need might have been thought to be greatest. The absence of wells or alternative water supplies was the worst drawback of most rural houses; many of them were (a few still are) appalling rural slums, though to the outsider the flowers around the door of a pretty cottage in a pretty setting may disguise the fact. John Mogey carried out an important rural survey in 1944. He remarked 'It has been estimated that 96% of all the houses in Fermanagh have no running water. The water-borne disposal of sewage is impossible without this service.' . . . 'Whole townlands were found in which there was not a single well' . . . 'general jealousy of the council houses, which are better than many farm-houses — and provided from the rates, too!' . . . 'Many farmers objected that, if the byre was reconstructed as ordered by the Ministry's inspectors' (to improve the quality of the milk) 'it would be better than the dwelling house. This was often a true observation.'

If conditions were bad in the open countryside, they were still worse in many of the small towns and villages. There was a code for the countryside, the Labourers (Ireland) Acts, which at least achieved the construction of sizeable numbers of dwellings, even though their administration was from the outset deeply imbued with the harsh philosophy of

the Poor Law Guardians and their overseers, the Local Government
Board for Ireland. There was another code for the cities, the Housing of
the Working Classes Acts, exclusively designed for urban slum
clearance; and augmented by the Local Acts which only large towns and
cities could promote. The smaller towns and the villages were, for the
most part, ignored, since they came under neither code. As early as
1903, Nicholas Synnott was writing 'The inferior houses in the small
country towns are often far worse than the cottages in the open country'
... yet, 'The labourer prefers to pay a high rent for a bad cottage in a
village rather than a low rent for a good cottage on a farm.'

Some councils did their best, in terms both of quantity and quality.
Between 1923 and 1937 a very moderate government subsidy was
available, at rates which fluctuated over the period, but only for houses
of ever-diminishing space standards: from 1933 onwards, a grant of
only £25 per house was available, and that only for houses not exceeding
the derisory size of 500 square feet. Stormont kept a tight rein on their
activities. For example, Downpatrick Urban Council built 24 houses in
1927; 15 in 1929; 25 in 1933; and on proposing a fourth scheme in 1936
was able to report that there were no rent arrears and no charge on the
rates from any of the earlier schemes. Yet, when the Council sought
sanction to borrow £12,500 from Belfast Savings Bank to finance 21
kitchen houses at £250 each and 16 parlour houses at £400 each, the
response for the Ministry of Home Affairs was:

> I am to state that the Ministry is unable to approve the application
> to erect 16 parlour houses of 908 square feet as the whole policy of
> Government is directed towards the provision of small houses for
> the poorer members of the working classes in appropriate sur-
> roundings.

So Downpatrick ended up building 36 kitchen houses of 600 square
feet at a cost of £250 a house.

But, it must be acknowledged, most councils showed little enthusiasm
for house-building at their ratepayers' expense. This has given rise to
some sharp, and not unjustified, criticism. R. J. Lawrence has written:

> In housing as in health services the pre-war record of local
> authorities was one of failure ... the rural district councils could
> have transformed the housing situation in their areas at little cost to
> themselves. In the towns ... the achievement of local councils can
> not unfairly be described as derisory.

These criticisms are echoed by Birrell and his colleagues, who write

> it is unlikely that the cost would have exceeded a 1d rate for each
> 100 cottages in each rural district ... The explanation given is that

the preoccupation with the geography of votes . . . governed what little public housing was built.

There is, to put it mildly, a strong prima facie case for believing that the sectarian politics of the majority, both in local government and at Stormont, played a part in the unsatisfactory and deteriorating state of Northern Ireland's housing between the wars. But in fairness it must be conceded that Ireland, both north and south, lagged far behind Great Britain in adopting the concept that housing should be seen as a social service, rather than a branch of the old poor law tradition.

\* \* \* \* \*

The German bombing raids on Belfast of April and May, 1941, in which 3,200 houses were destroyed and 53,000 damaged, constituted a turn of the tide for housing in Northern Ireland. Bardon has argued that the air raids 'exposed the ineptitude of both the Government and the Corporation' in a way so painful as to lead to major shifts both in public attitudes and in the response of those in authority.

A Planning Advisory Board was appointed, under the chairmanship of the Vice-Chancellor of Queen's University, Lindsay Keir; in January 1943 it appointed a Committee on Housing 'to consider and report on the general housing problem in Northern Ireland with particular reference to the clearance of slums and the provision of new housing in the post-war period.' The Secretary of the Committee, as to the Board itself, was a junior-to-middle ranking civil servant, John G. Calvert, later to play a major part in giving effect to its recommendations. Within eighteen months it produced a clear, lucid and extremely cogent report, the first-ever survey of housing conditions in Northern Ireland. It was a damning document, though its main conclusion, 'that to provide decent housing conditions, approximately 100,000 houses will be required', was deliberately much understated.

The Report acknowledged that practically all of the 53,000 houses damaged by the bombing had been repaired by September 1943; provided preliminary statistics on unfitness and overcrowding throughout the province (the latter unadjusted for the 9,000 evacuees from Belfast to the countryside); discussed slum clearance, the uses of flats, densities, the 'filtering-up' process, open space provision, the dilemma between low rents and minimum standards, and the need for community facilities in large new estates.

Sir Basil Brooke had formed a new Government at Stormont early in 1944, and had recruited to his cabinet William Grant, a former shipyard worker, who was determined to take positive action about housing conditions. Later that year a Housing Bill was introduced providing for new subsidies, and for the establishment of a Northern Ireland Housing Trust inspired, as Grant made plain, by the Scottish Special Housing Association, which had been set up in 1937, with the dual objectives of providing employment and improving housing conditions. This element of the Bill was hotly opposed by the Unionist old guard, who saw it as a reflection on the competence and integrity of the local authorities, as a derogation from the controlling powers of Stormont, and as an example of creeping communism. The objectors succeeded in obtaining a number of assurances from the Government which were to tie the hands of the Trust when set up. It was made very plain that the Trust was to be no more than an auxiliary to the local authorities with no powers to coerce them — a decision which was to have significant consequences in Derry, Enniskillen, and Dungannon.

Grant urged members to regard the Trust 'not as a fifth wheel on the coach but rather as a third horse to help the wagon up the hill.' It was to be required strictly to balance its books, and not to become a burden on the Exchequer: the Minister of Finance, Maynard Sinclair, laid it down that the Housing Trust's outgoings must determine its rents; 'and as it is intended that these should be as low as possible, a strict degree of economy in the Trust's finances will be necessary.' As to the private sector, 'nobody would be happier than myself' said Grant

> to see the usual laws of supply and demand in operation, and houses springing up everywhere in response to the working of the profit motive. But hon. members know that this is not the position, and that without a very substantial measure of Government aid, not a brick can be laid of houses which ordinary people can afford to rent.

And as to the councils,

> ... it is the statutory duty of every local authority in Northern Ireland to provide houses to meet the needs of its working people ... the fact that these requirements have in the past been more honoured in the breach than the observance (a not insignificant admission from a Unionist minister) does not mean that they should not be revived to meet our present needs ... I must give each local authority a clear direction as to what the Ministry regards as its duty in the provision of housing.

The pattern was accordingly set for the provision and administration of housing for the next 27 years. The task was to be shared between the private sector, building almost entirely for sale rather than for rent; the local authorities, which responded with varying vigour; and the Housing Trust. All three of Mr Grant's wagon-horses were to receive subsidies from the Exchequer. There were also certain subsidiary con-

tributors to the housing stock: of these the most significant was to be the
Ministry of Agriculture with its system of grants for the modernisation
or replacement of farm-houses. Over 9,500 farmhouses or farm workers'
dwellings were replaced or 'reconditioned' by this means between 1944
and 1972, often with advantage to their amenities, but brutal disregard
of their appearance. There was also a handful of charitable bodies, such
as the Soldiers' and Sailors' Land Trust, which embarked on building.
The better-off middle classes built new houses for themselves, with or
without subsidy. And, once materials became available, a fair number
of citizens set to and built houses for themselves, with their own hands.

\* \* \* \* \*

The Housing Trust, though not the largest provider of new houses in
the province — in its 26 years, it completed 48,500 dwellings, about half
of its original target — was unquestionably the most influential. From
the very outset, it was a body with a marked and individual character of
its own. Of the first five unpaid Board members, none was to serve for
less than twelve successive years. One, Lucius (later Sir Lucius) O'Brien,
served as chairman from 1945 to 1960, but remained on the Board for 22
years till 1967. Another, Herbert Bryson, served for 25 years, and was
chairman from 1960 to 1970. These two were the moving spirits; they
had already worked very closely as colleagues in the war-time welfare
branch of the Civil Defence Authority. They had a ready ally in Ronald
Green, an able civil servant who was at first assistant secretary with responsibility for housing, then Permanent Secretary to the relevant
government ministry, for most of the Trust's lifetime. Although they
would have indignantly denied acting as a Quaker pressure group, it is
not irrelevant that two of the three were Quakers, the third had close
Quaker connections, and all three had been (though not together) at
Bootham's School. John G. Calvert, sometime secretary to the Planning
Advisory Board and to its Housing Committee, served as general
manager for 21 years from 1946 to 1967. If ever personalities played a
commanding part in the formulation of housing policy and practice,
these did so, and the fact deserves remark, even if it is a little invidious to
single them out from the list of their colleagues and successors, many of
them distinguished.

Until the Civil Rights movement had begun to gather strength in
1968, no Roman Catholic was ever appointed to the Board: this was not
the fault of the Board members, who repeatedly pressed successive
Unionist ministers to appoint a Catholic: to be greeted with the
unvarying reply that 'the time was not right'. (For that matter, no trade
unionist, tenant representative, or member of anything but the philan-

thropic Protestant middle-class establishment was ever appointed to the Board). In practice, I am quite certain that the members of the Housing Trust acted at all times honourably and impartially; indeed, most Unionists thought the Trust far too favourable to Catholic claims. But some of the Trust's policies laid it unintentionally open to charges of favouring the better-off Protestant working class at the expense of the less-well-off Catholic working class.

The compactness and continuity of the Trust's Board was, I think, on balance, a great strength, though it has been suggested, not without some force, that more regular infusions of new blood and new ideas might have been valuable. Nevertheless, consistent and coherent policies could be pursued over long periods; the staff knew exactly what was required of them; decision-making was speedy and clear-cut. The Trust's business was conducted with efficiency, despatch, and economy; discretion bordering on secretiveness was the order of the day, and publicity was shunned; thriftiness and the careful counting of ha'pence were all-important. Indeed, Ronald Green once said in a public speech that 'never since the days of W. E. Gladstone had any public body to his knowledge managed their finances with such frugality'. The style of the Trust reflected the virtuous, austere, if sometimes puritanical, characteristics of the northern Protestant work-ethic.

The Trust could have transacted its business in no other way, given the financial constraints to which Stormont had subjected it; nor indeed would it have wished to; its members, in the spirit of the day, would have found deficit financing unthinkable, and would have regarded it as immoral to do other than keep the books in balance. Everything had to be paid for out of the subsidies received (modest by today's standards but then considered substantial); strictly regulated borrowings; and the rents collected. Unlike other housing authorities in the British Isles, the Trust could neither spread the rent-load over older stock built when costs were lower, as at least Scottish Special could, nor use the rate fund to subsidise the rents. This had serious consequences. When post-war wages and building costs began to rise sharply, above all when interest rates rose from the very low levels of the immediate post-war years, the Trust had only three alternatives: to raise the rents sharply: to lower the standards of its new dwellings: or to cease, or reduce, new building. At various stages in its history, at times of crisis, it adopted various compromise combinations of these courses. But at no time in its history was the Trust able to charge rents low enough to meet the needs of the worst-housed and lowest-paid; and, at no time was it able to bring the standards of its new houses up to the standards adopted in Great Britain. To quote Sir Lucius: 'The reason for the different standard was that Northern Ireland was really starting in 1945 where Great Britain had started in 1919, and it was wisely' (sic) 'felt that the 1945 British standard required too big an advance to be taken in one step.'

In fact, despite their comparatively small size and austerity, the Trust's houses (and estates) were exceptionally well laid out and designed, and introduced quite new standards to Ireland. The first estate, at Cregagh, was the work of that distinguished architect T.F.O. Rippingham; in 1948 James Cairncross, a Scots architect, was appointed Chief Technical Officer, and until the demise of the Trust (sadly, shortly followed by his own death) he made an unparalleled contribution to the quality and appearance of the province's housing.

It must be said, however, that not all the Housing Trust's legacies to its successors have been equally happy. The technical advances of wartime had, by 1945, brought about an unfortunate over-confidence in the miraculous potentialities of new methods and materials. At its simplest level, there was a mistaken belief, contrary to all experience of Ulster's climate, that flat roofs could now be relied upon to keep out the rain for as long, and as reliably, as pitched roofs. At another level, the Trust was an innovator in the use of concrete-based systems of building: as early as 1945-6, it had sponsored the arrival of the Orlit system and had entered into negotiations for the use of the Easiform and No-Fines systems. In the long term, the disadvantages of these concrete-based systems used by the Trust — as also, of the Sectra system used in Rathcoole, Rossville and at Divis Flats — and still more recently, the risks associated with timber-frame building — have become all too apparent.

Its provision of open spaces, careful retention of trees and hedgerows, and attention to landscaping and tenants' gardens, were quite without precedent; estates such as Belvoir and Seymour Hill are still amongst the pleasantest in the province. It provided modest community centres in its larger estates, together with shops — usually with flats over; sometimes, in the light of experience, a most unhappy arrangement — and sites for schools, churches and, occasionally, in its later years, pubs.

In 1958, the Trust, falling into line with current fashion in Great Britain, put out to contract its first two multi-storey flat blocks at Cregagh. When completed, they were adjudged a success, and thereafter, especially in redevelopment areas, an increasing proportion of the Trust's output consisted of multi-storey flats, whether in deck-access slabs or in point blocks. For the reasons discussed later in this book, some of these have proved successful, others disastrous. The last major innovation introduced by the Trust was district heating which, in 1969, the Board hopefully opined could achieve 'a uniformly high and efficient standard of trouble-free space heating and domestic hot water supply . . . throughout an area, at a relatively low cost to the users of the heat.'

From the outset, the Trust's Board resolved to adopt the Octavia Hill system of housing management, and at once sent off eight young ladies to be trained in Great Britain as woman housing managers. Each manager was expected to know each of her tenants individually, and to call weekly or fortnightly at each house to collect the rent and to discuss repairs or any other housing problems. Managers had full responsibility for allocations, transfers, and exchanges, and for the smooth and efficient running of their respective estates. This formidable body of women, a source of great strength to the Trust, was regarded by tenants with mingled awe and respect; indeed some of them were dragons, even if they were also in fact both competent and humane. Because of the importance attached by the Trust to thrift, good housekeeping, and the punctual payment of rent — and because the rents for Trust accommodation were perforce always somewhat higher than those in the private or local authority sectors — some managers acquired a reputation for picking and choosing the best tenants; who were seldom those most in need. The annual report for 1954-5 expressly refers to 'families with a bad domestic standard unsuitable for immediate transfer to a new estate amongst tenants who take a pride in their houses and surroundings.' There is no doubt that Housing Trust tenants felt themselves to be a cut above the rest — indeed, many of its ex-tenants still do; and the Housing Trust staff, too, sometimes felt themselves to constitute an élite, a cut above the rest, which led to a certain degree of complacency.

While this was understandable, it was unfortunately ultimately damaging to the reputation of the Trust, implying as it did not only an unacceptable kind of paternalism, but also a kind of discrimination — not necessarily on religious grounds, but sometimes open to that interpretation. Only in the last few years of its existence was the Trust seen to acknowledge the need to demonstrate publicly its impartiality in sectarian terms; a process accelerated by the appointment to the Board of James O'Hara, its first-ever Roman Catholic member, in January 1968. At that time, plans for the Lower Falls and Cullingtree Road redevelopment were being formulated; at that time also the Trust was becoming impatient at the obstructiveness of the Londonderry, Dungannon and Enniskillen authorities which, despite established housing need, were on various not very convincing pretexts seeking to block housing developments which might have upset established electoral patterns.

In its last report, the Trust referred to this obliquely: 'In a few areas efforts to overcome serious housing problems have been frustrated, and the Trust is convinced that this resulted in unfortunate consequences to the community as a whole'. It referred also to the setback caused by the onset of the troubles to its 'declared policy of creating integrated communities.' I have searched the earlier annual reports in vain for any previous reference to this so-called 'declared policy'; I think perhaps it was taken for granted: certainly the Trust was always ready to provide sites for Roman Catholic schools and churches where a need existed; and, for example, the Rathcoole, Seymour Hill, Suffolk and Twinbrook estates were consciously and deliberately designed to constitute mixed Protestant-Catholic communities.

Herbert Bryson has put it on record that, in 1969, James Callaghan told him that 'the Trust was the only organisation in Northern Ireland of which there was absolutely no criticism in Whitehall'. When it finally surrendered its functions to the Housing Executive on 3rd October 1971, it handed on 48,532 completed dwellings; 5,882 dwellings under contract; a land bank sufficient for 12,230 more; a housing account at credit; a staff of skilled and devoted housing specialists; and a high tradition of public service.

**\* \* \* \* \***

In the post-war years, some local councils welcomed the assistance of the Housing Trust, others viewed it with hostility and preferred to go their own way. Overall, the house-building record of the councils — the two county boroughs of Belfast and Londonderry; 10 borough councils; 24 urban district councils; and 31 rural district councils — was disappointing. Between 1944 and 1972 they completed a total of almost exactly 75,000 new dwellings; but this fell far short of making good the deficiency accumulated over the previous half-century.

The smaller councils were handicapped by the antiquated legislative structure within which they had to operate; and some of them were far too small, both in terms of staff and of rateable value, to undertake any but the most modest of schemes. The quality of the housing they did provide was often extremely poor. Some councillors preferred to employ the nearest small-town architect, engineer or surveyor, especially if he was somebody's friend or relation; the results were sometimes distinctly unsophisticated. Keeping the rates down was seen as paramount: some small councils had bizarre arrangements in order to spare the ratepayers even the cost of employing rent collectors.

Nor did the government see fit to interfere. Until the late 1950s, some councils were still building houses without running water, sewage, or even electricity. Dame Dehra Parker, when minister at Stormont with responsibility for housing, was a warm proponent of a small, cheap, sub-standard design, lacking all amenities, known as the 'Ulster Cottage'. She exerted considerable pressure on the Board of the Housing Trust to build such houses in rural areas, but this to their great credit they

resisted firmly, going so far as to threaten their resignation en bloc: and
no more was heard of the matter.

The borough and urban councils were considerably better placed in
most cases, since they commanded larger funds and could afford to
employ full time professional staff. But some were much more active
than others; and the largest did not always enjoy the best record, possibly in some cases for political or sectarian reasons. Indeed, Birrell and
his colleagues make the interesting observation that, of the 36 urban or
borough councils, the highest percentages of local authority housing
provision were to be found in the four non-Unionist-controlled councils
— Ballycastle, Downpatrick, Newry and Strabane. They conclude 'The
main explanation must be that the councils in these towns have been
very active, or at least more active than the Unionist councils, in
promoting a house-building programme.'

In some council areas, what building there was, was strictly segregated: provision was made for each community, but in such a way,
and within such electoral boundaries, that no ill-effects for the party in
power need be apprehended. In Derry, for example, new houses were
available for Catholics on the long waiting lists in the Rossville flats or in
Creggan, both in the South ward; but not in the North or Waterside
wards, where narrow Protestant electoral majorities would have been
imperilled. In other areas, such as Enniskillen, where the electoral boundaries did not lend themselves to this stratagem, little if any building
took place.

The record of the largest council, Belfast, was hardly better in the
post-war than it had been in the inter-war years: between 1945 and
1972, the average number of new dwellings built by the Corporation
averaged only 470 a year, desperately far short of the need, assessed by
the city surveyor in 1959 at 2,600 a year over a twenty-year period. It
must in fairness be said, however, that the government flatly refused a
boundary extension in 1947, and land within the existing boundary was
dwindling. Also the Corporation was quick to take advantage of the
availability of prefabricated emergency houses: of the 2,000 asbestos
Arcon bungalows imported by Stormont, regarded as temporary
dwellings with a ten-year life expectancy, 1,000 were erected in Belfast,
as were 800 aluminium bungalows, regarded as permanent. The
Housing Trust made a very large contribution to the city's needs by
way of overspill outside the boundary, particularly in the enormous
south Antrim estates which eventually coalesced to become Newtownabbey: though this was a missed opportunity to develop a proper
New Town.

But the reputation of the Corporation, whether for efficiency or
integrity, did not stand high. Its powers had been suspended, and com-

missioners appointed, from 1942 to 1946 as a result of the findings of an inquiry into allegations of corruption. Another public inquiry had to be held in 1954, this time into irregularities in the allocation of houses: the inspector, Bradley McCall, Q.C., found clear evidence that money was paid in expectation of favours, but no clear evidence that favours were in fact accorded: he did find, however, that 'many otherwise honourable and respectable people were prepared to lie, to bribe, and to cheat their way into a Corporation house.' Yet a third public inquiry was visited upon the city in 1962, when Robert Lowry Q.C. examined at great length, but without reaching any very clear conclusions, allegations of improper conduct made against no less than four municipal knights, their relations, and their associates.

The main thrust of the Corporation's efforts, such as it was, lay in the provision of new houses on whatever land was still available within its boundary, mostly either blitzed sites or pockets of hitherto undeveloped and usually undesirable land. Many of these were poorly laid out, to densities far too high for the families with children which were to occupy them, and all of the houses were small and far below Parker-Morris standards. On the other hand, there is no evidence of sectarianism either in siting or allocation: most of the estates were designed to be mixed, and in fact remained so until the turbulent population movements of 1969 to 1973. And from 1944 onwards the Corporation did operate a somewhat primitive points scheme based on need, though it was widely believed that this was not incapable of manipulation, whether by councillors or others.

The Housing Act of 1956 enabled the Corporation to start planning for a programme of inner-city redevelopment; though lengthy delays were caused by the discovery that considerable parcels of land, or ground rents, were owned by the churches, and so could not be compulsorily acquired without amendment to the entrenched provisions, designed to prevent religious discrimination, contained in the Government of Ireland Act. In 1962 the important Matthew Report was published: this, in essence, provided for a building stop-line around the city, and the relocation of future overspill in a New Town further up the Lagan valley. In 1965 a joint working party of City and Stormont officials produced a preliminary report on the need for redevelopment, and the kind of programme required. It was only in 1968, on the eve of the outbreak of the Troubles, that the city council at last adopted and set in hand a three-phase scheme prepared by its planning consultants, under which the aid of the Housing Trust was enlisted for the Divis and the Cullingtree Road sectors. The authors of these schemes failed to learn from the bitter experiences of redevelopment in Britain; and it is arguable that the widespread demolition which preceded these sweeping and ill-thought-out schemes contributed largely to the violence of the sectarian strife which marked the Troubles.

In January 1972 the Corporation handed over to the Housing Executive a total stock of 22,129 dwellings, of which about 5,000 were unfit houses acquired for redevelopment; and 1,446 new dwellings under contract. Between January and October 1972, the other councils handed over a total of 67,821 dwellings, plus 2,867 under contract. Many councillors were sore and indignant at losing a valued source of power and patronage; others were relieved to be freed from an onerous and contentious burden. Some council officials were helpful and co-operative in what was, technically, a difficult take-over: a few were positively obstructive. The travelling emissaries of the Executive who toured the town halls collecting records, ledgers and title-deeds (when forthcoming) had some entertaining tales to tell on their return.

Lastly, the Executive took over the housing stock and contracts of the three Development Commissions. It had taken twenty years after the end of the war for the New Town concept to cross the Irish Sea. In 1965, under the new Stormont legislation of that year, the Craigavon Development Commission was set up amidst considerable controversy, not least over the politically-loaded name 'Craigavon'. The Commission was to last for only eight years; had the venture been embarked upon ten years sooner, it might have been more successful, but in consequence of the combined effects of the Troubles and the economic recession, it must now be considered an unhappy failure. For this none of its chairman, S. J. McMahon, its reasonably non-political board, its planners, or its administrators, can fairly be held responsible.

The Craigavon Commission made considerable use of industrialised building, and was a pioneer in introducing full Parker-Morris standards to Ireland. Architecturally, some of its designs were more adventurous than successful. Housing, indeed, was not the foremost of the Commission's priorities: it was attempting, in contrast to Newtownabbey, to provide a whole new balanced community. It, and its officers, showed themselves unusually enlightened in their attention to planting, landscaping, and the retention of historic buildings. The well-planned facilities they laid out at Tannaghmore, Silverwood, Oxford Island, Kinnegoe, and the balancing lakes, constitute their most distinguished memorial. In December 1972 the Craigavon Commission handed on to the Executive a stock of 2,165 completed dwellings, and 574 under contract.

The life of the Antrim and Ballymena Development Commission was even shorter: just five years. It was not really intended to create a new town, but rather to plan and redevelop the two main towns and four largest villages within its area. Again, public sector housing took a somewhat subsidiary place. In July 1973, it handed on to the Executive 1,218 completed dwellings, and 440 under contract.

The Londonderry Development Commission, set up in February 1969, was very different. It is clear that, after the widespread publicity about minority grievances in Londonderry, the Government found it convenient to use the powers of the New Towns Act in order, quietly, to abolish the old County Borough and Rural District Councils. The chairman was Brian (later Sir Brian) Morton, and despite the appalling difficulties during that period of rioting, murder, bombings, squatting and intimidation, he and his very non-sectarian Board may take credit for a great measure of success. Despite the camouflaged official announcement, they knew exactly why it had been set up: 'The Commission regard the provision of new housing for the needs of the City, and the operation of a fair and impartial system for the allocation of such housing, as being matters of the first priority.' Despite all obstacles, it quickly set in hand a large programme, and by January 1973 a total of nearly 4,000 new houses had been provided. In June 1973, the Londonderry Commission handed on to the Executive a total stock of 15,374 dwellings, with another 457 under contract.

The three Commissions were dissolved, in two out of three cases protesting plaintively, on 30th September 1973, as part of the major reorganisation of local government which took place on that date. Despite their short lives, their contribution to the province's housing, taken overall, was a valuable one.

\*　\*　\*　\*　\*

Throughout the post-war years, the private builders for sale, large and small, remained the preferred instrument of the Stormont government for the solution of the province's housing problems; as they are today the preferred instrument of the British government. Between 1944 and 1972, 66,000 subsidy houses, and 9,000 non-subsidy houses, were completed by the private builders of Northern Ireland: the total of 75,000 being almost identical with the total output of the combined local authorities (excluding the Housing Trust) over the same period. To produce this result, a subsidy system without parallel elsewhere in the United Kingdom had been introduced soon after the war. Grants were paid on a sliding scale, depending on whether the house was for letting or owner-occupation; and on its size — houses of more than 1,500 square feet at one time, 1,050 square feet at another time; and of less than 500(!) at all times, were ineligible. The amount of the subsidy rose to keep pace with inflation: in 1972, the grants ranged from £300 to £575 for a house built for letting, from £150 to £385 for an owner-occupier.

This system undoubtedly encouraged speculative building on a large scale: though it must be acknowledged that an almost insatiable demand existed in any event; and it has been persuasively argued that the subsidy in effect did no more than raise the price by a corresponding amount, the taxpayers' money serving to increase the profit of the builder, rather than reduce the price to the purchaser. If the result was encouraging in quantity, the quality was often disappointing. There were some good houses, and some good developments, but a large majority comprised ill-designed and ill laid-out small boxes, usually semi-detached, crammed onto their sites geometrically without regard to landscaping or amenity. Few had ever enjoyed the attentions of an architect; the majority came from stock pattern-books.

Amongst the exceptions, the most interesting was the attempt to pioneer in Ireland the garden city concept first realised forty years earlier by Ebenezer Howard at Letchworth. Ulster Garden Villages Ltd. built over 1,500 houses, mostly at Merville Garden Village in Newtownabbey and in the vicinity, to the designs of the English architect E. P. Mawson. These were much more attractively laid out and landscaped than most; but the venture collapsed in 1950. Another sizeable contribution was made by a philanthropic Bangor solicitor, Fred Tughan, whose Victoria Housing Estates provided around 1,000 family houses, and Bangor Provident Trust around 200 houses for the elderly, as well as flats for nurses from the local hospital. And one or two of the large English house-building firms, such as Wimpeys, ventured into the local market; but withdrew again when the going got rough during the Troubles.

On the whole, the contribution of the private building industry to the housing problems of Northern Ireland was uninspired and uninspiring.

\* \* \* \* \*

So it came about that, by 1970, a first-class housing crisis was one of the principal contributory factors to the Troubles. In many areas there was an absolute shortfall of housing; there was gross overcrowding in some places, and a general mis-match between demand and supply; a disproportionately large percentage of the total stock was more than seventy years old, lacking all modern amenities, and rapidly approaching the end of its economic life; and in too many areas there were glaring disparities between the standards of housing enjoyed respectively by the majority and minority communities. The advantageous position of 1885 had been totally dissipated, not deliberately, but as a result of fifty years of apathy and neglect, followed by inadequate attempts to catch up in the post-war years. In some areas there was more than a suspicion of conscious and deliberate sectarian discrimination in the building and allocation of houses. No wonder that housing grievances fuelled the growth of the Civil Rights movement, and came to a head at Caledon.

# The Northern Ireland Housing Executive

The first meeting of the new Board was held, at Stormont, only a week
after the announcement of the names of its members. The urgency of
starting work could hardly be exaggerated: this was a dreadful period of
stress, the need to make progress as quickly as possible was overwhelming, day by day the housing situation was deteriorating as the old
conventional structure of government began to disintegrate. In that
same week, fire-bombs were found in a large number of Belfast shops;
Lord Scarman directed the immediate publication of a report on
residential displacement during 1969; a ballet company at the last
moment cancelled a long-standing engagement in Belfast because of
anonymous threats. It would almost be true to say that the new Board
met under the duress of events.

But root-and-branch reforms cannot be brought about overnight.
Progress was, in the early days, agonisingly and frustratingly slow. An
acting secretary, James Marsh, was seconded from the Ministry of
Development, an acting finance officer, Joe Jenkins, from the Housing
Trust: these were to be, for many weeks, the only employees of the
Executive. Inevitably, the meetings of the first few months were pre-
occupied by the twin problems of the transfer of functions from the
existing authorities; and the administrative structure, terms of service,
and transfer of staff. Nevertheless, an all-day meeting held on a Sunday
in May 1971 at the National Trust property at Springhill allowed time
for a first debate of future housing principles and policies, and some very
far-reaching conclusions were reached — on rent rationalisation, on
integrated estates, on house ownership, on rehabilitation, above all on
the undesirability of high-rise flats.

It was quite quickly agreed that the Executive should start by assuming the functions, and taking over the staff, of the Housing Trust, thereby providing itself at any rate with a headquarters and a ready-made administrative nucleus: and this took place in October 1971. The next largest housing authority, Belfast Corporation, was to hand over its functions on 3rd January 1972; those of the remaining councils were taken over in five tranches between April and October 1972; and those of the three Development Commissions followed last. In the meanwhile, the crucial top full-time posts in the new organisation had to be defined and advertised; interviews held; and appointments made. Of these, by far the most important was that of Director-General: and the Board counted itself fortunate in obtaining the services of Harry Simpson, then director of housing of Lambeth, widely known and respected as one of the most imaginative and experienced experts in housing in the British Isles. The first director of finance, Jack Brown, came from the Housing Trust; the first director of housing management, John Lazenbatt, from Belfast Corporation; the first director of development, Rae Evans, from Lambeth; the first director of administration, Peter O'Hara, from the private sector. All were in post by the early months of 1972, and the real work of the Executive could then begin.

It is always hard to tell how far events, or institutions, are shaped by personalities: but there can by no doubt that, between them, Desmond Lorimer as first chairman and Harry Simpson as first director-general exerted enormous, and wholly beneficial, influence on the development of the new organisation; and especially on its establishment, from the outset, as a genuinely fair, impartial and non-sectarian body, so seen by the great majority of the people of Northern Ireland. In many ways, the talents of these two men were complementary: Lorimer, the shrewd, capable, efficient man of business, inherently conservative with a small 'c', impatient of bureaucrats and politicians alike: Simpson, who had started as a rent-collector, the experienced and somewhat radical housing specialist with a strong social conscience, and an intense dislike of bigotry and prejudice in all their forms. They commanded great respect; and while many politicians, councillors, and even officials, of the old school disliked and resented the new body which had usurped their own powers of patronage, yet between them Lorimer and Simpson were successful in establishing to a considerable degree the independence and freedom of action of the Board without incurring the implacable hostility of those whose powers had been taken from them. In this task (at any time a difficult one, in the troubled time of 1971-72 an exceptionally arduous one) they were well supported by the first Board members and directors, between them representing a wide spread of backgrounds; and especially the vice-chairman, James O'Hara, who had served for two years on the Board of the Housing Trust, so importing an element of continuity with the best element in the previous regime. Chairman, vice-chairman and Board members were all part-time and, at this period, unpaid (at their own wish): yet were called upon to devote a great deal of time and energy to the daunting task which faced them, for this was a very bad time indeed in Northern Ireland. Two years had passed since the rioting, barricades, and population movements of the summer of 1969; it was on 15th August that year that a whole street of houses in Bombay Street had been burned out: despite genuine reforms, polarisation and antagonism had got worse not better: the 9th of August 1971 saw the imposition by Brian Faulkner's government of internment, followed by an enormous upsurge of violence — rioting, bombing, murder, intimidation, squatting; the burning of almost 300 houses in Farringdon Gardens and adjoining streets; the flight of over 2,000 families from their homes in Belfast within a period of three weeks. In August too, a province-wide rent and rates strike was declared in protest against internment, as part of a widespread campaign of civil disobedience. The resources of the Housing Trust, the Belfast Corporation and the Londonderry Development Commission were stretched to the utmost in the late summer and autumn of 1971 by the need to make emergency provision for the suddenly homeless; to repair constant bomb and fire damage to private houses as well as to the publicly-owned stock; to grapple with the problems posed by intimidation and squatting (both organised and unorganised), constant street fighting, and the intervention of paramilitary bodies on both sides; robberies and armed attacks on rent collectors; and a rent and rates strike affecting a third of the public sector. The Board of the Executive was powerless: until it had acquired housing functions, premises, staff, and a structure of command, it had to remain on the sidelines. Even the best-organised and administered of housing authorities might have been excused for cracking under the strain of those weeks; no circumstances could have been less propitious for the undertaking of a major reorganisation of a crucial welfare function — or, for that matter, the recruitment of new staff. More than once, bombs exploded in the close vicinity in the middle of interviews for senior posts: so furnishing a novel test of stamina — which candidates (which interviewers?) managed not to flinch when the bang interrupted the questioning. Nevertheless, the work went ahead with less dislocation than might have been expected; and by the early spring of 1972, the Executive was a functioning entity with a stock of some 70,000 dwellings.

The most urgent and immediate matter, of course, was the adoption in April 1973 — and equally important and still more novel, publication — of a single standard points scheme governing the allocation of houses.

The workings of this, however, were greatly distorted by the absolute priority which had to be accorded to emergency applicants; indeed, for a period of some years, there were many districts where only those on the emergency lists had a chance of being rehoused. This is turn caused friction between long-standing residents and 'strangers'; the sympathy accorded to refugees did not extend so far as to include acceptance of their claims to be awarded vacant houses in priority to natives of the town, village or district concerned. Although the early points scheme served well enough in the first years of the Executive, opposition to some of its provisions — especially from councillors for the dormitory suburbs around Belfast — made necessary a major review, and a number of adjustments, completed in 1976.

At the same time, it became necessary to consider how, if at all, allocation policy should reflect the uncomfortable existence of the sectarian divide. Should applicants be unrestricted or restricted, in naming their areas of choice? Should religious segregation be recognised de facto, or should an attempt be made to direct applicants into mixed ('integrated', in the then jargon) estates? Should applicants be asked, on a voluntary basis, to state their own religious beliefs — or their preference for a home in a Catholic, Protestant, or mixed estate? These questions were largely answered for the Executive: at a time when families were still fleeing from their homes for very fear, there was no possibility of expecting them to choose or accept new homes in areas where they would not feel safe.

Another early decision, reached with much reluctance, was forced upon the Board: the number of armed robberies of the Executive's rent collectors was such that, in fairness to staff, it became necessary in April 1973 to abandon the old door-to-door system, and adopt payment by post office giro. Between April 1972 and March 1973, no less than £15,000 was stolen in 44 successful armed robberies, leaving aside the number of unsuccessful ones. This change of policy, however, was a great loss, for with it went the former close and regular contact with tenants, one of the most desirable elements in good housing management, and one which the Housing Trust in particular had organised with marked success. The criticism has been made that the Executive could and should have carried on with door-to-door visits in areas which were not disturbed, rather than imposing universally an arrangement by which 'tenants pay their rent unobtrusively and safely', and that its comprehensive role actually 'hindered its effectiveness' in this respect. But, to one of those faced with the actual decision-making, this looks like academic carping. In the first place, the difficulties of administering simultaneously two quite different methods of rent collection, and presenting them without choice to the public, would have been very great.

Second, it is from just such kinds of differentiation as this that accusations of improper discrimination sprang. Third, what was to prevent the robbers from simply transferring their activities to the areas where the visitors were still carrying large sums of cash on their persons?

It was decided in 1973 that the Executive should rationalise rents across the entire province, so that identical dwellings would not command widely differing rents in different geographical locations. So great had been the disparities in policy and practice between the different predecessor authorities, however, that this proved more difficult than expected. Due to the need to impose individual increases by modest instalments, especially in years when the overall level of rents had to be increased, it took more than ten years to come near completing the process of rationalisation. And by then new inequities had crept into the system as a result of changes in design standards, in historic costs, and in the inflation rate: so that a new and more sensitive review of the rents scheme had to be undertaken in 1982-83.

It was also decided in 1973 that a province-wide rent rebate scheme should be introduced: this system was then a comparative novelty, though simple rebate schemes had already been introduced by the Housing Trust and Belfast Corporation. Their schemes were adapted and extended; they were later overtaken by the national scheme; and ultimately by housing benefit.

Another important and, in the event, influential decision was that the secretive and introspective policies of the old Housing Trust should be reversed. From the outset, the Board, firmly led in the right direction by Desmond Lorimer and Harry Simpson, determined to adopt a policy of the greatest possible openness; and gave very high priority to the establishment of a strong information unit, capable of maintaining effective liaison with public representatives as well as the press, and setting out to keep tenants and those on the waiting lists informed of their rights. At the same time, tenant consultation procedures were established and it was made plain that staff were expected to see that residents were fairly presented with the alternative courses of action when schemes affecting their districts were under consideration. All this was highly novel in the then very closed society of Northern Ireland; and had far-reaching repercussions in other branches of the public services.

Equally important was the determination of the new Board to equip itself to carry out the research, and obtain the basic facts and statistics, upon which alone sensible decision-making could be based. A strong research and corporate planning group was established, with instructions to take prompt steps to remedy the woeful lack of reliable information about housing matters in Northern Ireland. The first need was to carry out, at the earliest possible date, a House Condition Survey comparable to those produced in Great Britain in 1967, 1971, and every five years thereafter. This was a major undertaking; in the event, the first (and invaluable) Northern Ireland House Condition Survey was carried out in 1974: and similar surveys have been completed, and have proved their value, in every fifth year since then. It is unfortunate that the Northern Ireland surveys are not carried out in the same years as their British counterparts, which reduces their usefulness for purposes of comparison; but to have waited until 1976 before carrying out the first such survey would have been quite unacceptable, given the Board's pressing need for reliable factual information as to the extent and characteristics of the problems it had been charged to solve. Ever since then, the research and planning group within the Executive has performed an invaluable function, and one which a smaller organisation could ill have afforded; and has earned the healthy respect of academic and other commentators.

In the field of design and development, a number of fundamental decisions were taken very early in the life of the Executive. Four working parties, consisting of Board members and senior staff, had been set up at an early stage; I was asked by Demond Lorimer to chair the development working party which prepared an influential report, adopted by the full Board in March 1973, on a 'Strategy for New Building'. This statement of policy is printed in the Appendix and, to the best of my knowledge, has never been superseded: certainly throughout my own time as chairman the principles embodied in it remained little altered. It was agreed that, in urban areas, a policy of low-rise building to fairly high densities should be adopted; very high densities would be avoided and there would be no new high-rise or deck-access blocks of flats — though inescapably, those already in the pipeline had to be completed. (Some of them have had to be demolished already.) Harry Simpson and Rae Evans brought with them from Lambeth the minimum standards of layout, space and design laid down twenty years earlier by the Parker-Morris report; these had previously been employed in Northern Ireland only by the Craigavon Development Commission, and constituted a great improvement on earlier local standards. As an interim measure, standard house designs recommended by the National Building Agency were adopted. But it was also decided to set on foot the design of a completely new range of house-types, a process complicated by the introduction of compulsory metrication: so that the new houses, designed to metric dimensions and Parker-Morris space standards, were (when the first of them reached completion a few years later) different in very many ways from, and arguably very much better than, the houses built by the Housing Trust or the other previous authorities: though of course both costs and rents tended to be higher too.

A new contracts and tendering system had to be quickly established; and adapted to take account of the fact that, in troubled areas, many builders now found it impossible to obtain performance bonds from the insurance companies. The Report of the Rowland Committee (see page 51) and a number of other shortcomings which had come to light independently, particularly in the 'vetting' procedure adopted as a substitute for bonds, led to a major review of contracts procedure in 1980-81.

Staffing, appointment, promotion, and personnel matters raised many difficult questions. The Board succeeded early in its life in establishing generally amicable relations with the trade unions, staff association, and interim staff commission, with which it had to deal; but there were copious difficulties in assimilating the staff of the fifty-odd predecessor authorities, with widely varying pay scales and terms of service. After considerable debate, it was decided that local authority, rather than civil service, scales and terms, should prevail. There were many obstacles to be overcome nonetheless: and one very fundamental one. The Act establishing the Executive had conferred upon all those previously working for more than 50 per cent of their time in the housing field the right of transfer to the Executive, without detriment to pay or terms of service. Yet some of the local authority employees whom the Executive was thus bound to take on were the very people who had been administering the loaded and discriminatory housing practices — or those believed to be so — which the Executive had been set up to prevent. How to overcome this dilemma? Although the great majority of those taken over were certainly honourable and impartial public servants, it remained very necessary to guard against any repetition of the bigoted practices of the past, particularly in the fields of allocations, and of staff appointments.

The only solution available to the Board was, to set up strong central personnel and housing management units, under its own direct control, and to ensure that local discretion, and procedures, at area and district level, were subject to the closest possible checks and regulation. This was a cumbersome, laborious, slow and inefficient system; it led moreover to the involvement of the Board itself in a far greater degree of detailed supervision than any sane administrator would elsewhere have conceived possible; but there was no other means of securing what was, after all, one of the Executive's primary purposes. Happily, it has proved possible over the years to relax the degree of rigid centralised control to a considerable extent: but in the early years, that would have been to take an unacceptable risk.

More recently, allegations were made that the Executive had over-reacted, and was actively discriminating in recruitment against Protestants. In particular, it was said that there were disproportionate numbers of Catholics in the South Region, in the personnel department, and in the staff of the Executive as a whole. These allegations were investigated over a three-year period by the Fair Employment Agency, and all were disproved: indeed, in its 1985 Report, the Agency gave the Executive a clean bill of health, finding that 'by and large equality of opportunity is being provided ... for both Protestants and Roman Catholics.'

The Board faced also some difficult questions in relation to the employment of outside professional consultants — architects, quantity surveyors, engineers, and others: as also the question whether it should rely on a direct labour force to carry out repairs, or should rely on contractors. In a community as small as Northern Ireland, such decisions have large consequences for the livelihoods of many people. In the event, it was decided — much to the relief of the professions, and of the craft unions, involved — to carry on much as our predecessor bodies (taken in aggregate) had done; to maintain a balance between the employment of in-house professionals and consultants; to retain the direct labour units where they already existed, and to continue to employ private contractors elsewhere in competition with them.

Most of these were routine decisions which would have faced any new housing organisation in normal circumstances: but there were other pressing and difficult problems directly springing from the current Troubles. Should the emergency repair service, set up to provide swift first-aid in the wake of bomb-damage, be available to private sector tenants and owner-occupiers as well as to the Executive's tenants? Yes, it was decided: and so it still is: the emergency teams by now so experienced that they are often on the scene, with loads of hardboard and tarpaulin, before the bomb explodes. (Quite early on, its members requested, and received, a special footwear allowance; the best of boots or shoes do not last long on a constant footing of broken glass.)

What could be done to help owner-occupiers and others compelled by bomb, fire, threats or intimidation to leave their homes? Before long, a whole range of novel support provisions emerged. In the first place, the Executive (to some extent following the precedent set by Belfast Corporation) declared its willingness to buy houses, available on the market in the ordinary way, and rent them to those on the emergency lists who could not be allocated a house in an area acceptable to them: subject to price limits. This procedure, though useful, was necessarily slow, since the Executive had to go through all the procedures of valuation, and bidding on the open market, and was often outbid. Second, there was, and still is, a scheme for the purchase of evacuated dwellings (SPED): in certain circumstances, where the police are prepared to certify that the lives of an owner-occupier or his family will be at risk if he does not move, the Executive will buy at valuation, and later resell (if it can) the house in question. Third, the Executive was forced to come to the rescue of those seeking to buy perfectly good houses in the many areas where building societies, scared for their security, refused to lend. A home loans scheme was introduced in 1972, not dissimilar to the mortgage schemes run by many British local authorities, but designed primarily to support a large sector of the housing market which had been totally blighted by the (understandable) nervousness of the building societies and their surveyors: a task in which, happily, it proved successful.

The problems of squatting and intimidation, not yet extinct, have given rise to a long series of policy dilemmas. Some squatters, at the worst period of the Troubles a considerable proportion, have no moral justification for their illegal actions; they are thugs using strong-arm tactics to obtain for themselves priority over others more deserving. (The exposure on television of some especially outrageous cases in the end helped to turn public opinion against squatting as a means of queue-jumping.) But there are some — often abandoned unmarried mothers, or battered wives, or teenagers expelled from broken homes — whose cases are more pathetic than culpable. And, during the population movements of the worst fighting and rioting of the late 'sixties and early 'seventies, there were many families who squatted, in despair and desperation, in houses evacuated by equally frightened members of the other denomination. As with squatting cases, so with intimidation cases: some are more, some less, deserving of sympathy than others. Quite early on, it became clear that some who claimed that they had been threatened or intimidated had found an easy passport to a better house. (Just as, in the early days of the riots, the voluntary welfare organisations, offering relief, enquired helpfully, but naively, how much cash had been lost in the house; the first applicants gave honest answers, but as the word spread, so the sums alleged to have been hidden under mattresses sometimes grew astronomically). Over the years, no headache of the Executive has been greater than the necessity of steering a policy in squatting and intimidation cases which first, is fair and humane, second, is as little as possible open to abuse, and third, gives no encouragement to those who orchestrate such activities or take the law into their own hands.

Comparable problems sprang from the rent and rates strike of 1972, which was to drag on for years: there were still nearly 4,000 tenants on rent strike in March 1975: and there are still families whose accumulated arrears date back to that period. Those who called the strike were so sure of the justice of their cause that they felt no hesitation in calling on the whole Catholic community to withhold rent, in the belief that sooner or later an amnesty must be granted. In this they were mistaken; they failed to realise that any such amnesty would have been, of necessity, highly discriminatory against the law-abiding members of both communities. Serious consequences were to follow. First, there was to be considerable hardship for those less provident rent-strikers who had failed to put their money aside against the day of reckoning. Government was constrained to introduce a series of methods of rent recovery, including the systems known as 'rent direct' and 'B.A.B.' (Benefits Allocation Branch) which clawed back the arrears (in instalments) from those in receipt of benefits or wages from public funds. Whilst this was indignantly attacked by the left as a monstrous invasion of individual liberties, and ultimately moderated by a Labour Government, it was not really an unreasonable expedient so long as the instalments were not fixed unreasonably high. The nettle which had to be grasped was, unfortunately, a very political and even sectarian one: for, second, and most unhappily, rent arrears and militant republicanism came to be associated with each other in the Protestant folk-mind; so that, even years later, when rent arrears were far more likely to be badges of unemployment, poverty, and hardship, than of deliberate political protest, Protestant tenants continued to resent with bitterness subsidising, as they saw it, the deliberate withholding of rent and rates by Catholics. Third, the rent strike added sharply to the financial problems faced by the infant Executive.

It had originally been intended that the Executive, like the Housing Trust before it, should be more or less self-financing: it would be entitled to the same newbuild subsidies as the private sector, but should thereafter balance its building costs and its loan charges against its receipts from rents, so far as necessary by spreading its costs across old stock and new. Some rent increases were from the outset seen as unavoidable: from the earliest days, Desmond Lorimer preached that those who desired better housing conditions must be prepared to pay more for them. The position was complicated by the fact that the Executive inherited deficiencies on rent account from a large proportion of its predecessor authorities. This difficulty was increased by the effects of the rent strike; the additional costs associated with the continuation of civil unrest; rising costs of labour and materials; the unwillingness of government to contemplate rent rises at a time of sharply rising living costs and inflation (permission to increase rents by an average of 12 pence per week was turned down by the Ministry in March 1973!); together these drove the Executive, within the first five years of its existence, into a system of deficit financing which would have scandalised its thrifty and parsimonious predecessors.

Another major disappointment was to be the failure to achieve the over-ambitious newbuild programe of 10,000 new dwellings a year optimistically adopted by government and Executive alike at the outset of its existence. It had seemed, on the basis of the aggregate performance figures of all the predecessor authorities, that this might have been attainable, given the economies of scale and the more efficient per-formance expected of the Executive. But a number of factors were left out of account. Not surprisingly, the efforts of the local authorities had tailed off sharply in the last two years of their exercise of housing functions; so that there were many fewer new schemes on the shelf, and many fewer sites available in the land bank, than had been anticipated. The processes of inner-city redevelopment, with the painfully slow pro-cedures for vesting, clearance and decanting, could not be speeded up without unacceptable incursions into the legal rights of individuals. The processes of recruiting and staffing the new organisation, and bringing the land acquisition and design teams up to full productivity, took far longer than had been hoped. The continuing troubles, and the enforced population movements which continued throughout the early 'seventies, caused untold delays.

There was, too, the intractable problem of providing new houses to relieve the overwhelming pressure on Catholic West Belfast, to which thousands of families had fled from previously mixed districts. At first, it had been hoped that overspill housing at Ligoniel, at New Mossley, and in Newtownabbey (all to the north of the city) might have proved acceptable as mixed communities; but the hope was in vain. In March 1973, a meeting took place at Stormont from which there sprang a policy whose essentials were the speeding up of completion of the large Twinbrook estate, and the relaxation of the planning stop-line to permit the building of another large new estate at Poleglass, to the west of the city. The site was in territory considered 'Protestant'. The decision was a highly controversial one, and was to cause endless sectarian antagonism over the ensuing years — on a few occasions, inside the boardroom as well as outside it. It is now clear that the decision was, despite the unhappy circumstances surrounding its birth and development, a correct one; the Poleglass development, though still incomplete, has been a success in its own right, and has succeeded in relieving very con-siderably the pressures on inner-city West Belfast. But it was not possible in the short-term to do much to increase housing provision in the west of the city; vesting, planning and design procedures took long years; and in the meanwhile, the programme continued to lag behind the extent of need, expecially in and around Belfast.

Great efforts were made. In June 1974, Gerry McSheffrey succeeded Rae Evans as Director of Development, with a remit to accord increased output higher priority even than improved quality; Desmond Lorimer personally chaired weekly progress-chasing meetings intended to iron out the snags and delays; even so, newbuild completions were never to exceed 7,676 in the best year, 1977. And that figure was not achieved without a measurable cost: quality of design and layout suffered to some extent: the houses were sometimes built more because of the instant availability of sites than because of the existence of demonstrable need in the areas concerned. With hindsight, Harry Simpson's warnings against the the dangers of playing the 'numbers game' in order to placate politicians and public opinion were proved justified. In 1974 also, he was appointed to the important post of controller of housing with the Greater London Council; though it would not have been right to stand in the way of so notable a promotion, his loss was much felt by Board members and senior staff alike. He was succeeded by a local man, formerly a hospital administrator, Bob Spence.

At this time, there was a perceptible shift in public opinion away from new build towards modernisation and rehabilition of the existing stock. This took three forms: in the country areas there was a sudden upsurge of demand for the improvement of the old rural cottages. Some local authorities had continued to build only slightly updated versions of the 19th century labourers' cottages, lacking bathrooms, indoor lavatories, even running water, sewage and electricity, right up to the date of the Executive's takeover. It was often the very same councillors who now, in the name of progress, demanded that their constituents be immediately provided with all modern amenities: in all cases an expensive and difficult, in some localities an impossible, demand. In the cities, the revulsion against the processes of large-scale, wholesale, redevelopment had gathered force, and was stiffened by the territorial imperatives of sectarianism. The emotional movement of protest against what was called the 'Rape and Plunder of the Shankill', for example, was in part fed by genuinely held belief in the desirability of regrouping a scattered community; but in part also by a desire to hold Protestant ground against the risk of invaders from the adjacent overcrowding of Catholic West Belfast. This was a heady mixture, in evidence in many other confrontation areas, and fuelled too by the very definite shift in emphasis in Great Britain from redevelopment towards rehabilitation. The third element in the change of policy which took place around 1975 was the pressing need to bring back into use the thousands of homes, especially though not exclusively in Belfast, which had been evacuated, vandalised, bomb-damaged, blocked-up, or otherwise rendered unusable by the bitter fighting, shooting, rioting and bombing of the past unhappy years.

In most of the central areas of Belfast, the sectarian boundary-lines, laid down a hundred or more years ago, stood unaltered; but around the edges, and especially in the post-war suburbs to the north-west of the city, massive population movements had taken place. Sometimes the aggressors used fire and bullet to take over new territory: sometimes the dispossessed set fire to their homes as they left, on occasions pouring wet cement down the lavatory bowls in order to render the sewage system unusable by the invaders. Whole estates lay bullet-scarred and largely unoccupied; but such was the pressure of need, families were anxious to move in again as soon as the new sectarian boundary-lines had to some extent stabilised themselves. Squatters began to move in, often under the protection of paramilitary organisations, and to carry out self-help repairs. In these circumstances, it became imperative for the Executive to regain control; but before it could hope to do so, it must render these estates at least minimally habitable again.

But this was no easy task. Reputable contractors had no desire to risk their lives, and those of their men, in such contentious areas. Protestant workmen were, not without good reason, afraid to venture into some areas, Catholic workmen equally afraid to enter others. Since in Belfast, slaters and tilers are traditionally Catholics, and since bricklayers are traditionally Protestant, this situation posed almost insoluble problems. Foremen, supervisors and clerks of works were at particular risk, and subject to exceptional pressures. The position in parts of Derry, and some other strife-torn provincial towns, was little different. Yet all — including government — were agreed that the work must somehow be done.

It was in this situation that lay the roots of the Rowland Commission of Inquiry. By 1974, disquieting rumours had got about, not only of escalating costs for rehabilitation work in the strife-torn estates, not only of excessive profits and fraudulent activities, but also of actual involvement by paramilitary organisations in unsavoury rackets of every kind. Questions were first asked in Parliament in the autumn of 1975. There was clear evidence that costs had run out of control; and, unsurprisingly, that supervision on the ground had been lacking. There was little or no hard evidence however — again, unsurprisingly — of actual paramilitary involvement or racketeering. The rumours continued; the reputation of the Executive began to suffer sharply. At length James O'Hara, who had succeeded Desmond Lorimer as chairman in January 1976, with my full support (I had by then succeeded him as vice-chairman) decided in December 1977 himself to call for a public inquiry. Many experienced people advised against this course; but I believe now, as I believed then, that it was the right decision, and that the air could have been cleared in no other way. It was sad, nonetheless, that the laborious sittings of the inquiry were to overshadow unhappily the last year, otherwide a fruitful and successful one, of James O'Hara's three-year term of office.

The Report of the Rowland Commission, when it was finally published in June 1979, exonerated the Executive from the gravest charges of collaboration with paramilitaries, while making a number of criticisms of the contractual and other procedures used by it at a time of exceptional stress. Some of these matters had already been remedied: a number of individuals had left the employment of the Executive: action was taken with some promptitude to act on the findings of the Inquiry. It did not, I believe, have any long-term adverse effects on the standing or performance of the Executive, unpleasant as the episode was to live through at the time.

In the meanwhile, the mutual confidence between ministers and civil service on the one hand, Board and staff of the Executive on the other, had not been unscathed. Throughout the Labour administration of 1974 to 1979, housing had been accorded a high degree of political priority, and funds were almost unlimited: it was rather the Executive's capacity to spend them efficiently that was in question. In parallel with the proceedings of the Rowland Commission, ministers and Department became more and more concerned to obtain better value for money in the housing field. D.O.C.S. (Department of the Civil Service) efficiency experts were sent in to examine the management structure of the Executive — the first of an interminable series of consultants' reports by which the Executive was to be afflicted over the years. By 1976, Ray Carter (the minister) and Ken Bloomfield (the permanent secretary) had reached the conclusion that the Executive was unwieldy, cumbersome and overcentralised: and that an extensive process of delegation of decision-making, and regionalisation, was required.

This conclusion was viewed with suspicion and dislike within the Executive for two principal reasons. In the first place, the centralised system of controls had been deliberately established in order to prevent the growth, at local levels, of discriminatory practices (whether in recruitment, allocations or elsewhere) of the kind whose existence, or supposed existence, had brought the Executive into being. It was feared by some, myself included, that it was too soon to loosen this central grip without real risk of a resurgence of undesirable practices: or, at any rate, allegations of their existence. Secondly, in the volatile state of Northern Ireland party politics at that time, it was feared that a process of regionalisation might render too easy the break-up of the Executive into six separate entities, which would then be at the mercy of local politicians throughout the province; who might be expected to undo much of what had been achieved.

In the end, regionalisation was imposed with a pretty high hand on a most unwilling Board; but the fears of its opponents proved, in the event, unfounded. That this was so resulted largely from the fairly peculiar structure of regionalisation ultimately devised — one which left an unresolved dichotomy between the areas of influence of functional directorates at the centre, and the delegated authority for the execution of policy now vested in six regional controllers; both, always subject to the unchallenged responsibility, in matters of policy, of the Board. This worked out surprisingly well in practice, due partly to the common sense and goodwill exhibited by all the senior officers concerned; and partly to the quiet skills of a senior civil servant, John Murray, seconded into the Executive for two years as director of reorganisation, though more widely known (ultimately with respect and affection) as 'the cuckoo in the nest'. To some extent, it has met the criticisms of over-centralisation, bureaucracy, and 'facelessness' to which the Executive has always been subject; but it cannot be said that all such criticisms have been allayed; and it may be that further delegation of responsibility to the regional controllers, still falling short of the delegation of policy-making, could yet be salutary.

One subject on which opinion was for long deeply divided within the Executive was the question whether or not houses should be offered for sale to tenants. In the latter half of 1978, the members of the Board succeeded in reaching agreement on a compromise, with the approval of Labour ministers, under which houses would be offered for sale, with moderate discounts and subject to clawback of profits on resale, in those parts of the province where urgent housing need had been met; in effect, about two-thirds of the province. This scheme had not really got off the ground when it was overtaken by the fall of the Labour government, and the return of the Conservatives, in May 1979. It quickly became plain that the Executive would be expected to give effect to the new government's much more sweeping scheme for house sales, with its much more generous discounts, and its applicability right across the board irrespective of local circumstances. There were signs of a revolt: most, if not all, members of the Board were less than happy about abandoning the carefully thought-out compromise so laboriously reached only a few months earlier. I personally had great reservations. But the Government's mandate was undeniable, as was its sweeping majority at the recent general election: and ultimately even those members of the Board who had been most deeply opposed to large-scale house sales were constrained to acknowledge that, as a matter of democracy, the newly elected government was entitled to the final say.

This was a period of many changes. As chairman, I had succeeded James O'Hara in January; Philip Goodhart became minister with responsibility for housing, under Humphrey Atkins, in June; and at this

**Plate 14**

There is a long, formal and royalist tradition of Protestant gable-painting; this coronation portrait of King George VI and Queen Elizabeth dated from 1937. It had much faded by 1963, when the photograph was taken; since then, all of Little Ship Street (in the docks area of Belfast) has been demolished.

**Plate 15**

*Above*, a pair of recent gable murals in South Belfast, dating from 1984, commemorating the Rev. Robert Bradford, MP for the constituency, murdered in 1981. *Below*, Glenalpin Street, in the same area of Belfast, decorated for the annual Twelfth of July celebrations of the Battle of the Boyne: even the kerbstones painted red, white and blue. The plaque to the left of King Billy reads 'We will never forsake the blue skies of Ulster for the grey mists of an Irish Republic'; that to his right, 'Ulster is not for sale – No surrender.'

**Plate 16**

**Plate 17**

Republican murals are a much
more recent tradition; owing
something to the Paris *émeutes* of
1968; less stylised, more explicit,
publicising present-day violence
rather than the battles of the
seventeenth century.

**Plate 18**

**Plate 19**

**Plate 21**

*Left and above*, Bombay Street, a Catholic street off the Falls Road, burned out by Protestants from the nearby Shankill Road on the night of 15th August 1969. *Left*, a vigilante guards the wreckage. *Above*, the shells of burned-out houses bitterly inscribed 'We only defend' — 'We do not burn our neighbours out.'

**Plate 22**

*Above*, the Glenard estate in North Belfast photographed soon after its completion in 1938. It quickly acquired an unhappy reputation due to squatting by victims of the riots of 1935, followed by a prolonged rent and rates strike. All the street names were changed before the war; but trouble flared again in the summer of 1971. *Below*, Farringdon Gardens, on the night of 9th August, when Protestant families fled as a result of intimidation, setting their homes on fire as they left.

**Plate 23**

**Plate 24**

*Above*, next morning: picking up the bits.

*Over the page:* Though less speedily and dramatically, vandalism produces the same results as bomb damage. The pretty houses at Aughton Terrace, Donegall Pass had to be demolished soon after this photograph was taken. (**Plate 25**)

time, the post of director-general was abolished. Bob Spence retired, and John Gorman was appointed chief executive and vice-chairman. It became plain, quite quickly, that under a Conservative government, the housing programme was not to be exempt from cuts either in cash or in manpower terms: programmes were slashed: moratoria were imposed: rents were raised sharply. This was a period of very great strain; had it not been for the inflow of money from the relaunched house sales programme, the Executive would soon have been forced to abandon its newbuild programme altogether.

This situation brought forth a two-fold response. In the first place, a major campaign was mounted to demonstrate factually that housing need was far sharper in Northern Ireland than in Great Britain; and to enlist public opinion generally, and that of all the local political parties, in support of the restoration of housing funds, especially for Belfast. This was ultimately successful: when David Mitchell and James Prior succeeded Philip Goodhart and Humphrey Atkins in January 1981, they accepted the arguments and restored housing to the top of the local list of social priorities. This was a great relief, even though funds still remained more tightly restricted than could have been wished.

Accordingly, the second branch of the Board's self-help policy retained its importance: much energy was devoted to searching for additional funds wherever it seemed they might be found. The attempt to find support (through the use of the Executive's accumulated Home Loans Fund) in the City of London did not meet with treasury approval and had to be shelved. The attempt to obtain financial aid from the EEC in Brussels was, if indirectly, more successful; though in the end, opposition from West Germany to the principle of using community funds for housing purposes blocked the original proposals, while leaving open a route by which it would be possible for government to increase its housing allocation to Belfast. More directly successful was the approach to the building societies movement; in previous years, there had been a net outflow of investors' funds from Northern Ireland, but it proved possible to reverse this dramatically, much to the benefit of overall housing conditions in the province. Similar partnerships with the Builders' Federation, with its New Homes Marketing Board, with the Co-Ownership Housing Association, with the housing associations movement, and energetic experiments with self-build schemes, homesteading and equity sharing, kept alive a disproportionately buoyant level of housing activity despite the depths of recession, the continuing Troubles, and the continuing retrenchment of public expenditure.

It would be wrong to conclude, however, that this diversion of effort towards collaboration with (in some respects, direct involvement in) the private sector led to neglect of the problems of the Executive's own tenants. The financial year 1983-4 was largely dominated by two initiatives: the introduction, in November 1983, of the single system of housing benefit (in substitution for the former dual system of rent rebates and housing allowances) more swiftly and smoothly, and with more care for the interests of those in need, than had been the case in Great Britain. And, the preparation (after prolonged and contentious public con-sultation) of a new scheme to redistribute more equitably the total rent burden as between the occupiers of different categories of accom-modation. At the same time, the Executive's systems for administering maintenance, both short-term and long-term, came under close scrutiny; and a major review of strategy was undertaken with a view to releasing a greater proportion of total funds for the modernisation and up-grading of purpose-built stock.

This, then, was the position reached when I handed over to my suc-cessor as chairman, after a first term of three years, and a second term of two years and three months, on 31st March 1984. In the thirteen years of its existence, the Executive had broadly succeeded in establishing and maintaining a reputation for fairness and impartiality; it had completed 56,926 new dwellings, with another 3,256 under construction, all still (despite government policy) to Parker-Morris standards; urgent housing need in most parts of the province outside Belfast had been met, and in some places over-provision was beginning to make an appearance; though unfitness rates were still unacceptably high — far higher than in England — yet a sizeable reduction had been brought about; despite booming house sales, waiting lists were falling and the rate of relets rising; private sector newbuild starts, especially at the lower end of the market, were increasing steadily, and new modes of tenure, such as equity sharing and co-ownership, had opened the possibility of home ownership to many who previously could not have contemplated it; the quality, design and layout of the Executive's new developments, especially in the cities of Belfast and Londonderry but also in many of the smaller towns and villages, had proved practical and popular, and were widely admired. It was possible to feel that, though a vast amount remained to be done, a vast amount had been achieved since the first Board meeting of the Executive at Stormont on 13th May 1971.

# House, or Home:
# Need, or Desire?

Is there such a thing as a 'right' to a house? And, if so, is it the right merely to the basic necessity of crude shelter: or is it the right to a nice house in a particular place? Twenty years ago, the question could hardly have been posed; but today many people consider that they have an actual entitlement, legal or moral, to be provided with a house by the community. And, perhaps, not just a house but a home; and, not just for one life but for several generations; and, not just any house, but a good house with all mod. cons.; and, not just anywhere, but in the nicest possible surroundings and convenient to jobs, shops, friends and family.

There is some theoretical basis, at any rate, for the claim to shelter; the United Nations Declaration of Human Rights expressly states — 'everyone has the right to a standard of living adequate for the health and well-being of himself and his family, including food, clothing, housing and medical care . . .' And, of course, it has been accepted since the latter half of the 19th century that sub-standard housing carries with it serious risks of disease, epidemic and child mortality, as well as other grave social ill-effects: so that it can be argued that the provision of good-quality housing is at least as much for the protection of the community as a whole, as for the benefit of the individual occupier. Nevertheless, the right to a home, like the right to a job, while entirely legitimate as an aspiration, is hard to provide in practice, especially in times of recession, unemployment, and financial stringency.

And, just what standard is required to secure 'the health and well-being' of 'everyone . . . and his family'? By third world standards, a tent, a packing-case shanty, a cave, even a large-dimension drainpipe, may meet this standard. In the developed countries, the itinerant who wandered the roads (as James Stephens put it in 1912) might long for 'a real nice house with clean windows and a shiny knocker on the door, and smoke in the chimney.' Public expectations are now such that people in atrocious housing conditions will flatly refuse offers of accommodation in dwellings which for one reason or another are seen as undesirable, even though they may be quite modern, with good space standards, and all conveniences. The country-dweller who, a few short years ago, was perfectly content to accept a tilley lamp, a coal-fired range, a bucket in an outside shed for lavatory, old car seats for kitchen chairs, and an old-fashioned wireless set, now has very different aspirations. Why should not he, like the town-dweller, expect to enjoy indoor lavatory, bathroom, hot press; electric light and power; central heating; cooker, hoover, fridge, deep-freeze, washing machine, spin dryer, washing-up machine; television set, video, record deck? All these over and above the taken-for-granted commodities of a snug, dry, weather-tight, spacious house, with up-to-date fittings and ample indoor and outdoor storage space.

All this serves to emphasise the important distinction, in housing terms, between 'need', 'demand', and 'desire'. Nothing is more fundamental to a balanced understanding of housing problems. Need can be objectively measured, with a fair degree of accuracy, by the use of sophisticated pointing systems. Demand can be quantified pretty accurately. But the validity of desire for change is, for all practical purposes, incapable of comparative measurement. Yet it would be a rash housing administrator indeed who left demand and desire altogether out of his calculations, and concentrated exclusively on the provision of units of accommodation to meet proven need.

Indeed, the very definitions of these terms are in permanent flux. As Donnison and Ungerson remark in *Housing Policy,* 'demands for housing are complex and constantly changing. *They are also insatiable.'* And as they also explain, the aim in the early post-war years was to provide a *separate* home for every *family* that *needs* one; while by the mid-sixties that aim had become a *good* home at a price they can *afford* for everyone who *wants* one. And, one may add, by the eighties this had been jacked up further still: while the objective of providing *each* member of *every* household with a *separate bedroom* was still far from having been attained, there was a growing demand from single people, amongst them young adolescents fleeing the nest, for a *separate home* (needless to say, a *good* one at an *affordable* price) for every *individual* (rather than family or household) who *wants* one. (My italics throughout). Although they are likely, at most times and most places, to be extremely difficult, if not impossible, of attainment; and although they pose expensive and often insoluble problems for those concerned with the provision of housing; there is nonetheless nothing inherently unreasonable about these aspirations, which have always been those of the better-off sections of the community.

Housing desire can take many forms; one of which is the desire to stay put. Very many people look on a house as a permanent family home, not necessarily for one generation only. Country people particularly, be they farmers or labourers or even country-house gentry, feel a strong attachment to land and place, especially in Ireland where, since Mr Gladstone's Land Acts, the tenant farmer is totally unknown. To a lesser extent this attitude has travelled into the towns and cities: very many people in Ulster do think of their house as a permanent family *home* and centre of gravity. But of course, as children are born, grow up, leave home, in the normal cycle of family life, this means that inevitably the house may at some periods be overcrowded; at others under-occupied: a wasteful and unsatisfactory position from the community's point of view: and, economically speaking, great nonsense.

In Northern Ireland as elsewhere, the average middle-class couple takes a far more practical and down-to-earth line. The pair will probably start their married life in a small rented flat; buy a small house when the first baby arrives; move to a larger house as the family expands; move back to a smaller house or flat when the children leave home; and the survivor may hope to end his or her days in an Abbeyfield bedsitter. So, counting the homes in which they spent their own child-hood, and leaving out of account moves because of change of job, each such family is likely to occupy at least five or six dwellings in the course of one life-cycle. And at no time will the family have seriously either under- or over-occupied its home for the time being. This is no longer an entirely middle-class way of life; very few young couples who take out mortgages as first-time buyers remain in the same house for the whole 20 or 25 year life of the mortgage; whenever they can, they trade up-market within a few years. All of which is entirely logical and sensible.

It is, at the very least, arguable that the same principle should be compulsorily applied to the public sector stock as a whole. If it were possible to move people around like pawns at frequent intervals, so as to ensure that nobody was occupying more or fewer rooms than he or she needed at any given moment, then housing shortages and waiting lists would disappear almost overnight. And that is the solution which was employed in the communist bloc during the period of acute post-war housing shortage: on a child leaving home, or the death of a member of the household, those remaining could be pressingly required to move to smaller accommodation. I was told, on a recent visit to Leningrad, that this is no longer the case. Interestingly, the Stormont minister responsible for housing, William Grant, proposed the adoption of similar measures in introducing his Housing Bill of 1944; but this proposal aroused violent opposition on the back-benches and was, perhaps unsurprisingly, dropped.

It is plainly unacceptable compulsorily to deprive widows and widowers of their homes; to uproot elderly people who do not want to leave their patch or parish; to trample on everyone's toes, and to invade the reasonable liberties of the individual. From the outset, the Board of the Housing Executive decided as a principle to accept that a house is not just a house, it is a home. This was a deliberate and conscious decision, taken very early on: the inexperienced members of the new Board might not have thought of it for themselves, but their first director-general, Harry Simpson, from long years of experience, knew that it was a fundamental dilemma, on which the Executive needed to have a reasoned view. I am quite sure that it was a correct decision. Nevertheless, the balance of advantage is not as clear-cut as it may seem; for the liberties of those who *have* homes are being provided at the expense of those on the waiting-lists who lack them. There are many countries, and not only communist ones, where the ability to house everyone suitably might be thought to deserve greater priority than the personal liberties of those who already have homes.

From all this I conclude that there is a need to provide greater incentives for the voluntary resolution of mismatches between house and household. The ever-increasing number of small households, against the predominance in the stock of family-sized dwellings, lends this increased urgency. As the waiting-list has been falling over recent years, so the transfer list has been rising. The National Mobility Scheme (of which Northern Ireland forms a part), and the establishment of registers of those seeking exchanges, have helped a bit; but not yet enough. One expedient which has been left unused is the financial disincentive: the threat to cut housing benefits in cases where tenants insist on occupying premises much in excess of their needs, and where more suitable alternative accommodation is available. Harsh as this may seem, the benefit to overcrowded families might well outweigh the hardship to the under-occupying tenant.

The desire to stay on in the family home, even though it means severe under-occupation, is one thing: the desire to move, quite another. It is entirely understandable and reasonable that most people should aspire to live in the nicest possible house, and in the most pleasant possible surroundings. I strongly suspect that, if they had absolute freedom of choice without the constraints of jobs and schools, half the population of Northern Ireland would choose to live in an attractive small seaside town such as Portballintrae or Donaghadee. (Of course, in the process, they would destroy what they were looking for; the Executive has to be constantly on guard against inflated demands for additional houses near the coasts, or in villages of uncommon charm and character.)

How far should a housing authority be swayed by the desire, rather than the need, to move? Many thousands of people who are already quite adequately housed, with all the modern amenities, but who find their surroundings dreary and unattractive, or dislike their neighbours, put down their names on the transfer list for better estates; or even to better houses in the same estate. Many of those who have been longest on the waiting-list — sometimes for many years — refuse all offers of dwellings except in one particular favoured estate; if relets are few, they may never be rehoused there at all.

There are, of course, many genuine and pressing reasons for wishing to move: for example, to be nearer children or parents. But in a large proportion of cases there is no pressing *need* to move, no real reason apart from the quite legitimate desire to live in a nicer house or in better surroundings. There are some cases in which it is comparatively easy to gratify these wishes; others, where it simply is not practicable. Some of the most indignant and unreasonable complaints received by the Executive fall into this latter category. I well remember an eight-page letter accusing the Executive of discriminating unfairly against him, from a highly-pointed applicant who had turned down three offers of newly-completed houses, two of them in the estate of his first choice, because they were not in the particular street in the estate which he preferred.

It will also be true, in every street, estate or development, as in every town or city, that some houses are more desirable than others. A pleasant outlook; a group of trees, or an old hedgerow; even a small group of good neighbours: can make one house much more attractive than others apparently identical. But not everyone can have the nicest homes, nor is it possible to frame a scheme (even if it were a good idea, which it is not) to see that the nicest people get the nicest houses, and the nastiest houses go to the nastiest people. So that desire must be tempered by practicality. And there is an obverse to this: every street, estate or development has also its least desirable dwellings. The proximity of a shop or a toddlers' playground where rowdy teenagers gather at night; an adjoining factory; a blank gable that invites ball-games; a problem family as neighbours — be they burglars, paramilitaries, gypsies, tinkers, or just rowdy and anti-social — may be enough to render one house, or a whole group (comparatively) highly undesirable.

This is of course particularly the case in estates which have gone downhill and turned into hard-to-let or problem estates. Here, the better tenants will desire, with increasing eagerness and justification, to move elsewhere, however good in physical terms their existing accommodation may be. But if their desire to move is gratified, the condition of the whole estate is likely to spiral further downward, since either the house may be re-allocated to a family with lower standards, or may prove unlettable and have to be bricked up. So that, very naturally, housing managers and social workers alike are reluctant to grant requests for transfers out of such estates. Which again, in its turn, gives rise to understandable complaints and grievances.

It is, I think, impossible to find any perfect theoretical resolution to the dilemma. As a general principle, the reasonable and legitimate desires of the individual should, whenever possible, be met, even if there is little or no element of need to reinforce his or her desire. But: the interests of the larger community must be considered too: and where the desires of the individual are plainly in conflict with the interests of the community, then perhaps the latter should prevail. This is a difficult example of the conflicts which can arise, in a free society, between the rights and interests of the individual and those of the larger community of which he is a member. There are those who would argue, persuasively, that the rights of the individual should prevail. I would not be dogmatic on this subject. In the large majority of cases which fall between the two extremes, there is nothing for it but to make pragmatic judgements on a basis of common sense; and so long as such judgements are made fairly and impartially, without improper preference for the claims of one individual — or prejudice against those of another — nobody need suffer injustice.

The acceptance of the principle that a house is more than just a unit of accommodation, it is a family home; and of the principle that, so far as practicable, individuals should enjoy not only freedom of choice, but also the right to have their desires as well as their needs taken into consideration; carries with it considerable implications for the provider or manager of housing.

A newly-built house, the day before its first tenants move in, is of itself no more than a box or shell — Le Corbusier's *machine à habiter* — designed to accommodate a group of human beings, age anything from babyhood to second childhood; and perhaps their dog, cat or budgie. It is neither Protestant nor Catholic; male nor female; Conservative nor Labour, Unionist nor Republican.

But, within a week, a month, a year, after its first allocation, that dwelling will have become a home, with strongly pronounced characteristics of its own: including perhaps holy pictures, or statues, or a sacred heart upon the wall; or else biblical texts, or a picture of King Billy crossing the Boyne, or bowler hat and sash in the wardrobe; so that politicians may well from then on speak of it, without blushing, as a Catholic (or a Republican) house; or as a Protestant (or a Unionist) house.

And, moreover, though the bricks, mortar, timber and slates of the new house may be intrinsically neutral and characterless, the same can never (in Northern Ireland) be true of the plot of land upon which the dwelling has been built. A.T.Q. Stewart was I think one of the first to apply to the Northern Ireland problem the concept of the 'territorial imperative' to whose importance in the animal world Robert Ardrey drew attention a few years ago. To quote from Dr Stewart:

> The two 'religious' communities are not intermingled — that is patently not what has happened — but they are interlocked, and in ways which it is probably impossible for anyone except the native of Ulster to understand. This gives rise to a situation in which the 'territorial imperative' is extremely insistent. The quarrel is therefore very much concerned with the relationship of people to land, and that relationship has indeed been considered the central theme of Irish history.
>
> Of its very nature it consists in particulars, the location of a road, a stretch of wall, a church or cluster of houses. Yet the problem is invariably discussed in abstract terms. The war in Ulster is being fought out on a narrower ground than even the most impatient observer might imagine, a ground every inch of which has its own associations and special meaning.

It is with this complicating factor, and its implications for the providers and managers of housing in Northern Ireland, that the next chapter is concerned.

# Sectarianism, Violence and Housing

Visiting politicians of all parties find the sectarian divisions in the housing estates of Northern Ireland incomprehensible. A surprising number of them (again, of all parties) appear to believe that, by tolerating segregation of the two communities, the Housing Executive is itself guilty of perpetuating such divisions. Indeed, some of them are so naive as to believe that, if all Catholics and all Protestants were compelled to live in mixed estates, the fears and antagonisms of the past three centuries would immediately disappear. Would that it were so simple!

Some years ago, during the delusive détente of the early 1960s, I had an illuminating experience. At that period, the private rented sector still provided most people with homes; my family firm of solicitors administered several trusts whose assets included streets of houses; it was then normal practice to offer the tenancy of any house coming vacant to any friend or acquaintance who might want it and seem likely to prove a good tenant. The firm then employed an elderly and, as I thought, ultra-timid law clerk whose son had just got married, and who was in want of a house. It so happened that I was in a position to offer the tenancy of a better-than-average parlour house, which had just become available for reletting, in the Ardoyne district of Belfast. I was greatly taken aback by his response: 'Oh, no, sir, that would never do, there were bad troubles in that street before the war, it wouldn't be a safe place for them to live at all.' I thought him unreasonable, ungrateful, and characteristically pusillanimous; I assured him that those bad old days were dead and gone for ever; I urged him to think again; but he refused to change his mind. He was proved dead right, and I was proved dead wrong: that street was one of the first to burst into open conflict in the renewed troubles of 1969: within a few weeks, every family of his denomination had been burned, intimidated or frightened out, and the whole street had become once again the exclusive territory of the other denomination.

Many other people had been less cautious and less far-sighted than he. By 1968, large parts of Belfast, and of most other Ulster towns, had become genuinely mixed in religious complexion. This did not of course apply to the traditional heartlands of the two communities: not many Protestants felt comfortable living in the Catholic areas of the upper and lower Falls Road, Smithfield, the Markets area, or the Short Strand district on the far side of the river; not many Catholics felt comfortable in the streets off the Shankill Road, or around the Sandy Row, or the shipyard workers' streets of Ballymacarrett; though there have at all times been a few exceptions, many of them resulting from mixed marriages.

These heartlands had first come into existence for historical reasons: the influx of unskilled labourers, of navvies, and of workers in the textile mills of West Belfast, in the years just before and after the Great Famine, had been mainly Catholic; the skilled craftsmen who found work in the foundries, the engineering works and the shipyard were mainly Protestant. Hostility between the two factions, blazing up at intervals into open violence, has been intermittently in evidence ever since the Reform Bill riots in 1832. And the patterns of violence have been extraordinarily consistent; on almost every occasion of sectarian violence, Protestants have attacked the homes of Catholics, and vice versa: in 1835, in 1841, in 1857; in 1864, in 1872, in 1886; in 1907, 1920-23, 1935. Much has been written in recent years about these forerunners of the most recent troubles; there have been many public inquiries, all of them inconclusive. Perhaps three quotations, widely separated in time, from Bardon's *Belfast, an Illustrated History*, will serve to set the scene:

In 1857:

> On Monday night, while mobs hurled stones and insults at each other ... Catholics at Millfield wrecked a spirit-grocer's store and beat two Methodist ministers with sticks. On Tuesday night Protestants from Sandy Row made a determined attack on Quadrant Street in the Pound smashing windows with long poles and setting houses on fire ... while Catholics wrecked a Methodist church on the Falls Road ...

In 1872:

> One of the worst features of the riots was the large-scale eviction of Catholics living in Protestant areas and Protestants living in Catholic areas. The religious dividing lines running through

Belfast became much more abrupt and ... the evictions caused much suffering ...

In 1935:

The balance of deaths had been on the Protestant side but the Catholics had suffered most. Most of the wounded were Catholic, and 514 Catholic families were driven out of the York Street area. ... The exodus of Catholic families from the Dock area led to the mingling of people of both denominations in north-west Belfast, but the two communities did not merge completely, and in 1969 and 1971 isolated families here were to find themselves terribly vulnerable when sectarian conflict erupted once again.

It is plain that, at any rate in the older parts of Belfast, fear — and well-justified fear — constitutes the principal reason for the segregation of housing on religious lines. There may of course be other reasons too: the desire to live close to other members of the family; the wish to be near chapel, parish hall, and denominational school: or, as the case may be, church, orange hall and state school. In the middle-class residential areas, in the newer estates and suburbs where the old territorial imperatives were less deeply ingrained, these reasons held less sway: there were on the periphery of Belfast, in 1968, very many areas where Protestant and Catholic lived quite peaceably together.

The same pattern held generally true of the provincial towns: in some, such as Derry, Armagh, Dungannon, Lurgan and Newry, the historical boundaries in the older areas between the mainly Protestant and the mainly Catholic districts survived; but the new estates on the outskirts tended to be segregated too. In other places, especially in new estates, the religious divisions had by 1968 largely broken down. There are still a fair number of such towns, villages and estates: but it is noticeable that good relations between the two communities are more likely to exist where one faction has a clear ascendancy in numbers over the other, rather than where numbers are roughly even. In general, and throughout Northern Ireland, the 1950s and 1960s had seen a considerable relaxation of the old defensive patterns of habitation, and a much increased willingness on the part of neighbours of different loyalties to live in harmony with each other.

All this was, however, to change sharply in the summer of 1969, when large-scale population movement started; there were ugly incidents on either side of the Crumlin Road, and around Unity Flats, in July; more and more families decided to move: in August the British army arrived, interposing itself between the factions, but not soon enough to prevent a Protestant foray from the Shankill which burned out almost every house in Bombay Street, off the Falls. So-called 'peace lines' of corrugated iron were established in many parts of the city, in an attempt to keep the combatants apart. The paramilitaries on both sides recruited their forces and brought in arms. Many hundreds of families left their homes, some voluntarily, some involuntarily, during the summer and autumn of 1969. A steady trickle continued to do so for the rest of that year, and throughout 1970: in particular, Protestants were expelled from the formerly mixed estates at Moyard and New Barnsley, while Catholics were expelled from most parts of East Belfast (except the enclave surrounding St Matthew's church in the Short Strand area), from Springmartin and the Donegall Road.

The second great wave of movement occurred in August 1971, following the surge of disorder consequent upon the introduction of internment. This was much more fully documented by the Community Relations Commission; in an influential report, *Flight,* published only a few weeks later, the Commission estimated that, in the three weeks after 9th August, at least 2,100 families fled from their homes; and this was certainly a considerable underestimate. The Commission considered that about 40% of the total movements were Protestant, about 60% Catholic.

Amongst its findings and comments were the following:

> To give up a home where one has lived for years, and which is itself a symbol of security, for the insecurity of squatting, which many did, is an act of desperation: to damage one's house on leaving, or allow others to do so, is an act of despair. Each of the statistics recorded in this report represents an individual tragedy and a personal bitterness which remains as a legacy of what has taken place.

In August 1969

> there was a direct confrontation across the territorial boundaries between solidly segregated areas ... On this occasion (i.e. August 1971) ... the major upheaval has transferred to the mixed areas which were formerly thought to serve as 'buffer zones' guaranteeing stability. This re-sorting of mixed areas into segregated areas is an extremely ominous development ... Explanations as to why this is taking place may vary from conspiracy theories to the complex question of the balance of fear between sections of the community and the fear-threshold within them.
>
> Protestants are tending to move out into the newer housing areas of the city's margins and Catholics are crowding into the Falls/Andersonstown sector of the city and the older housing in North Belfast. Spontaneous and organised squatting is re-segregating housing in such a way as to undermine the credibility for the community of non-sectarian housing policies.

Nobody who lived in Belfast through those dreadful days will forget
them. The sounds of gunfire and explosions a mile away on the Falls
Road were all too audible, the flames and palls of smoke all too visible,
from my own home in the peaceable middle-class Malone Road. There
was a sting to the poster of the period, 'Malone Road Fiddles While Falls
Road Burns'. We did not fiddle, but there was not much else we could
do. I recall an alarming expedition, one glass-strewn Sunday morning,
to try to rescue two elderly Protestant sisters from their house in the confrontation zone at Ainsworth Avenue; they refused to move. And for
several days an entire young Catholic family from Spamount Street took
refuge from the fighting at our home, till it was safe for them to return.

The human problems caused to the families most affected were heart-
rending; the problems posed to the various welfare authorities, and not
least those responsible for housing, were appalling. All the normal rules
of civilised conduct, of law and order, had broken down; every con-
tingency was perilous and unpredictable. Firemen were shot or petrol-
bombed as they tried to do their, already dangerous, work. Tall
buildings — church spires, factories, monasteries, blocks of flats —
might harbour snipers; two slaters were shot by the army while repairing
bomb-damage to roofs. Previously unarmed vigilantes had turned into
armed and organised paramilitary armies, some of which sought to take
over the control and allocation of housing. In the Belfast Corporation's
Westland Road estate, new houses nearing completion were squatted in
systematically: the site foreman was prevailed upon, no doubt under
some degree of duress, to hand out keys for distribution to the local Protestant paramilitary force. Equally, in Beechmount on the Falls Road,
notices were placed in the windows of new houses announcing 'allocated
by Provisional IRA to . . .' A prominent Protestant paramilitary leader
in East Belfast was nick-named 'Sir Brian Morton' after the well-known
estate agent of that name. Barricades of burned-out cars, lorries, buses
and wreckage turned some estates into no-go areas for all but their
residents; a third of the population was on rent strike. The army had to
protect school-children of both denominations, passing through hostile
territory on their way home from school, from stone-throwing mobs.
Housing assistants, rent collectors, maintenance and repair squads, all
were at risk in their daily work.

By the end of 1971, the fulcrum of housing discontent and housing-
related violence had shifted mainly, though not entirely, to Belfast. The
campaign against sectarian discrimination in housing had had its roots
in central Ulster — Caledon, Dungannon, Armagh, Coalisland; and in
the west, particularly Londonderry and Enniskillen. To some extent,
the reforms announced in 1969 had defused these grievances: the
imposition of points schemes, however crude; the promise to set up a new

Central Housing Authority and the passage through the Stormont parliament of the legislation required to bring it into existence; above all, the substitution of the Londonderry Development Commission for the former city and rural councils; each had gone some way to ease the position.

Conditions in Londonderry were still very bad, however. The waiting-list was hovering around 2,000 families — equivalent to around 9,000 people — or one-seventh of the population; there was gross over-crowding, with two or three families sharing a single parlour house; no family with less than five years' seniority on the waiting-list had a hope of an allocation, and many had to wait far longer. Although there were years when the old council had built no houses at all, it had at least called the Housing Trust in aid to build the Creggan estate for Catholics, and to redevelop the Leckey Road-Rossville Street area; indeed the high Rossville flat-blocks, built in the early 1960s, were at first perfectly acceptable. But these were for the families displaced by redevelopment, not for those on the general waiting-lists, and did little to remedy the sense of bitter frustration of the minority. Protestants had a far wider choice of estates, smaller families, and a shorter wait. One of the last actions of the Londonderry Rural Council was to pre-allocate almost entirely to Protestants the not-quite-completed Ballynagard housing development at Culmore Road in order to pre-empt the possibility that the Commission might use it to relieve Catholic overcrowding.

The Commission set about its task energetically, and was seen to act fairly; it resumed building at Shantallow where the old Corporation had refused to allow the Housing Trust to build on specious grounds of bad drainage; it built Gobnascale, implemented the area plan, and opened up new sites in every part of the city irrespective of electoral con-siderations. But the violence of 1969, of which the focus was to a large extent the Rossville flats, led (as in Belfast) to organised squatting, intimidation, and a massive movement of population, mostly of Pro-testants from the west to the east bank of the river Foyle, although simul-taneously there was a reverse flow of Catholics moving from east to west bank in search of safety. The difficulties of housing staff on the ground were compounded by organised squatting in new houses before their handover; the wholesale intimidation of contractors; the no-go areas from which police and army were excluded, and the rent strike; the armed struggles between the different factions within the IRA; and the general resentment of all authority.

In towns which had not only Catholic majorities but also Nationalist councils, such as Strabane and Newry, the Troubles were much less directly related to housing; both because these councils generally had much better building records, and because if there were any allegations at all of discrimination, they were of discrimination against, rather then by, Protestants and Unionists. But that is by no means to say that housing managers in such areas faced no problems. The large Derrybeg estate on the outskirts of Newry, 350 houses built to high density in 1964 by the old urban council, first became a paramilitary stronghold, and was then the scene of much bitter in-fighting between Provisional and Official IRA; with the result that transfer applications were received from more than half the tenants, supported by an avalanche of medical certificates. A gradual drift of Protestant families north of the Camlough Road, and of Catholic families southwards, ensued. In the surrounding rural areas, the onset of sectarian murders gave rise to a similar trend. The rent strike received almost 100% support amongst the Catholic community; and many homes were damaged, some destroyed, in the sequence of fierce confrontations, major riots, and large bombs, to which Newry was subjected.

There were bitter clashes in many parts of Craigavon, situated between hotly Protestant Portadown and hotly Catholic Lurgan; greatly increased in violence by the arrival of many families of refugees from the squatting and intimidation of Belfast, for the new town was one of the few places (Antrim was another) where new housing was reasonably easily available at short notice for the tide of homeless; there was polarisation, there was paramilitary activity, and ultimately some parts of the new town became effectively uninhabitable and had to be demolished. In other towns and villages where relations between the two communities had formerly been peaceable and harmonious, such as Downpatrick, Ardglass and Portaferry, the sudden influx of city-bred refugees from Belfast, some with paramilitary affiliations, greatly upset the balance and calm of formerly amicable mixed communities.

Throughout this period, the staff concerned performed prodigies; but the newly-formed Housing Executive and its Board could do little, at any rate until its first director-general took up his duties, and the housing functions of Belfast Corporation became vested in it, in January 1972. In the meanwhile, the Housing Trust in particular had made great efforts to provide emergency housing, both by importing timber-framed units and by speeding up existing contracts, to meet the acute needs especially in over-crowded West Belfast. But it was only as the Executive gathered strength and confidence in 1972 that the real issues could be thrashed out. Desmond Lorimer and Harry Simpson called in aid the leaders of all the churches, whom they approached privately, sometimes with frustrating results. And government was not much more helpful on the issues of squatting and intimidation: when William

Whitelaw arrived, he was unable to be of much help, since both police and army declined, firmly but politely, to undertake the unpalatable task of evicting the squatters, though theoretically and unenthusiastically prepared to offer a degree of protection to any bailiffs brave enough to do so. Out of the infinite number of day-to-day conundrums posed by the Troubles of the immediately preceding period, there are, I think, five questions with long-lasting policy implications which demand discussion here. They are: squatting; segregation versus integration; dealings with paramilitaries; the so-called 'peace' walls; and, allegations of imbalance in housing provision as between Catholics and Protestant areas.

As to squatting, it must be said at the outset that the form it has taken in Northern Ireland differs materially from that to be found in London, Amsterdam, and other cities, where it is the simple consequence of a drastic shortage of suitable accommodation. Between 1969 and 1972, most of those who squatted in Ulster left perfectly adequate accommodation to do so — they moved not from need but from fear. In the early days at least, until strong-arm men moved in to impose their own selfish and sectarian imperatives, most squatters were viewed with much sympathy by the authorities; indeed, Belfast Corporation twice went so far as to grant a general amnesty to all squatters. In many later cases, it proved possible to legalise tenancies where the previous circumstances of the squatter would in any case have warranted rehousing under the points scheme.

But the need to act with humanity towards individuals had to be balanced against the need, first, to discourage further and wholly unjustified squatting on the part of those anxious only to help themselves; and second, to regain control over the housing stock, and enforce the priorities in the new allocation system adopted by the Executive. So no further amnesty was granted; individual cases were looked at with humanity, and legalised where reasonable grounds for doing so could be found; rent and rent-books were refused, but 'use and occupation' payments were accepted; in an area where squatting ceased entirely, all tenancies might be legalised: but in areas where squatting continued, legalisation would be confined to those with entitlement from their previous home under the points scheme, and eviction proceedings would be taken against the rest.

Here, of course, lay the nub of the difficulty: the legal procedures for eviction are enormously long-drawn-out and complicated. Judges and magistrates tend to sympathise, understandably, with the individual in his battle with a large authority; and often grant long stays of execution. But even where an order is granted, there may arise the utmost difficulty over its enforcement: especially in an area dominated by paramilitaries. Under the system in force, the eviction itself is the responsibility of the Enforcement of Judgements Office, which in Northern Ireland has taken over the functions exercised by sheriffs and bailiffs elsewhere.

The evicting officers are entitled to call on the police for protection; but, given the risks of serious disorder, and given the unhappy associations of evictions in Ireland going back to the old Land League days of the last century, there is little enthusiasm amongst the security forces for this procedure. The result has been that it has proved possible to deal more effectively with unjustified squatting in Protestant areas, where the rule of law runs at most times and in most places, than in some of the republican estates where its enforcement poses greater difficulties. So that it has become a Protestant grievance that Catholic squatters appear to be more leniently treated than Protestant ones: despite the resolve of the Executive to institute proceedings impartially against all squatters.

No problem, has over the years, exercised more of the time and anxiety of the Housing Executive Board. Squatting still goes on, though now on a much smaller scale than in the past, and almost entirely in the over-crowded areas of Belfast and Derry. It is most damaging in those cases where it constitutes, strictly, overholding rather than squatting; that is, the refusal to vacate a condemned house whose demolition must take place before a redevelopment scheme can proceed. In such cases, the Executive accepts its obligation to rehouse the squatter elsewhere, but never in one of the new and most desirable dwellings, since that would constitute a striking incentive to further squatting on the part of those anxious to jump the queue for new homes. It should be added that, where squatting now occurs, it is sometimes as a result of complicity between an outgoing legal tenant and a friend or relative; sometimes too, money may change hands. Also, of the statistics for current squatting, some represent cases of unauthorised transfers or exchanges. Some, too, will be pathetic hardship cases. But there is still a hard core of cases where those in most need of the house, and who have been duly allocated it, are deprived of their home by the arrogance and selfishness of a wholly unprincipled squatter: and in such cases, neither the Executive nor any other responsible housing authority can look the other way.

As to the integration-segregation debate, neither wandering members of Parliament nor other visiting firemen can alter what appears to be, for the foreseeable future, the unalterable. It was with great distress and mortification that the Board members of the old Housing Trust, and particularly their last chairman, Brian Rankin, watched the final collapse of their well-intentioned attempts to create wholly integrated estates; especially at Twinbrook, which had been patiently and laboriously designed to provide a model: with sites for churches, schools, and community centres for all denominations. The Board of the incoming Executive was, in fact, very slow to give up hope of reviving and fostering such schemes. It was only after much trial and error that it gave up the task as, for the present, in Belfast at any rate, hopeless; and only with much distaste and dismay that it decided to include a question in the housing application form asking whether the applicant would prefer to live in a mixed, a Protestant, or a Catholic estate.

Two bitter experiences of failure led to the conclusion that this kind of experiment in positive social engineering would not work in the Northern Ireland environment: indeed, might prove actually counter-productive.

The first of these arose at Farringdon Gardens, in North Belfast. In August 1971, 194 houses were completely burned out, and another 100 severely damaged, in this and adjoining streets (Cranbrook Gardens and Velsheda Park) by Protestants fleeing from the formerly mixed, though mainly Catholic, Glenard estate. (Although it was no doubt unconscious, this was to follow the example of Rostopchin, who set Moscow on fire on 15th September 1812 in order to deny it to Napoleon and his army.) 'A voluntary, interdenominational body, the Ardoyne Housing Committee, was formed for the purpose of restoring these homes and inviting back to them their former occupants, thus re-estab-lishing an integrated community.' This was an ambitious objective; on the one hand, there was no certain prospect that the Protestant families would be prepared to return; on the other hand, the Committee com-manded far too few resources to complete the work. In July 1972 it was agreed that the Executive should take over the work in hand, and endeavour to restore, rebuild and upgrade the area. A scheme had been very swiftly prepared by outside consultants at the instance of Rae Evans; the Board gave its blessing; work started without delay; but the objective of restoring an integrated community ran into difficulties as soon as the first houses were available for occupation. The spokesmen for the Catholic community in the locality were, it became clear, acting as a front for, if not actually members of, the IRA. Equally, it became clear that the Steadfast Tenants' Association, spokesmen for the Protestant ex-occupiers, were a front for, if not actually members of, a Protestant paramilitary organisation. Many difficult meetings were held by the Executive with the delegates of both bodies; at one of them, Harry Simpson opened his remarks by saying — 'I will be absolutely straight and open with you, gentlemen' — to meet the response 'Yes, you better had be' from the leaders of both groups, each fingering the gun in his pocket. It soon became plain that Protestant and Catholic would never again be willing to live here as next-door neighbours; with reluctance, the Catholic spokesmen ultimately agreed that they might be prepared to countenance Catholic tenants on one side of the street, Protestants on the other. But the only Protestants prepared to contemplate putting their heads into a noose of this kind were the most ardent and fiery paramilitaries themselves, intent on 'steadfastly' retaining a foothold in formerly Protestant territory; their wives and children were almost all unwilling to accompany them; and it ultimately became evident that the prospects for restoring an integrated community to Glenard were non-existent, so that the scheme as projected had to be dropped. But even that did not solve the problem of intimidation in the area. When Harry Simpson suggested that, if segregation there must be, it should be peacefully carried out by using the Housing Executive to effect the redistribution of houses, the pitying response of the local representatives was 'You can't do that, that's just English logic, Mr. Simpson.'

The second failure, of a somewhat but not wholly different kind, was at Horn Drive, in the comparatively recently-built Lenadoon estate at Suffolk on the western outskirts of Belfast. This too had been a mixed estate, with a predominance of Protestants at the lower end of the hill, close to the mainly Protestant village of Dunmurry, and a predominance of Catholics at the upper end where the estate fronted to the Glen Road. In a way, the Protestant part of the estate was seen by Catholics as a salient projecting into 'their' territory north of the Stewartstown Road. The flood of refugees from other mixed areas into Catholic West Belfast exerted exceptional pressure upon this salient; and many of the Protestant families moved out; but this was territory which their defenders were not prepared to concede; so that it became the scene of many confrontations.

Once again, the Housing Executive was faced with the unpalatable dilemma: if it surrendered to the Catholic pressures, and agreed to rehouse the remaining Protestant residents elsewhere, there was an end to the last vestige of a mixed estate in this part of West Belfast. If it refused to do so, it laid itself open to the charge of aligning itself with the Protestant paramilitaries in keeping Catholic families in great need out of houses which most of the Protestant occupiers had already left. The Executive chose the former alternative; but this was unacceptable to the local UDA, and the security forces desperately tried to maintain the status quo pending some peaceful solution.

This dispute came to a head during the period of the brief ceasefire declared by the Provisional IRA between 27th June and 9th July 1972; indeed, it was the failure to resolve it that caused the ending of the ceasefire. Between those dates, Desmond Lorimer, Harry Simpson and John Lazenbatt used their utmost efforts to find a solution, and attended (very uncomfortable) meetings with all those concerned — police, army, IRA, UDA. Some quotations from Deutsch and Magowan's *Northern Ireland: A Chronology of Events* for that year will demonstrate the pressures under which all concerned were working:

Friday 23rd June:

> The 1st Battalion, Provisional IRA in Andersonstown Belfast issued a statement accusing the British Army of making no effort to curtail the activities of Protestant gunmen at Horn Drive, Suffolk.

Saturday 24th June:

> Heavy shooting continued in Suffolk.

Sunday 25th June:

> At Suffolk and Andersonstown more than 500 shots were fired at Army posts. The shooting was described by troops as 'suicidal' and ambulances were seen speeding to the area.

Friday 7th July:

> The Catholic Citizens' Defence Committee stated that ... they would be moving Catholic families into some houses in the Lenadoon area which had been vacated by Protestants ... In the evening, the move was attempted but the Army prevented it because of tension in the area ... Local residents said that, if the Army would not move the families, then they would move them forcibly themselves ... UDA representatives warned that if Catholics were given the empty houses left by Protestants, they would burn those houses down. Local Provisional IRA leaders demanded that the tenancy agreements which had been issued to the Catholic families by the Housing Executive should be implemented but Lt-Col Tomlinson pointed out that his permission was required ... A postponement of any action for 24 hours was agreed but the Provisionals warned that they would rehouse the families themselves after that time limit. In the tense atmosphere that existed, Belfast Corporation stopped all bus services ...

Saturday 8th July:

> Three top-ranking Provisional IRA members, Mr Seamus Twomey, Mr Seamus Loughran and Mr Gerry O'Hare met Army officers, including Lt-Col Mike Tomlinson, inside the Lenadoon Avenue Army post in order to settle the rehousing of Catholic families in the area.

Sunday 9th July:

> At 11.00 am at the Army post at Musgrave Park, Belfast, Pro-
> visional IRA leaders, including Seamus Loughran, Adjutant 1st
> Battalion, met Lt-Col Mike Tomlinson, UDA representatives and
> members of the Northern Ireland Office, Mr Neil Cairncross and
> Mr Denis Trevelyan, and representatives of the Housing Executive
> and the RUC, in a further attempt to settle the question of re-
> housing Catholic families in the Lenadoon area. No positive agree-
> ment was reached and both sides decided to report back to their
> senior officers. Mr Seamus Twomey, Commander of the Belfast
> Brigade, Provisional IRA, decided to give the Army until 4.00 pm
> to move Catholic families into the Horn Drive area. At about 5
> o'clock, troops on duty at Lenadoon Avenue fired rubber bullets
> and CS gas at a hostile Catholic crowd of about 3,000 who threw
> missiles at them after the troops had prevented a lorry loaded with
> furniture from proceeding to re-house Catholic families in Horn
> Drive, Suffolk. Members of the UDA watched the confrontation
> behind the Army line but took no part in it.
>
> Mr Seamus Twomey told the Army Commander on duty that
> he considered the British Army had now violated the truce.
> Shooting started and the troops moved into defensive positions as
> over 300 rounds were fired at them. The soldiers were ordered to
> return fire at identifiable targets.
>
> At 9.00 pm an official announcement from Kevin Street head-
> quarters of the Provisional IRA in Dublin said, 'The truce between
> the IRA and British occupation forces was broken without warning
> by British forces at approximately 5.00 pm today at Lenadoon
> Estate, Belfast. Accordingly, all IRA units have been instructed to
> resume offensive action.'

Not even the most starry-eyed and idealistic of integrationists, I think,
could have achieved his aims in that situation.

The upshot of this unhappy process may be seen from the map in the
endpapers, which shows the distribution in autumn 1985 of wholly or
predominantly Protestant and Catholic areas respectively, in and
around Belfast. The pattern is a complicated one: not at all like that in
Derry where almost all Protestants, apart from one modest enclave
beside the city walls, have abandoned the west bank of the Foyle. In
Belfast, as in a number of other places, the words of A.T.Q. Stewart,
quoted on page 61, are very apposite: "The two religious communities
are not intermingled — that is patently not what has happened — but
they are interlocked, and in ways which it is probably impossible for any
one except the native of Ulster to understand."

On the Protestant side, the major residential areas are in East Belfast, on the Shankill Road and Ballysillan, and on the outskirts at Rathcoole, Lisburn and Dunmurry, Belmont, Castlereagh and Dundonald; but there are clearly-defined patches of Protestant territory at the Donegall Road, Sandy Row, Donegall Pass, and the Shore Road; and smaller enclaves at Suffolk, Lower Ardoyne, Torrens, Taughmonagh, Tiger Bay, and Whitewell. On the Catholic side, the major residential area runs along the line of the Falls Road from the city centre all the way to Poleglass and Twinbrook; with sizeable subsidiary Catholic residential areas in Upper Ardoyne, the New Lodge district, Lower Ormeau, and the Markets; and enclaves at Unity Flats, Ligoniel, Greencastle, Fairyknowe, Bawnmore, and the Short Strand.

There are three main mixed districts, still principally middle-class areas of owner-occupation: all three formerly mostly Protestant: the Antrim Road, the Ormeau Road, and the Malone ridge (including Stranmillis, the University area, and the Holy Land). In each of these a discernible pattern has appeared over the past decade: Catholic familes have by degrees moved in, and Protestant families have by degrees moved out. This process is a complex one; it reflects in the first instance the greater pressure of demand on the Catholic side, since so many other formerly mixed areas became 'unsafe' in 1969-1972; it reflects also the fear of Protestants, especially those serving in the security forces, that their new neighbours may include unidentifiable members of, or sympathisers with, the IRA. So, gradually and usually without overt intimidation or fighting, streets in the mixed areas have been changing complexion: thus providing, on the one hand, a very welcome and much-needed safety-valve for the hard-pressed Catholic population; but on the other, a loss of traditional territory viewed with dismay and apprehension by many Protestants, even quite moderate ones. It is not unlikely that the denominational map of the city will look considerably different in 1995, even should there be no further unforeseen external influences.

The map shows also the principal present lines of confrontation. Some of these, such as the peace line between the Falls and the Shankill, have remained static for a century or more. Others have stabilised themselves comparatively recently. Others again are in a state of flux, with territory being won, lost, and fought for, as part of a continuing process. There are still blocked-up and bullet-pock-marked houses, regarded as uninhabitable by both sides, along some of these frontiers; often the abandoned homes of owner-occupiers, depressing reminders that peace is not in sight. In most cases, the trouble along the interface is intermittent, bursting into open conflict only at times of special tension — around the 12th of July celebrations, or the anniversary of internment, or when political feeling is running exceptionally high. In a few cases, there is endemic trouble, mostly between gangs of teenagers. Practically nowhere, and practically never, does the possibility exist of encouraging, still less imposing, integrated housing in the public rented sector.

This sequence of events leads logically to the third of my three policy issues: how far representatives of a housing authority should, how far they should not, engage in direct dealings, negotiations, or meetings with the representatives of paramilitary organisations.

At first glance, it would appear that they ought never to do so. But that is not, in practice, a tenable stance. Membership of the Provisional IRA is illegal; membership of Sinn Féin, or of the Protestant UDA, is not. There is a presumption that every man is innocent until he is proved guilty; what is more, even if convicted, he is supposed to leave prison with a clean sheet, having purged his crimes. There can be no doubt that paramilitaries have at times been the most effective — indeed, ultra-forceful — spokesmen for their respective communities: even if they may not speak for all. (Although I have been less subjected to their company than my predecessors, I too have sometimes been disconcerted: as when I was told, with venom, 'Yez ought to be shot' by a spokesman who had himself been shot, and who had certainly shot others — or arranged for them to be shot.) The difficulty is compounded when, as has quite frequently happened, the spokesmen concerned can claim to have been democratically elected — whether to Parliament, to the Assembly, to the local council, or to the committee of a tenants' or residents' or community association.

The question is one of some legal delicacy, and it can have unexpected ramifications. It has got more difficult, not easier, since Parliament has imposed a statutory obligation on housing authorities to consult with tenants and their representative organisations. It is still further complicated by the see-saws of power which may take place between rival organisations, or rival individuals within the same organisation. In at least one instance, the orderly and sensible progress of a major redevelopment scheme was greatly retarded because control of the tenants' association for the area alternated, over a period of years, between front men for the Provisional and the Official IRA, with each, immediately on election, disclaiming and overturning all the policies and decisions of the outgoing committee.

Still greater difficulties can arise in dealing with builders or other commercial concerns, such as the (now defunct) Andersonstown Co-operative Society, believed to be under the control of the paramilitaries. If such an organisation can be demonstrated to be in the ownership and under the control of proven members of an illegal organisation, then there is no problem. If only evidence falling short of proof exists, then how can such a firm be denied the right to tender for Housing Executive contracts? The conclusion may not be very palatable to some politicians or even to some ministers, but I conclude that the law, including the laws of evidence, must be paramount; however distasteful and politically undesirable it may seem, a housing authority (like other welfare services) must not pick and choose those with whom it will do business, but must make itself available to all those who cannot be proved to have strayed beyond the protection of the law.

As to the so-called 'peace walls': these expensive, unsightly and inherently undesirable articles have become the subject of regular controversy. There can be no argument as to their ancestry; they are descended on one side of the family from the comparatively flimsy barriers of corrugated iron, wire mesh, and barbed wire, erected by the British army in 1969 to assist in the arduous task of keeping the two factions apart; on the other side of the family, from the defensive barricades built at the same period first around Catholic, then around Protestant, enclaves and estates for protection against intruders. Of course, it is no part of the Executive's business to make judgements or take decisions on questions of security; but of necessity, much thought has been given, in the years since then, to the best method of treating the so-called 'sectarian interfaces' between the two communities. Some favour a wide strip of bare waste ground; and indeed, some such *cordons sanitaires* have come into existence almost spontaneously. They are, however, unsightly, and further they allow a wide field of fire, as well as providing a ready-made open battleground. Some favour a landscaped park: but this gives too much cover to malefactors, and lends itself to the refinements of jungle warfare. Some favour building houses right up to the dividing line: but there is a real risk that the dwellings on one or the other side of the line will find no takers in a confrontation area. Some favour a wide dual-carriageway carrying a maximum traffic load; and this has much to commend it, apart from noise, pollution, and the danger of far-reaching traffic jams every time there is trouble. Where the two communities are at close quarters, a well-built wall, of adequate height, suitably treated to minimise graffiti, is clearly the least unsatisfactory solution.

The weaker (or the more peaceable) party in any given locality invariably welcomes, if it does not actually demand, a wall on such a site. The stronger (or more aggressive) party invariably opposes its construction, or calls for its instant removal, on the grounds that it will perpetuate division and inhibit any possible return to integration of the two communities. These arguments have been employed several times in recent years, in particular at Cupar Street (on the Shankill/Falls interface) and at Cluan Place (between the Catholic Short Strand

enclave and the rest of Protestant East Belfast). When looked at closely
in the light of the actual facts on the ground, the arguments against the
building of walls may be seen to have grown pretty thin. In most cases,
they have in practice performed pretty successfully the purposes for
which they were erected. But, both the existence and non-existence of
such walls provide local politicians with ammunition for the proposition
that the Housing Executive is biased against their respective factions.

Indeed, such accusations of generalised bias continue to be made
against the Executive, though almost exclusively by those at the two
extremes of the local political spectrum: Sinn Féin, and some members
of the Democratic Unionist Party. Pretty well all those who occupy the
middle ground, whatever their other criticisms, are prepared to accept
the general fairness and impartiality of the Executive: from Workers'
Party, to SDLP, to the several Labour, Socialist and Communist
groupings, to the Alliance party, to (a majority of) the Official
Unionists.

Nevertheless, the accusations of bias that exist must be taken
seriously, and cannot be ignored. They are in fact mutually contradictory. Both spring from the polarisation and population movements of
1969-72, as they were accurately described in the 'Flight' report already
quoted: Protestants tended to move into the newer housing areas on the
margins; Catholics 'are crowding into the Falls/Andersonstown sector
of the city and the older housing of North Belfast.' From this analysis it
follows that however long the waiting lists in Protestant areas, the
pressures of need have been highest and most urgent in Catholic areas.
And, as a body dedicated to the principle of responding to need, the
Executive has worked hard — at Poleglass and elsewhere — to try to
relieve that pressure.

This has led to allegations of a Republican plot, to which the
Executive is said to be party, to 'de-protestantise Belfast'; alleged to be
proved by a higher density and put-back rate in Catholic redevelopment areas than in Protestant ones. The principal proponent of this
theory has to date declined every challenge to produce the figures upon
which his allegations are based; he asserts that his proposition is self-
evident from the figures furnished to him in reply to Parliamentary
questions. But those questions did not compare like with like: they
ignored the availability in some districts, and unavailability in others, of
non-housing land: above all, they ignored the existence in the Catholic
areas of the high-rise high-density blocks of flats conceived not by the
Executive, but by its predecessors. There is no such plot, nor ever has
been; and only blinkered adherents of the conspiracy theory could even
entertain the idea.

At the other extreme, spokesmen for Sinn Féin have attacked the

Executive for bias against the Catholic community because it has not devoted a *higher* proportion of the resources available to the relief of overcrowding and low standards in the republican areas of the city. In this they have sought to enlist the support of Ken Livingstone; and at the same time, rather inconsistently, accused the Board of the Executive of being obedient hangers-on of the British government in general and the forces of law and order in particular. There is no such bias either: as anyone prepared impartially to examine the evidence will see.

Indeed the Poleglass scheme represents a firm stand by the Executive, with full support from successive governments, in defence of those in greatest need. The history of Poleglass deserves a book in itself: it has indeed been the subject of considerable academic discussion: suffice it to say here that, after the population movements of 1969-71, it became urgently necessary to find means of relieving the overcrowding of West Belfast where the majority of Catholic victims of eviction or intimidation had taken refuge. Many alternatives were considered, but the only feasible one, it was concluded, was the building of a very large new estate outside the planning stop-line (that is, in farmland designated for Belfast's green belt) on the boundaries of West Belfast. But this was hotly Protestant territory, adjacent to Dunmurry and Lisburn, whose residents saw themselves in danger of being swamped both socially and electorally. The scheme aroused passionate hostility, with many threats that force would be used. After much public debate, the holding of a public inquiry, the somewhat ambivalent findings of the planning commission, and a vast amount of heated controversy, the scheme was allowed to proceed as planned by the Executive, save that government halved its size from 4,000 to 2,000 dwellings. This decision pleased neither side: the decision to go ahead was regarded by the Unionist factions as discriminatory against Protestants, and a departure from impartiality in housing provision: the decision to halve the size of the new estate was regarded by the Republican factions as discrimination against Catholics. Nevertheless, the decision was a defensible one in terms of need, in terms of politics, and above all in terms of planning — for the larger any new estate, the greater the risk that it will go wrong; in early days, the Board of the Executive had proposed a maximum of 400 houses in any one estate as the normal rule (see Appendix).

At all stages of the debate, the Board of the Executive stood firmly in favour of the Poleglass development, on grounds of urgent and pressing need. Exceptional pains were taken both by the Department and the Executive over its planning, layout and design, in the hope of ensuring that it would not turn out another over-large and soul-less housing estate. Special precautions were taken to prevent squatting, threatened by the IRA, in the part-completed houses. It was one of the most satisfying days of my life when, on a snowy morning in November 1980, I was there to see the first thirty families moved in, as part of a complex and carefully organised operation. To date, the scheme has been a notable success — no squatting, little vandalism and no graffiti, and the swift growth of a genuine community spirit. It is not quite exclusively Catholic, though mainly so: and it has succeeded beyond all hopes in relieving the intolerable pressures in West Belfast.

Nevertheless, and through no wish of the Executive, there do remain considerable disparities between housing standards in different areas of Belfast. The most striking example is the contrast between the over-crowded Lower Falls, and the nearby half-empty wastelands of the Shankill. The pressure groups for the residents of the latter maintain that it was the processes of redevelopment alone that emptied the Shankill; and that if new houses were built, staunch Protestant families, in their thousands, would be vying to return from 'the newer housing areas on the city's margins' to which, as *Flight* found, so many of them had fled. The evidence, however, is all the other way: the Shankill is now a predominantly elderly and backward-looking community; it is certain that most of those who voted with their feet for the outer suburbs a decade ago prefer to stay where they are now.

This brings about an exceptionally harrowing dilemma for the Executive. The Falls and Shankill may be likened to two adjacent mill-dams, the first full to the very brim with water and in danger of bursting its banks, the second at a far lower level. If the sluice-gate between them could but be opened, the water-levels of both could be equalised, and each kept at a more satisfactory level. But what a sluice-gate to open that would be! For in terms of local history, the desecration of traditionally Protestant and Unionist territory in such a way would be quite unthinkable. It might seem to a man from Mars the simple and obvious solution; but not even the staunch Protestant opponents of Poleglass in the Lisburn area, though they were well aware of the argument, dared to advance it.

Nor did the Housing Executive; nor would it, in my view, be either right or wise to do so: for there are, at any rate in Ireland, some historical imperatives which nobody can defy with impunity.

One such is the connection between politics and sectarianism; another such is the connection between sectarian politics and places. Impartiality is not the same as insensitivity. It would be an insensitive politician indeed who sought to divorce housing in Northern Ireland entirely from matters of religion, politics, and geography. And he would not last long.

# Allocations, Siting and Discrimination

Allegations of political or sectarian discrimination in housing, before the Executive was set up, centred on two charges: first, that some councils or councillors improperly allocated houses as and when available to those of their own party or creed, in preference to those of other parties or creeds, without regard to the comparative needs or circumstances of the applicants. Second, that some councils manipulated the siting of new housing estates in such a way as to secure electoral advantage for the party in power, or, at the least, to ensure the perpetuation of its majority.

As I have remarked in chapter one, I think there is clear evidence that some housing authorities in Northern Ireland engaged in one or both of these practices; but that the majority of authorities were not guilty. However, these two issues are plainly quite fundamental to the success or failure of any present or future housing body in the province in establishing a reputation for fairness and impartiality. So long as the Board of the Executive is broadly representative of all the major strands of opinion in the province, and so long as no one group or party has an overall majority on the Board, allegations of the deliberate siting of new estates to gain political advantage are hardly likely to gain much credence. But the impartiality of the allocation scheme, and its public acceptance as being impartial, are absolutely central to the purposes for which the Executive was set up.

The Executive's original points scheme was framed in 1972-3, and introduced on 1st January 1974. Some aspects of this scheme, particularly in relation to the relative priorities to be accorded to different categories of applicant, gave rise to criticism and concern; and in April 1975 the Board appointed a strong sub-committee, under my own chairmanship, to carry out a thorough review of every aspect of the scheme, and to take evidence from all interested parties. Widespread consultation took place with the Housing Council, public representatives, tenants' and community associations, numerous other organisations, and many individuals; as usually happens in such cases, a substantial part of the evidence was conflicting and mutually contradictory. The committee reported back in January 1976; with only a few subsequent modifications, its findings have constituted the basis of the revised scheme in force since October 1977 (the delay was caused by the necessity to re-point every applicant then on the list).　Both the original scheme, and its successor, were based on the principle that need should be the paramount, though not the sole, criterion; time on the waiting list, and geographical claims, were accorded subordinate points. The arguments for putting need above all else are very strong, and have been almost universally accepted, but their validity is not in fact self-evident. There are those who argue that seniority on the waiting-list should be the determining factor, and they have a case: it was said that, in Londonderry in the 1960s, an applicant could take many years to reach the top of the list — in extreme cases, by the time a family's turn came for the allocation of a house, the children were grown up and off hands, and a flat or old people's dwelling would have been more appropriate. Others argued that absolute priority should be given to local residents; one highly-pointed applicant, living in a caravan, wrote to me:

> So far this year, quite a number of new houses have been allocated in X, and when it comes near our level and we feel at last a house is within reach, alas someone comes over our heads with higher points and snatches the house from under our noses.

A few, usually themselves applicants, considered that dwellings should be allocated to the most deserving rather than the neediest:

> Dear Mr Brett . . . I would like it to be known that I am not a child or person of low intelligence who cannot manage a little place of my own. I have already stated my lifetime's service up to retirement, and for those particular points I think I am as much entitled as those with a higher rating.

However, there was no large volume of support for any of these alternative proposals: and there was very general support for the view that patronage, nepotism and favouritism should be, as I believe they have been, eliminated.

The measurement of need, and the drawing of priorities between almost equally needy cases, is in itself a matter of considerable difficulty. How much weight, comparatively speaking, should be accorded to overcrowding; sharing; lack of amenities; disrepair? Opinions differ widely. And such differences of opinion can take on a sectarian dimension. If overcrowding and sharing command large numbers of points, then families with numerous children are likely to obtain priority over families with few children: and most people would say they rightly should. But, because of their church's attitude to contraception, Catholics generally have more children than Protestants. It has been a long-standing Protestant grievance, and sometimes advanced as a justification for the old discriminatory practices, that where houses are few and waiting-lists long, Catholic applicants may thereby gain a built-in and unfair advantage over their more thrifty and less polyphilo-progenitive fellow-citizens. This grievance is strongly felt and goes deep; it will continue to smoulder so long as 'need', defined to include overcrowding, remains the predominant criterion: until the day is reached — and perhaps now it is not so far off — when there are enough family houses to supply the needs of both communities. But there is a certain element of unreality about this particular grievance, since in practice large families are not in the same queue as small families — so long as houses of different sizes are allocated in relation to differing needs.

In fact, the review of 1976 did recommend that the balance of points should be shifted somewhat in favour of those sharing accommodation, or suffering overcrowding, as against those whose claim to points rested on disrepair or the lack of amenities; but at the same time, tightened up the definitions of the several categories.

There are several other difficult and controversial areas in the construction of any scheme. One of these is the position of young married couples: for whose claims there is strong emotional (perhaps even sentimental) public support. But it would be to stand the criterion of need on its head to allocate houses to young childless couples in preference to those with children; there is the further difficulty of reaching a satisfactory definition of such a group (could one, should one, discriminate against those living in sin?); and the still further difficulty of deciding which members of such a group should have preference over which others. The solution must lie partly in encouraging young couples to enter the private sector, where necessary taking advantage of new forms of tenure such as equity sharing; partly in seeking to provide more small units of accommodation for the small households (single people too) who form an ever-increasing proportion of those on the waiting-lists.

Indeed, this change in the profile of the waiting-list is a matter for much concern. When the Executive was formed, unarguably it was the families with young children who had the greatest need and the greatest claim for consideration. Now that need has, to a considerable extent, been met; and single people — some very young, some middle-aged, some elderly — are vociferous in expressing their hitherto comparatively low priority claims. But how are they to be accommodated? In the high-rise blocks now thought unsuitable for families, perhaps? But, in the peculiar circumstances of Northern Ireland, would not this solution run the risk of creating new and lawless communities of criminals, prostitutes, drug-addicts, glue-sniffers: still worse, barrack blocks for whole platoons of young paramilitaries?

The most difficult question faced by the Review Committee, and perhaps the thorniest political problem to face the Housing Executive since its inception, was that of local preference. In the decade after 1969, there was a steady pressure from people wishing to leave inner Belfast, and to bring up their children in comparatively prosperous and peaceful areas such as, for example, North Down. But politicians both at the exporting and importing ends viewed this process with deep alarm. From the point of view of an inner-city councillor or MP, he is all too likely to be left with a depopulated wasteland, sparsely inhabited by an ageing and discontented community, victims of violence, vandalism, and decay, and increasingly unwilling to vote for him. From the point of view of the public representative of the importing area, whether or not he welcomes outsiders (and most Ulster people distrust 'strangers', especially those of a different religious persuasion), the pressure of demand may mean that highly-pointed outsiders reduce to nil the availability of housing for local people. So, both parties want to set up barricades — to keep people in, or out, as the case may be. Which is very understandable, and in a way reasonable: but it cuts right across two other important principles: first, the desirability of increased mobility in the population; and second, the right which individuals ought to enjoy (within reason) of choosing their own areas of first and second preference.

I think that, as a result of prolonged consultation with the Housing Council and local authorities, and by restricting the areas of preference of those who seek housing without reference to points as priority emergency cases, the balance between need and local preference is now about right. But it is a delicate and sensitive one, which may require further adjustment in one direction or the other from time to time.

It is inevitable that there will always be some dissatisfied customers, whatever scheme is adopted, since the necessity for a scheme at all results from a mismatch between demand and supply. The Review Committee received many suggestions for increases in the number of points awarded to particular categories of claimant: had all these suggestions been adopted, the Executive would have ended up with an inflationary situation where nearly every applicant's points had been doubled, yet nobody was any better off. It is satisfactory to be able to record that,

**Plate 26**

*Housing personalities: left to right, above,* Harry Simpson, first Director-General of the Northern Ireland Housing Executive, Desmond Lorimer, first Chairman, and the author, May 1974; *below,* Bob Spence, second Director-General, James O'Hara, second Chairman, and Don Concannon, Labour Minister with responsibility for housing.

**Plate 27**

**Plate 28**

Working conditions; *above*, in the boardroom at College Square East, the members of the original board; *left to right*, Pat McArdle; Frank Kinghan; Hugh Brown; James O'Hara; Desmond Lorimer, Chairman; Harry Simpson, Director-General; the author; Jimmy Donnelly; Eddie Elliott; (absent on this occasion, Mrs. Mildred Jones).

*Left*, outside the boardroom; just after the explosion of a 300lb car bomb on 9th November 1972. Between 1972 and 1984, there were 49 such bomb or arson attacks on Housing Executive offices. Damage to Executive property during the same period was assessed at £2,788,485, leaving aside loss of records and disruption of work. During the same period, five members of the Executive's staff were murdered, seven were wounded (in several cases gravely) and twelve were attacked but escaped injury.

**Plate 29**

**Plate 30**

Unhappily, demolition was not all the work of the bombers. The 294 Turf Lodge flats on the Falls Road, *above*, built by Belfast Corporation in 1966, and the 284 Weetabix flats on the Shankill Road, *right*, (built by the Corporation in 1972, and so-called from their resemblance to cereal packets) had both to be demolished as uninhabitable within a few years of their erection. *Below*, condemned terrace housing in McClure Street, Belfast, awaiting its turn for demolition.  Pla

**Plate 31**

**Plate 33**

**Plate 34**

Rehabilitation, much in fashion during the mid-seventies, posed problems of its own. *Left*, the contrast between unregenerate and rehabilitated houses in Essex Street, Belfast. The effect was striking, but the cost disproportionate. Bathrooms could only be provided in the smaller houses by cannibalising a bedroom; or else by adding an obtrusive extension. *Above*, a traditional back entry in East Belfast; *below*, new bathroom extensions in a similar entry; acceptable perhaps in an end-of-terrace house, but elsewhere squeezing out light and air.

**Plate 35**

**Plate 36**

Vandalised, boarded-up and uninhabitable house in Legahory Green, in the new town of Craigavon, photographed in 1982; note the aptly sardonic graffito: 'Welcome to the home of your dreams': now demolished.

though very many allocation cases have been referred to, and investigated by, the Commissioner for Complaints, and though he has found evidence of mistakes or maladministration in a few, he has in no instance to date found the Executive guilty of political or religious discrimination. Indeed, the existence of the Commissioner provides a welcome and salutary safeguard for those members of staff responsible for allocations.

Such protection is very necessary. There is no doubt that the Executive's points scheme is more rigid and inflexible than any comparable scheme in any other part of the British Isles. This has real disadvantages; it minimises the exercise of skilled discretion by housing managers, whether in relation to cases of exceptional hardship which do not fit tidily into any of the existing categories, or in relation to the matching of applicant families to the homes or estates for which their backgrounds best suit them. But though it is a heavy one, this inflexibility is a price worth paying in order to reduce to an absolute minimum the areas within which the exercise of individual discretion may be vulnerable to charges of abuse, of favouritism, or of discrimination. And a safety-valve is provided by the much greater degree of flexibility and discretion allowed to managers in dealing with transfers and exchanges; indeed, it is Executive policy to use transfers in such a way as to benefit whole chains of tenants by meeting the respective needs of each.

One area where the absence of discretion in making allocations gives rise to both difficulties and complaints is that of the unsatisfactory tenant; the 'problem family'. Few people want to live next door to a burglar, a bomb-maker, or a brothel. But against this, since it is the sole provider of public authority housing, the Executive is under a duty to provide housing for all who seek it; not excluding pimps, prostitutes, paramilitaries, and even politicians. It cannot refuse to house known criminals, drug addicts, vandals, itinerants, skinheads, glue-sniffers; but is bound to treat every application on the basis of its needs — and points — irrespective of its deserts. There is a real difficulty here; and one which has exercised the Board on many occasions. It is undeniable that a small nucleus of such tenants can drag down the standards of a whole estate, rendering it almost (sometimes, entirely) unlettable. Yet what is the alternative? It can only be the designation of certain estates as 'less-favoured'; the creation of dumping-grounds, ghettoes, or (as the Germans call them) 'sin-bins' for anti-social families. In any community, this course would be very questionable, and open to strong moral objections. In the context of Northern Ireland, and a deeply-divided community, it simply cannot be contemplated: for it implies that somebody (who?) would have to make qualitative judgements regarding the desirability of some applicants as against others. It is my understanding that some British housing authorities do, secretly, make such judgements, and categorise tenants on a scale from 'desirable' to 'highly undesirable'; then match them to houses or estates similarly categorised; and get away with it. (Dr Spicker writes: 'The practice of grading applicants . . . is said to have declined, though as it was not done publicly in the first place, it is difficult to know how true this is.' And also: 'Carmarthen gives points for cleanliness, and Great Yarmouth deducts points for dirtiness, which is not quite the same thing.') In Northern Ireland, every such judgement would be open to the innuendo that it had been reached on political or sectarian grounds: and that would strike at the very roots of the impartiality and integrity which the Executive is charged to display.

A major area of concern in relation to allocations, which has not received much public attention in recent years but may yet come to do so, is the question whether those who could well afford to house themselves, either by purchase or at the upper end of the private rented sector, are being unnecessarily subsidised by the rest of the community. From time to time one hears dark tales of council houses with two shiny new Mercedes cars, or a gleaming new yacht, parked outside; the implication being, that public authority housing is too readily available to those well able to fend for themselves; and that some sort of upper means-limit should be imposed.

Some years ago, the Executive did some research into this subject, which indicated that only a minute percentage of tenants fall into this favoured class; and of those who do, it is probably only for a very short span in the family life-cycle, at a time when several grown-up children are earning but still living at home. In a few other instances, tenants may be individuals who have built up small businesses of their own, and have chosen to invest their savings, together with any capital generated by the business, not in buying a home but rather in building up the business itself. This seems a fair choice, and one of which Mrs Thatcher herself could hardly disapprove. There seems little good reason at present to impose any kind of income (or capital) limit on the resources of those eligible for housing, apart from the existing rule that the owner-occupier of an existing house may not be admitted to the lists unless the house is inadequate for the applicant's needs, or there are urgent and compelling reasons for its sale.

Nevertheless, as the stock of houses available for letting inevitably dwindles in consequence of sales to sitting tenants at generous (perhaps over-generous) discounts, the time may not be far off when public authority housing will have to be reserved for those unable to afford any alternatives. Many people would regard that as a retrograde step; there is certainly as much to be said for a housing service available to all as for a health service available to all. But it is not hard to see the logic of the direction in which present house sale policies are pointing us.

One other category of query regarding allocations policy brings me back full circle into the field of sectarianism and discrimination: the complaint that a house in a Protestant estate or village has been allocated to a Catholic; or, much more rarely, vice versa. For example: letter of May 1983 from a village branch of a constituency Unionist Association;

> ... Out of a total of 25 houses only 8 are habited by Protestants and there seems to be a policy by the Housing Executive to 'import' people, even people who have been owner-occupiers from any-where as long as they are not Protestant to fill each vacancy as it occurs ... Why are relettings not allocated on a fairer basis so as to reflect the balance of the neighbouring community ... Enough is enough and this must stop now ...

My response:

> I know of no evidence to support your statement that young local applicants are being deprived of housing. It appears from the evidence I have that all recent allocations have been made to app-licants with specific family ties in the ... locality. It also appears that they have been made strictly in accordance with need, strictly in accordance with the Executive's Allocation Scheme, and without reference to the religious or political beliefs of the app-licant: and this is as it should be.

This is plainly the only proper response, on the point of principle; but even here it must be said that grievances of this kind are not always founded only in bigotry and prejudice: they may also be founded in genuine fear. There are some areas, mostly near the border, where a suc-cession of murders, bombs and death-threats put at real risk not only those who are courageous enough to serve as part-time members of the police or Ulster Defence Regiment but also peaceable householders who see themselves as being subjected to ever more intolerable pressures from an encroaching local majority. In such cases, there is a difficult conflict between sensitivity to a genuine predicament, and adherence to an important principle. It is sometimes possible for a good housing manager to find ways of reconciling the two, by skilful use of his stock: but not always. And in such cases, the principle and the rules must prevail.

Finally, I return to the question whether the Executive is open to the charge of building new houses or estates in such a way as to influence the outcome of elections. There is no doubt that this policy was practised by some of its predecessor authorities, including Londonderry, Dungannon and Fermanagh. And indeed, many councillors would still stoutly defend it, on the grounds that they are under no obligation 'to cut a rod for our own backs'; and further, that they have done no more than many local housing authorities, Labour or Conservative, in various parts of Great Britain, especially in marginal constituencies or wards.* There is, undoubtedly, some truth in these arguments. There is some truth also in the argument, passionately propounded to me by Harry West (former M.P. for Fermanagh and minister) that the siting of every single house must, of necessity, have electoral consequences in those parts of a divided community where a few more votes one way or the other can influence the outcome in any given constituency or ward.

But the answer is, that the Housing Executive, like any other housing authority elsewhere, should be solely concerned with meeting need when it acquires the sites for new developments; it may look at the price, it may look at the convenience or otherwise of the proposed site to local amenities, it may look at ground conditions; but it should never even glance over its shoulder at the electoral consequences of building here rather than there. *That* is the concern of the Boundaries Commission: and of no-one else.

I firmly believe that, in the matter of allocation and of the siting of new houses, the Executive since its inception has displayed complete impartiality; and that its work in both fields would stand up to any investigation by any fair-minded observer.

---

* See the report, *Who gets Council Houses in Wales*, Welsh Consumer Council, 1985.

# The Physical Fabric
# of Housing

Although those in need of housing services come, like their homes, in all
shapes and sizes, I have found it useful to try to visualise in human terms
a typical customer; one to whom housing bosses owe the very highest
degree of duty. I see that person as an elderly man or woman with a
recurrent bowel complaint, living alone in a condemned kitchen house
without amenities, who is obliged on freezing winter nights to leave his
or her warm bed and go outside at frequent intervals to the primitive
and rat-infested privy at the end of the back yard, or to make insanitary
indoor alternative arrangements. I am not quite sure whether he or she
lives in town or country; but I am quite certain that all those concerned
with housing provision stand towards such a person in the relationship of
trustees.

There are still many thousands of such houses in Belfast (the worn-out
survivors of those so much admired by the Royal Commission in 1885),
in the small towns and villages, and scattered over the Ulster countryside. There are still far more of them, in relation to the total housing
stock, than in Great Britain. One of the major benefits of the establishment of the Housing Executive has been its ability, for the first time in
Northern Ireland, to mount adequate programmes of research; and successive House Condition Surveys have established the position on a
squarely factual basis.

The tables on the next two pages demonstrate, starkly, the extent of the
discrepancy in standards: they are extracted from an article written by me
which appeared in the *Belfast Telegraph* on 17th November 1980: I hope it
is not too immodest to suggest that their publication proved to be a
turning-point for housing policy in Northern Ireland. (I was told that

Table 1:

## Household conditions — Belfast & major British cities

| City | Percentage of households* living two or more rooms below the bedroom standard | Percentage of households with no inside flushing W.C. | Percentage of households without exclusive use of a bath or shower |
|---|---|---|---|
| BELFAST | 3.7 | 24.2 | 23.0 |
| Birmingham | 1.3 | 6.2 | 5.7 |
| Leeds | 0.4 | 2.2 | 4.8 |
| Liverpool | 1.4 | 11.1 | 10.1 |
| Manchester | 1.4 | 7.8 | 8.4 |
| Newcastle-upon-Tyne | 0.6 | 4.8 | 5.4 |
| Sheffield | 0.9 | 7.7 | 7.4 |
| Greater London | 0.9 | 3.5 | 10.0 |

*Percentage differentials between Belfast and the average of the above seven British cities:*

| | |
|---|---|
| Overcrowding | 411% |
| No Flushing W.C. | 550% |
| No exclusive use of a bath or shower | 258% |

*Households which have two or more bedrooms less than their family requirements, i.e., overcrowded

when, a few weeks later, the then Secretary of State, Humphrey Atkins, met Belfast City Council, every single councillor produced a copy of the article from his pocket and laid it on the table.) I am in no doubt that the facts and figures contained in it were influential in securing the restoration of housing funds which came soon after. And, not before time.

The gridirons of working-class streets, of which Belfast is mainly composed, originally built to a density nearly double that of Leeds, were indeed good houses in their day. Many of them have provided a home for three generations of the same family: many of them have been brightly painted and well cared-for by their tenants (if not their landlords).

Elderly people especially look on these tiny kitchen or parlour houses, proudly and affectionately, as 'wee palaces'. And the neighbourliness of street life is remembered sentimentally, if some of its disadvantages tend to be forgotten.

But their defects are self-evident. They were mostly jerry-built in the first place; they mostly lack damp courses; often the chimney is shaky, plaster and woodwork are in poor order, there are damp patches in the

Table 2:

## Dwelling conditions — Northern Ireland & England

| Characteristic | Northern Ireland 1979 | England 1976 | Belfast 1979 | Greater London 1979 |
|---|---|---|---|---|
| Percentage of all dwellings lacking: | | | | |
| 1. Internal W.C. | 15.7 | 6.3 | 24.5 | 3.5 |
| 2. Bathroom | 15.4 | 4.7 | 23.2 | 4.5 |
| 3. Wash hand basin | 15.9 | 5.8 | 26.2 | 6.8 |
| 4. Kitchen sink | 3.6 | 0.3 | 0.6 | 0.6 |
| 5. Hot water supply at 3 points | 17.0 | 6.9 | 26.7 | 8.6 |
| Percentage of all dwellings lacking at least one basic amenity | 19.9 | 8.7 | 28.6 | 9.1 |
| Percentage of all dwellings statutorily unfit | 14.1 | 4.6 | 15.1 | 9.7 |

| Percentage Differentials: | Northern Ireland and England | Belfast and Greater London |
|---|---|---|
| No internal W.C. | 249% | 700% |
| No bathroom | 328% | 516% |
| No wash-hand basin | 274% | 385% |
| No kitchen sink | 1200% | 100% |
| No hot water supply | 246% | 310% |
| Lacking at least one basic amenity | 229% | 314% |
| Statutorily unfit | 306% | 156% |

walls, slates are cracked and letting in the rain, bricks are spalling and mortar has crumbled away; space and storage standards are very low; kitchens are cramped and inconvenient; no bathroom, no indoor lavatory, no wash-basin or even tap apart from the kitchen sink.

The older rural cottages and smallholders' farmhouses often share all these defects: plus, in many cases, the absence of running water and mains sewerage: even, occasionally, of electricity. Somehow, such disadvantages seem more bearable amidst green countryside than in a grimy city; but there are still too many people, some of them struggling to bring up families of children, living in such disheartening conditions. A neatly-kept and white-washed cottage, with honeysuckle at the door, may nonetheless be in desperate need of modernisation (and at least, in the country there will usually be room enough for enlargement) or replacement. But resistance to change goes even deeper in the country than the town: one houseproud tenant of such a cottage, when offered an indoor lavatory, replied — 'What! Have one of those nasty dirty things inside my nice clean house! The proper place for that kind of filth is the wee house at the end of the garden.'

The most depressing kind of poor housing, however, is that to be found in some post-war blocks of flats. Some, not all; of the high-rise blocks inherited by the Executive from its predecessors, about half seem to work perfectly well and to be well-liked by their tenants. The other half include some of the worst disaster areas in the province. And it is by no means clear how or why this has come about, despite much research into problem estates of this kind in England, the United States, and elsewhere. In particular, I remain unconvinced by the arguments of Alice Coleman in *Utopia on Trial* (1985). She analyses statistically a number of specific design faults shared by unsatisfactory developments, and unequivocally attributes all the failures to these. I think her conclusions much too sweeping, and her book is much weakened by the lack of any analysis of the characteristics of those blocks of flats which seem to work successfully. High blocks at Cregagh, Seymour Hill, and Dundonald, for example, seem to work well and to be acceptable and even popular; whereas blocks on the Protestant Shankill Road as well as Catholic Turf Lodge and Moyard had to be demolished as unlettable after only a few years; and the high-rise blocks at Rossville in Derry, the Divis complex in West Belfast, Unity Walk and the Artillery flats in North Belfast, and the blocks in Protestant Larne, give rise to constant trouble and demands for their demolition. In earlier days, there were no doubt too many families with small children, and too many destructive adolescents; but experience soon taught the Executive not to allocate high flats to such families. In some cases, but not others, paramilitary take-overs can be blamed for the unpopularity of flat complexes.

Some defects are easily identified, if not so easily put right. The cold-bridge effect in deck-access blocks, leading to severe condensation, has now been clearly diagnosed. The perils inherent in the use of various cement-based non-traditional methods of construction have become widely realised. The consequences of poorly-installed plastic plumbing systems are all too evident. The inadequacies of chute-based rubbish disposal systems are now apparent; though the original designers cannot fairly be blamed for failing to foresee the packaging revolution, which has doubled our output of rubbish in two decades. But there are other things which are not so clear. Why is it that district heating has been a complete disaster in Northern Ireland, and in many parts of England too: yet it appears to work efficiently and economically in Scandinavia?

Why is it that, in almost every country in Europe, and throughout the Eastern bloc, blocks of flats which would here be problem estates are found perfectly acceptable and satisfactory?

The inescapable fact seems to be, however unpalatable to any liberal-minded observer, that it is the people who live in the flats, not the flats themselves, that make the difference. With a measure of self-discipline and thoughtfulness for others on the part of *all* tenants and their families, most blocks could be reasonably comfortable. (I emphasise *all* tenants; for one family of vandals can wreck a whole block; and I say *most* blocks, since some like the now-demolished Turf Lodge T-block could never have worked.) The class factor, however regrettably, cannot be wholly ignored. Some ladies club together to lay carpeting on the common landings; some others would not dream of sweeping them. Nicely brought-up little boys do not pee in the lifts: badly-brought up little boys, for some reason, take particular delight in doing so, and worse. And so with graffiti, vandalism, mugging, glue-sniffing, joy-riding, and the other mischiefs which can render intolerable the lives of decent and respectable neighbours. In the very long term, perhaps education in civics and in the art of community living will do the trick. It could be cynically remarked that a staircase is as much more sophisticated than a ladder, as a lift is more sophisticated than a staircase: and living in flats accordingly requires a degree of sophistication considerably greater than living in a street, or a cottage.

I realise that, in making these observations, I lay myself open to charges of élitism, class prejudice, and so on. It seems to me however that it is time they were said, plainly and openly, by one whose leanings have always been, and still are, more to the left than to the right. I have much sympathy with the many decent people who live in the Divis complex; I have little with those who are, in the expressive lawyers' phrase, 'the authors of their own misfortune'; I have none whatever with the wholly destructive aims and activities of the Divis Demolition Committee. However disagreeable the Divis complex may be (and there are major improvements in hand) at least every tenant has the benefit of indoor lavatory, wash-basin, bathroom, hot water at three points; and I place their claims on my conscience a long way below those of the typical housing customer identified at the beginning of this chapter.

I must add, that I think it most unfair to lay the blame for conditions in Divis on the architects and housing administrators of twenty years ago. They set out to provide the residents of the old slums which formerly stood on its site with what they, and their spokesmen, insisted they wanted: everybody to have new homes, with all modern amenities, but all within the confines of St Peter's parish. There was no conceivable way of reconciling these three objectives without building upwards:

there simply is not room within the parish boundaries to provide a new house to modern space standards for every former resident. Councillors, representatives of the church, and of the local community, were offered a free trip to Sheffield to see the then recently completed deck-access blocks of flats there: was this what they wanted? Yes, they said, if that is the only way of reconciling our objectives, that is what we want. It is easy now to be wise after the event; but for my part, I place the responsibility where it belongs: on those who insisted they must have the unattainable. And there is a moral here, not to be forgotten when it comes to considering just how far tenant participation in decision-making can sensibly go.

Worn-out terrace housing; primitive rural cottages; unacceptable inner-city flat-blocks; these are the worst deficiencies in the present housing stock. To them must be added two other subjects of growing, though still subsidiary, concern. The first is the need to upgrade and modernise low-rise flats, maisonettes and houses in the public stock, dating from the first decades after the last war, when standards were lower, and designs and materials of far less good quality, than in later years. The second is the need to arrest the deterioration of thousands of owner-occupied houses whose owners, in many cases no longer earning, cannot afford the cost of maintenance and repairs, even with the aid of grants. As John Greve wrote, far-sightedly, in 1969, 'Thousands of owner-occupiers of old houses are buying small but hungry white elephants.' This brand of domestic zoo-keeping has been becoming more and more popular, with government encouragement, ever since; and the consequences for the health of the overall housing stock are becoming more and more worrying.

These then, in brief summary, are the ingredients of the current housing problem of Northern Ireland. There are, I think, five possible solutions: not necessarily as alternatives, any combination is admissible. First, extensive new building on virgin greenfield sites, where they can be found. Second, redevelopment; that is, the acquisition and demolition of unfit housing, and its replacement on the same site. Third, large-scale use of generous grants out of taxpayers' funds to private owners, tenants and landlords — indeed, possibly to public housing tenants too — to enable them to carry out desirable improvements or necessary repairs. Fourth, a major campaign to rehabilitate and modernise, rather than to replace, old dwellings. Fifth, and I do not really believe this is a solution, to leave the whole problem to private enterprise to sort out in strict accordance with the laws of supply and demand.

The first alternative is quick, simple, reasonably economical, and technically by far the easiest. It has been used almost continuously since

1945. But it has great disadvantages: apart from eating up valuable land, it too often results in peripheral estates situated too far away from places of work, schools, shops, pubs, and community facilities. And indeed, in most parts of Ulster the need for this kind of new housing has been almost exhausted; it is likely that Poleglass (on the outskirts of Belfast) and Ballymagroarty (on the outskirts of Derry) will be the last large new greenfield estates of this kind for many a year to come.

In my view, the last alternative — that of pure laisser-faire — can be discarded immediately. No doubt the private sector can make a large, indeed perhaps a much larger contribution, but the essence of the problem concerns people who can afford neither the unsubsidised rent nor the undiscounted purchase price of the kind of homes they need. Market forces, without support from public funds, would drive them within a few years into the kinds of hut, shanty, and hovel which, thank goodness, are no longer to be found in most of the developed countries of the west: it would be a desperately retrograde step, with potentially catastrophic social consequences.

A combination of repair and improvement grants to the private sector with rehabilitation of old houses in the public sector has much in its favour; indeed, it is now in England received public policy; but in my view there are weighty counter-arguments too: and great dangers in abandoning redevelopment and new build altogether: especially in the circumstances of Northern Ireland. I am strongly in favour of rehabilitating the larger and better of the old dwellings in the stock; as also, all those with any degree of architectural or historical merit. But there is an increasing volume of evidence pointing to the conclusion that neither grant-aid nor rehabilitation is always just as good value for money as used to be thought.

To begin with, there is the question of cost: a full modernisation and upgrading job may cost, in Belfast, as much as £18,000, whereas a completely new house to Parker-Morris standards could be built for perhaps £23,000 to £25,000 on the same site. The alternative of converting two old kitchen houses into one single larger one works out far more expensive in practice, usually considerably more than the cost of a single new dwelling. Is this value for money? The life of a well-built new dwelling should not be less than 75 years and it may well have to last for a hundred. The life of a worn-out jerry-built 75-year old house, however well modernised and refurbished, is unlikely to be much longer than another 20 or 30 years. Rehabilitation may merely be an expensive way of postponing the still more expensive day when replacement is indispensable.

But the strongest argument against the wholesale rehabilitation of two-up two-down parlour or kitchen houses is the quality of the result.

On the restricted sites on which most such houses stand, there are only two possible ways of providing modern amenities. One is to sacrifice one of the bedrooms to become a bathroom; in which case, the house can no longer be used for a family, and is suitable only for a one- or two-person household. The other is to extend the dwelling beyond its existing shell by encroaching on the already restricted yard-space. A two-storey extension, with new kitchen below, bathroom above, may be reasonably satisfactory internally; but it drastically reduces light and air both to the house to which it is attached, and to its neighbours. And it leaves practically no yard at all: where before there was perhaps just space to swing a cat, now there will not even be room (in the expressive East Belfast phrase) to trot a mouse. There were good reasons for the insistence in the old Public Health Acts on minimum space standards for backyards; apart from ventilation, they provided space to hang out washing, space for a pet, space for a pot or two of orange lilies or sweet william or easter lilies, according to taste; space to seek at least momentary refuge from a nagging wife, a drunken husband, a heavy parent; and space to provide light and air to back windows.

Moreover, such a house, even when well rehabilitated, will still have only two bedrooms, and so will be ill suited for growing families. It may be quite acceptable for a boy and a girl to share a bedroom until puberty, but by the time they reach their teens children of different sexes need separate rooms. So, though the rehabilitated house may be very suitable for elderly couples, single people, or childless families, it will never again make a suitable family home: nor is it likely to meet the aspirations of modern young couples. There has been a discernible trend in recent years for waiting list applicants to turn down the offer of a rehabilitated house, and insist on waiting for a new one. It would be disastrous if the blighted inner-city areas were to turn into enormous permanent old people's colonies, with no young people at all, no children, and no hope of becoming self-regenerating communities once again. It is necessary to balance the desires of present residents against the needs and aspirations of the younger people who will constitute the householders of the future.

Though there are of course those who take the contrary view, I personally think the case for preferring redevelopment, renewal and new build, is unanswerable, especially in Belfast; but also in many of the provincial towns and villages which have pockets of worn-out and substandard housing near their centres. But such developments, unlike their predecessors, must henceforward be small and manageable; they must be sensitive to the needs of local communities; and to the local environment. Particularly successful examples of this kind of redevelopment scheme have been carried out in Killyleagh, Donaghadee and

Downpatrick, all in Co Down. There have been quite a few others — at Newry, at Gilford, at Glenarm, at Omagh — but there remains a need for many more. I hope that these will be the kind of new building schemes which will predominate over the next decade; and that numbers will not be allowed to fall off because of the laborious procedures involved in consultation, persuasion, land acquisition, decanting, and finally building on constricted sites in small parcels.

So then: what sort of dwellings should be built? There is little doubt what most Ulster people want; single-storey or two-storey houses of traditional appearance and construction: preferably of red-brick in the city, white-washed or roughcast in the smaller towns and villages: with reasonable space standards and all modern amenities. (There are, however, some curious quirks of local taste to be borne in mind. Internal bathrooms constitute an odd example. Hardly a five-star luxury hotel can have been built since 1945, anywhere in the world, which does not make use of this sensible space-saving expedient. Yet many Ulster householders, who have never had any bathroom at all before, seem to regard it as a gross dereliction of their rights that they should not be able to air the toothbrush on the window-sill: and for some enigmatic reason, this view is particularly widespread amongst Catholic tenants, while Protestants generally find internal bathrooms perfectly acceptable.) Certain crucial decisions were taken by the Board very early in the life of the Executive; indeed, as noted on page 43, I was the principal author of the paper 'Strategy of New Building' (Appendix), approved in March 1973, on which policy has been founded for more than a decade. No more high-rise developments; a predominance of medium to high density layouts; full adherence to Parker-Morris standards (when the Conservative government in 1980 ditched them, the Executive elected to go its own way); the design of a series of basic house-types, with proven internal layouts, capable however of adaptation in detail and in materials to different environments.

Some early hopes failed to materialise; others were over-ruled from Stormont; others again were much altered in the light of experience. I personally was an advocate of a return to the three-storey terraced town houses which had served previous generations so well. Although a certain number of these have been built, especially along main-road frontages where two-storey houses would have seemed mean and out of scale, they have proved less popular than I had hoped: mainly because of the not inconsiderable extra cost of rent, floor-covering, curtaining, furnishing and heating. They have their place in the range, nevertheless, especially for large households, and on particularly sensitive sites.

Several Board members joined me in the view that the then-fashionable district heating schemes should be embarked upon with caution: and that, save in flat blocks where the problems of coal storage and ash disposal would have been insuperable, every dwelling should have a fireplace and a chimney. Putting it at its lowest, we said a tenant should have the right to burn his furniture or even our bannisters rather than freeze to death. But, though the Board backed us, our officers did not; the desire for an open fire was then seen by the architectural profession as nothing but sentimentality; and the Ministry flatly refused to approve the modest expenditure involved — under £200 a house — in providing every new dwelling with a chimney, on the grounds that it would have constituted an unacceptable duplication of provision. It remains my own view, whatever the technical experts may say, that lack of ventilation is the cause of much unnecessary condensation; and that the installation of chimneys would have served a double purpose. However that may be, the wheel has come full circle, and chimneys are now to be inserted, at a cost not much below £2,000 a house, in those dwellings from which district heating is to be removed. It gave me great pleasure, in December 1983, to write an I-told-you-so letter to our Minister, pointing out that in this instance the Board had been wise not after, but before, the event — but had been over-ruled by the bureaucrats and technocrats: and inviting him to draw the appropriate inferences for the future.

In another instance, Board members ultimately prevailed over the advice of officers and civil servants that it was impossible, in high-density urban developments, to orientate every house so that it received either morning or evening sunshine in the main rooms. With ingenuity, and sometimes a slight loss of density, this can be achieved: and it is to the especial credit of one Board member, Mrs Moyra Mitchell, that it became established policy to build no house without some share of sunlight.

New systems of building, and in particular the timber-frame construction systems then coming into vogue, were approached with increasing caution. Experience with earlier systems (see page 29) had not been very happy; though there were great theoretical attractions about any system which might simultaneously generate increased local factory employment, and provide satisfactory housing more quickly, or more cheaply, or both: yet there were real risks too, and the benefits were uncertain. In order to provide sufficient guaranteed work to justify the establishment and tooling of a new factory, one particular competitor would have had to be granted so substantial a contract as to accord him a near-monopoly for a considerable number of years. Not only would this have run counter to the well-established principles of tendering for public works, it raised other worries too: no adequate quality control system for the factory floor, comparable to the supervisory on-site role of the clerk of works, had yet been devised. And then, the still larger question: is timber as a primary structural material really well-suited to the rainy and humid climate of Northern Ireland? Fire and war may not have been the only reasons why no single Elizabethan timber-frame house survives in the whole of Ireland, though it is known that many thousands were built. Those with experience of the ravages of the unseasoned timber, wet rot, dry rot, woodworm, or death-watch beetle, tended to shudder, despite the reassurances of the industry and its marketing men. Since in housing it may take decades for the most expensive misjudgements to become apparent, there is much to be said for sticking to methods and materials which have proved themselves reliable in the past. On the whole, whilst not refusing to consider new products, the Executive tended to be more conservative, and less inclined towards innovation and experiment, than its predecessor the Housing Trust. And I must admit to having been, in this respect, amongst the most conservative of its members.

Another decision of significance was, that unsupervised old people's dwellings should not, in future, be built with less than two bedrooms; the purpose being to ensure that, when an elderly person fell ill, there would be room for a friend or relative to come and care for him or her. This policy decision will soon have to be revised if the Executive is to try to meet the ever-growing demand for small dwellings for one- or two-person households, and to provide more flexibility of accommodation between old and young. An equally contentious question will be whether such small dwellings should, like family houses, have fireplaces and chimneys; there is a strongly-supported school of thought whose members think that this is what elderly people are mostly used to and prefer: another which says that heavy coal and hot ashes are too dangerous for them to handle, and that electricity, however dear, is safer. If there is to be a new generation of dual-purpose small dwellings designed to meet the needs of both young and of old, questions such as this will have to be rethought all over again.

Given my personal interest in Irish architectural history, and long-standing commitment to conservation, it was hardly surprising that, throughout my time with the Executive, I took a close interest in the appearance and the aesthetics of its output. I started out with high hopes that it might, in the normal exercise of its proper functions, become a powerful instrument for conservation. I under-estimated the extent of the conflict between well-intentioned conservation, and the considerations of speed, economy, and practicality. I had hoped that, in particular, its regional and district offices might have been sensibly housed in some of the many neglected but attractive buildings in which the towns of Northern Ireland used to be rich. In this ambition, I met

with much opposition. In Ireland, too many people, from architects to
trade unionists, think only what is modern is good. I had a short-lived
success in the city of Armagh, where one of the noble terrace of houses
known as Seven Sisters was converted, at considerable cost, to provide
office accommodation; only to be quickly bombed and judged beyond
restoration. And another in Lisburn, but there a splendid mid-18th
century town house, even after adaptation, was considered unsuitable,
and sold in favour of more modern premises. Of the new red-brick
purpose-built housing offices in Downpatrick and Enniskillen I can only
say, humbly, that I am ashamed; both are quite inappropriate to the
historic town-centres in which they stand. I can but plead in self-defence,
first, that the Board was in each instance assailed by strong technical and
professional advice that only a 'modern' building could efficiently meet
the needs of the town in question. And, second, that I felt it not right
to force my own minority views down the throats of my colleagues,
lest every other Board member should in consequence claim the
right to ride his own hobby-horse at full gallop through the executive's
programme.

I must acknowledge, ruefully and with regret, that in my time the
Executive's contribution to the preservation of the traditional townscape of the province was a lot less than I could have wished. There have
been a few, but alas too few, worth-while conservation undertakings,
such as the restoration of a terrace of late-Georgian houses in Joy Street,
Belfast: and I have an uncomfortable feeling that even this scheme was
only approved by a reluctant Department of the Environment as a sop
to the importunacies of a conservationist chairman. I did not feel that
many politicians, civil servants, Board members or even officers of the
Executive really sympathised much with my own views. I did my best,
however, to atone for this by seeking to secure — perhaps with
somewhat more success — that its new houses fitted reasonably happily
and harmoniously into their historical and geographical framework.

The various ranges of house-types were designed by a team of the
Executive's own staff architects, principally Ken Shaw, Bob Strang and
Roy Reid, and the fifth range in particular was a great improvement on
the preceding types. About half the Executive's output has over the
years been produced by its own design groups; about half by private
firms of consultants using the basic range of house-types with appropriate (and it must be said, occasionally inappropriate) variations to
meet the exigencies of the particular site. Some consultants had to be
weaned gradually away from their predilections for monopitch roofs,
corner, triangular, and thin vertical-strip-windows, and such-like
'features'. Two or three firms or individuals — it would perhaps
be invidious to name them — have been particularly successful in

establishing local versions of a modern vernacular, an objective very close to my own heart. This, however, did not come about quickly or easily.

Early schemes on particularly sensitive sites in Tandragee and Banbridge, though popular with the public, smacked too much of 'reproduction' architecture, with Georgian glazing-bars, quoins, and generally somewhat pasteboard theatricality. The breakthrough came at Shore Street, Portaferry where a curving line of old fishermen's cottages, beloved of conservationists, was satisfactorily replaced by a new terrace which reproduced the massing, the scale and the colouring of the old, while being quite contemporary in detail. In general, the Board has much preferred this kind of formula to the stagey use of mock-Georgian features: though in some places, especially in proximity to older Georgian houses, criss-cross glazing bars at least have seemed appropriate.

Since its inception, the Board has devoted much time and attention to the scrutiny of scheme designs, whether by way of plans, elevations and drawings; scheme booklets; or slide presentations. Some administrators might be tempted to say, a disproportionate part of its time; but I remain firmly of the opinion that this concentration on quality has well justified itself. Certainly, the designs of the last few years have seemed to be practical, well-liked, and popular with tenants — subject to some criticisms, most of which relate to the layout and the characteristics of the surrounding space rather than to the houses themselves.

In fact, this is an area of much debate and some dissension. The Executive's early schemes were, for the most part, laid down on the 'Radburn' principle, involving separation of pedestrians from traffic. In practice, this usually meant that all vehicular traffic was to the rear, with only a footpath in front; which proved most unpopular with tenants who, reasonably, whether car-owners or not, at least wished that the wedding limousine and the funeral hearse could come to the front door (just as they very properly required, what some architects forgot, that the stairway must be capable of allowing a coffin to be brought downstairs without the indignity of having to stand it on its end). Now we are into the era of shared surfaces; which work well so long as they are sufficiently intimate and small in scale, but less well if they are too large. And this involves the debate on the ratio of car-parking spaces required. In present times of recession, few inner-city dwellers have cars, but the planners argue that, over the lifetime of the houses, their numbers may largely increase, and provision must be made for them now. Probably they are right, but present tenants do not appreciate the point. Some tenants long for, and tend lovingly, their individual garden plots, front, back, or both; others do not want any garden at all. Most tenants dislike

the currently fashionable brick-enclosed planter-boxes, which nevertheless do serve a useful purpose in softening otherwise unduly harsh surroundings. Most tenants want infants' play-space, but never outside
their own houses. Some tenants want the highest possible densities,
others want more breathing space and air. It will never be possible to
please everybody. The quality and appearance of many of the
Executive's developments, and especially redevelopments, have been
vitiated by the fact that the vested areas have not extended to include
the main-road frontages, comprising largely worn-out (and often
derelict) shops. This arises from government policy resulting from
pressure to retain traditional local shopping areas. The consequences,
unfortunately, have been discreditable to all concerned; and have
resulted in a new environment whose heart is sound enough but whose
face is hideous. This is something which requires reconsideration.

It is noticeable that the courtyard-type layouts, now almost universally employed by the Executive, owe something to the concept of
'defensible space' developed in the United States in recent years. There
has been a conscious and deliberate attempt to encourage the growth of
small communities in each courtyard, rather than the anonymity of the
long grids of streets of the past. Yet there are those in some tenants'
associations who argue for a return to the old street pattern; though they
take little account of the needs of modern motor traffic, and the hazards
it poses for playing children. Nevertheless, and on a fairly experimental
basis, the Executive has responded here and there by trying to rebuild as
nearly as is practicable on the old street lines: it remains to be seen how
successful in the longer term such schemes will prove.

Time will tell in particular whether the houses built in the last few
years will retain their popularity. Every generation tends to think its
immediate predecessors foolish and shortsighted; blames them for their
egregious mistakes; and knows better than its parents. It takes quite a
time for the cycle of fashion to perform one full revolution, and it may be
that, unconsciously, though we have been trying very hard to learn from
the mistakes of our immediate predecessors — the high-rise and deck-
access flat blocks, the untried systems and materials, the heating systems
that did not work, and so on — we have been making even worse
mistakes. I hope not; and if we have, I do not yet know what they are; but
I am resigned to the possibility, perhaps even the probability, that the
next generation will blame us bitterly for something.

There are difficult questions, constantly changing, not only as to the
kinds of dwellings to be built, but as to the mix of different sizes of accommodation; the locations where they should be built; and perhaps most
controversial of all, the numbers required. All these factors require
much research and analysis; but in the end, they require predictions of

the inherently unpredictable, and decisions which must be taken (if anything whatever is to be achieved) at risk. Population projections, forecasts of rate of household formation, estimates of the availability of relets, these and many other relevant figures must be assessed. But in the last resort, the closure of a single large factory can radically alter overnight the pattern of housing demand over a wide area; as can the opening up of new employment opportunities; or many other unforeseeable factors. The over-provision of houses in Craigavon and Antrim new towns resulted directly from the recession in employment there. The same thing could happen elsewhere: East Belfast depends largely on the employment generated by the shipyard and aircraft factory, both all too vulnerable to cycles of recession. There is an element of gamble about the siting of new housing, as also about the selection of a housing mix: an expanding community requires a higher proportion of family houses, a declining one a higher proportion of accommodation for the elderly. And this last can pose particular problems; it is no use building groups of old people's dwellings at the top of steep hills, or miles from shops, surgeries and churches. Yet relatively flat sites close to all amenities are, in most towns and villages, hard to find: they have mostly already been snapped up for commercial development. And in many places, particularly in the west of the province, sites available even for normal family housing are hard to find — since neither hilly nor boggy sites make for successful estates, and rocky ones pose formidable problems for water supply and sewerage. It is not nearly so easy to find satisfactory sites for new housing as the casual traveller, seeing green fields at the town's edge, might suppose.

The question of the numbers of dwellings required is even more complicated: waiting-lists supply only a very crude and unsophisticated indicator of real housing need. Much depends on the question whether one chooses to take a long or a short view. If one selects the latter alternative, then the numbers of housing starts required may fluctuate wildly from year to year reflecting completions, relets, private sector performance, rent levels, interest levels, mortgage availability, inflation, unemployment rates, willingness to accept sharing or over-crowding in the interests of economy, or sheer despair. And whatever happens, the supply will reflect the demand several years too late — because of the irreducible time-lag between programming new houses and having them ready for occupation.

Alternatively, one may take the very long view; and simply look at the total stock of dwellings, the foreseeable number of households, and the rate at which old houses will require to be replaced by new ones. There is an element of crystal-ball gazing in this approach too: but at least, its conclusions will be based on a time-scale long enough to iron out the

peaks and troughs of war and peace, recession and prosperity, demand
and supply. I started out in 1956 calling, on a wholly empirical basis, for
a minimum programme of 5,000 new public sector houses a year for
Northern Ireland. I was happy enough to increase the target figure in
the pushful years between 1971 and 1979; some politicians, and Shelter,
have from time to time called for a revival of the figure of 10,000 a year
with which, optimistically, the Executive started out; but I have never
seen that figure statistically justified; and when the Conservative cutbacks of the latter year arrived, I continued to press for a minimum programme of 5,000 houses a year. The pressure was successful: in 1981 the
Executive was allowed to set itself a target of 5,250 houses a year for the
ensuing five years, but in 1983, monetary pressures tightened, private
sector performance began to pick up, waiting-lists fell and relets rose
despite house sales: and the target figure was cut, first to 4,000 then to
3,000 houses a year, ostensibly to meet changing circumstances.

I was, and remain, unconvinced: though I must perforce accept that
in a time of cash limitation, new building may not be the only or highest
priority. I recognise the dangers of 'the numbers game' as it is called: I
recognise the serious risks of overprovision: I do not regard the number
of houses started or completed in any financial year as a status symbol, or
a token of virility. Nevertheless, I still think the greatest lesson of the past
century is the need to maintain, so nearly as possible, an even and steady
flow of new houses from year to year over a long period. And I still think
a figure of 5,000 new houses a year is correct for the foreseeable future: I
reinforce my argument by proposing the assumptions that, even if
nearly 50,000 houses are sold to their occupiers, there is likely to remain
a need for not less than 150,000 houses of acceptable standard for rental
in the public sector. If each new house has a useful life of 75 years, then a
rolling programme of 3,000 new houses a year would suffice to replace
them all. But that presupposes that we are starting from a satisfactory
base-line: which we are not. With at least 10 per cent of the present stock
below the unfitness plimsoll mark and more old houses constantly
deteriorating, a good deal more is required. In any event, it leaves out of
account the fact that, between 1900 and 1945, only rock-bottom
numbers were built; and it will take till the end of this century, another
15 years at least, to catch up with the backlog by adding an additional
30,000 dwellings at the rate of 2,000 a year; giving a starts programme at
the rate of 5,000 a year.

As the 'better' houses in the public stock are sold off to the 'better'
tenants, so the older residue will increasingly urgently require replacement. Moreover, all the demographic projections suggest that the trend
towards smaller households, and an increasing rate of new household
formation, will continue; so that the balance between dwellings and

households will be overturned unless the total stock increases at a corresponding rate.

There are two further arguments for continuing a sustained new build programme in a time of recession. First, and this is an argument which certainly swayed James Prior and David Mitchell when they decided in 1981 to accord housing priority over other competing claims for resources, a high building programme generates very considerable direct and indirect employment. Second, it is precisely at a time of recession that prices are lowest, and the taxpayer can obtain the best value. Tenders from work-hungry builders are exceptionally keen; contracts tend to be completed far more quickly and economically by those anxious to obtain payment at the earliest moment. Certainly, in the mid-1980s, and despite wide variations in pricing between country towns and inner-city Belfast, the costs of new dwellings, in real money terms, have been lower in Northern Ireland than for many years past. The social and economic arguments therefore coincide in favour of a very deliberate policy of keeping a high new build programme in a period of depression and high unemployment.

In fact, the most obvious and damaging criticism which can be levelled at the Housing Executive is that it has over a quite lengthy period produced fewer new houses than did its predecessor bodies between them. The Executive, in its first thirteen years, completed an average of under 5,000 a year: but between 1966 and 1970, the Housing Trust, the Development Commissions, and the Councils, between them completed a steady average of nearly 7,500 a year; and in 1971, topped the 9,000 mark. It was then hoped that the Executive, with all its resources and all the advantages of scale, could have bettered that figure with comparative ease.

There are in truth good reasons why it failed to do so. First, the concentration on better quality was to some extent at the expense of quantity — if the Executive had gone on building high-rise or deck-access flats, it could have produced far more units. Second, the shift from greenfield to redevelopment carried an inevitable penalty. Third, the over-impetuous shift of fashion from renewal to rehabilitation brought about a sharp cut in newbuild numbers (without, be it noted, a corresponding increase in rehabilitation completions). Fourth, there were the direct and indirect effects of the Troubles. Finally, it is fatally easy to build large numbers of houses in places where they are not really needed: but confoundedly difficult to compete with all the other pressures on space, and build them in the places where they really *are* needed.

But to my mind, the most important question of all is whether the Executive has got right the balance between quantity and quality. For an expenditure of one million pounds, it is possible to build a single

palace (as at least one South American police chief has in fact done out of
his bribes); or ten luxurious mansions for £100,000 each; or forty good
houses for £25,000 each; or fifty rather less good houses for £20,000 each;
or five hundred shacks, little better than hen-houses, for £2,000 each.
This is the point at which cost becomes a very material factor; and where
the value-for-money argument comes into play.

Various politicians have at different periods argued that the best is the
enemy of the good; that the country was spending more than it could
afford on extravagantly generous new housing; that it would be better
value to build larger numbers of smaller houses at lower prices. This
argument has not been the sole property of any one party: it was
advanced by the late Anthony Greenwood, and by Harold MacMillan,
as well as, more recently, by Mrs Thatcher. Some tenants would agree;
the higher cost of a house implies higher rents, too, and to the extent to
which housing and other benefits fail to overcome the poverty trap, this
can have unfortunate consequences for less well-off families. There is no
doubt that, behind the lace curtains of nice new Parker-Morris houses,
there can be grinding poverty, contributed to by the need to buy on the
never-never new curtains, floor coverings and furnishings, and to heat
much larger spaces than were necessary in a previous kitchen house.

But I remain very firmly convinced that *some* minimum standards
there must be; and that the Parker-Morris criteria, laid down almost a
quarter-century ago, are today too low rather than too high. I believe
that it is foolish short-sightedness to build down to minimum standards,
when aspirations and expectations have been steadily rising all through
this century, and seem far more likely than not to go on doing so for the
next century — and the house we build today may well have to last so
long. As Donnison and Ungerson put it,

> A new source of housing obsolescence has appeared, for those
> households, which do not have the space to accommodate cars,
> freezers, dishwashers or washing machines will eventually perceive
> themselves as deprived — and not without reason ... Housing
> which prevents people from sharing in this way of life will become
> the slums of tomorrow.

And finally, I believe very firmly that some system of adequate
housing benefit is indispensable; and that people who cannot afford the
full cost of housing themselves, whether in the private or the public
sector, are entitled to expect the community to provide them with a
house which reasonably meets their *needs* — not just the least bad accommodation they can afford. Though having said this, I must acknowledge
that there has never been any adequate public or political debate as to
the definition of 'needs'. How is subsistence level to be defined? Is it to

include a colour television set, black-and-white, a wireless, a stereo, a video? Is it, at any rate in country areas, to include a car? Successive governments have driven up rents, reduced benefits, and promulgated the concept of a basic subsistence level, without ever saying what is the minimum level they expect. There has been a real failure here: and it is time that government and the political parties tried to discover a consensus on the subject.

One other argument has particular force in Northern Ireland: the deficiencies of the past. For the reasons I have explained in chapter two, the standard of the housing provided in Northern Ireland, while it was comparatively high in 1885, has lagged steadily behind the rising standards of the rest of the United Kingdom ever since 1900. By now, in Britain, a large proportion of the total stock has been built to reasonable standards of space and amenity; but only the output of the last decade falls into that category in Northern Ireland. There is still a great deal of leeway to be made up, probably even more in terms of quality than quantity. I remain absolutely and unalterably convinced that the province in general, and Belfast in particular, still requires a major injection, over a considerable period, of both quantity and quality in the housing field.

# Tenants:
# Their Rights and Wrongs

I never thought it right to take my telephone number out of the directory, since I hold strongly to the view that the chairman of a public body ought to be accessible as a sort of court of final appeal to those with complaints or grievances. For the same reason, I tried to reply personally (and by return) to as many as possible of the tenants' letters I received. Some of the telephone calls to my home, and some of the letters too, were rather odd: it is only to be expected that, out of nearly 200,000 tenants, a certain proportion will be cranks, or paranoid, or just slightly mentally unbalanced. On one occasion, I had a telephone call from a lady saying she was speaking on behalf of God, and that He had seen me on the telly, and that He said I was a right decent fellow, and I was to allocate a house in East Belfast to His representative's sister's daughter without delay. On another, I had an agitated call from a lady who complained that, whenever she had a bath or washed her hair, the water splashed over the floor and might cause her electric wiring to short unless I provided her with a waterproof floor covering. A good many of the letters have been odder still: an anthology of them, carefully selected, would make a book far more entertaining than this one. But, of course, the great majority of them have been genuine and reasonable, if not always polite.

The very first letter I received as chairman of the Executive was a bitter complaint from a tenant that nobody had come to re-hang the door of his living-room, which did not fit properly — yet he was himself an unemployed joiner! It is right that tenants should expect a housing authority to honour its legal obligations to keep their homes in good repair; and should have legal redress (to which, increasingly, they are now having recourse) if it should fail to do so. Yet, for all that, too many able-bodied tenants have come to expect to have done for them what they could very easily, and far more cheaply, do for themselves. Every private home-owner knows how many minor running repairs a house, however well-built, needs in the course of a year to keep it in good order. Those who have the taste or the talent for do-it-yourself will take on all but the most daunting tasks: I used to have a neighbour, a highly-skilled orthopaedic surgeon, whose principal recreation was renewing and improving his plumbing. Few owners, other than the aged or handicapped, will face the cost and inconvenience of bringing in builders if they can possibly do the job themselves. In the past, tenants of private landlords had no expectations that any repairs whatever would be done: and resigned themselves to looking after their homes themselves. Public housing authorities, including the Executive and some of its predecessor bodies, took a more responsible attitude, and (certainly since 1945) have done their best to carry out their obligations. But they have been largely defeated by the steady rise in tenants' expectations.

No subject is more fruitful of grievances than that of repairs and maintenance performance: while many of these grievances are reasonable and justified, others are wildly unreasonable. People can wax extraordinarily indignant about really trivial defects; and, of course, complaints about repairs are the staple diet of local authority politics. There was a sudden, quite unforeseen, and phenomenal increase in the number of repair requests received by the Executive in the autumn of 1982; there was no obvious cause, such as a spell of hard weather; an overspending of several million pounds seemed unavoidable, and was only in fact avoided by a seven-week moratorium on all but the most pressing repairs. It subsequently became plain that the unexpected rise in demand had not been unconnected with the elections for the Stormont Assembly: candidates were competing with each other in collecting up complaints — 'Is there anything the matter with your house?' was the canvasser's cry on every doorstep. And since then, the Assembly's adjournment debates have provided a ready opportunity, with no minister or responsible person present to contradict, for attacks on the maintenance record of the Executive in this constituency or that.

Of course, some of these complaints are justified: but not all. In an attempt to meet the pressure, the Executive divided repair requests into three categories — urgent, to be completed within four days; significant, to be completed within six weeks; and comparatively unimportant, to be dealt with as part of a scheme for the estate concerned. The time limits are in practice pretty well adhered to; yet the percentage of the third category of requests is surprisingly small. Some repairs are carried out by the Executive's own direct labour force, others by contractors, and there is no striking disparity between the performance of the two. Others again, though not a large proportion of the total, are carried out through a self-help repair scheme under which the tenant can arrange for approved work to be carried out to a maximum value of £125 and then send the bill to the Executive. In addition to the normal run of demand-generated response repairs, there is a very substantial annual programme of planned maintenance. A fair assessment of the validity of the criticisms is made more difficult by widespread public confusion, not least amongst politicians, between 'repairs' and 'improvements'. Many of the complaints turn out to be about the latter and not the former; for example, the housewife who complains bitterly that she cannot get a new stainless steel sink unit, when her existing porcelain sink and wooden draining board are in perfectly good order, and have years of useful life to go before they are due for replacement.

The National Consumer Council, in a study of repairs in 1979, found that though local authority tenants tend to receive a speedier repairs service than owner occupiers, the former are, paradoxically, less satisfied with that service. This finding was quoted in a survey commissioned by the Executive in 1983 from the Housing Research Group of Glasgow University which found that the economic circumstances of tenants had as much to do with repair demand as the characteristics of the dwellings themselves. They also found that tenants in Northern Ireland lacked the extra cover which recourse by the housing authority to the general rate fund provided in Great Britain; and that maintenance expenditure and numbers of repair requests were not excessive, indeed expenditure had dropped in 1981/82, and compared unfavourably with performance in Britain when seen as a percentage of rent collected. There has been, in consequence, an increase in the proportion of total funds allocated both to maintenance and to improvements; but whether this will be effective in stemming the tide of criticism remains to be seen. A cynic could come to believe that tenants' grievances about maintenance are as unalterable as farmers' complaints about the weather.

The other major perennial grievance, of course, is at the amount of the rent. And indeed, it is a very intricate and controversial subject: everybody can tell when rents are too high, but few and far between are the citizens who can propose a water-tight method of determining what a fair rent may be.

Apart from the rather complex system used in the United Kingdom there are five principal theoretical alternatives. The first is, to provide all housing free; as with the national health service in earlier and happier days. Of course, if this were possible, food and drink should be free too: but this is not quite so unrealistic and anarchistic a view as might be thought: it remains the objective of the Soviet Union to provide free housing for all its citizens, though it has not yet achieved that aim. It still operates the second alternative, that is, the levying of rent as a fixed percentage of income: in the USSR, this is as low as 2.5%, though in most other eastern bloc countries, it is somewhat higher. For purposes of comparison, it is interesting to note that the present Conservative government has fixed rent levels at around 8% of average earnings. In many west European countries, the percentage of income devoted to housing costs is considerably higher. The third alternative is to charge differential rents related in part to the costs of construction, maintenance and management, in part to the income of the occupiers under a compulsory means-testing system. This is the system employed in the Republic of Ireland. The fourth is to allow rents to be determined solely by the market forces of supply and demand: this, like the fifth alternative, is not in Britain a political possibility at present. The final alternative would be to charge full economic rents, covering not only the costs of land acquisition, site development and construction, but also management and maintenance costs, amortised over the expected life of the dwelling. Any such calculation is highly sensitive to fluctuations in interest rates. It was calculated in January 1983 that the historic cost rent of a new 5-person 3-bedroom house in inner Belfast would then have been no less than £92.50 per week. By January 1984, due to falling interest rates, this had dropped to £69.50 per week. In theory, rents might be set so as to rise and fall in harmony with mortgage rates. But that would be to throw away one of the greatest advantages of the British system: the pooling of costs in such a way that properties built in times of lower costs or interest rates subsidise the rents of properties constructed at a time of inflation, high costs and interest rates.

This unique system means that in Britain the rents of new houses for young families do not, as in the rest of Europe, constantly outpace the rents of older housing occupied by more affluent middle-aged people.

In Northern Ireland, as in Britain, the present system is a compound one, based on the pooling of all costs and subsidies: the Government decides how much of the total cost of housing is to be borne each year by taxpayers, how much by tenants: the Executive is responsible for the distribution of the total rent burden as between the different types of dwelling in the overall stock: and the government sets the level of the housing benefit which is related, not to the dwelling, but to the circumstances of the individual tenant and his ability to pay. The only significant differences between the system in Great Britain and the system in Northern Ireland are, first, that unlike English housing authorities, the Executive can neither use ratepayers' money to subsidise tenants, nor tenants' money to subsidise ratepayers; second, that the Government has power (has indeed used the power) to issue a direction to the Executive as to the amount of rent it is required to collect.

This is a complex and sophisticated system, which would have seemed quite unbelievable to our great-grandparents, which seems unbelievable still to people in many parts of the world. In the past, there was nothing to moderate the harsh operation of the laws of supply and demand: the first Rent Restriction Acts date back only to 1915, when they were brought in to deal with unrest amongst Glasgow munitions workers: the first subsidies date only from the post-first-war years: the pooling of historic costs dates only from 1936; rent rebates, and now housing benefit, are more recent still.

Just as the repeal of the Corn Laws in the 1840s had provided the industrial masses with cheaper bread at the expense of the farmers, so the Rent Restriction Acts provided the tenants of private housing with cheaper homes at the expense of their landlords. In the process, they brought into existence the belief that a 'fair' rent must be something less than an economic rent; a belief which found particularly easy root in Ireland, with its long tradition, until the passing of the Land Acts, of resistance to rack rents. (A 'rack-rent' is a highly ambiguous article. The Oxford English Dictionary gives two meanings, mutually con-tradictory, without expressing a preference between them: 'a very high, excessive, or extortionate rent; a rent equal (or nearly equal) to the full value of the land.' Unsurprisingly, tenants tend to prefer the former usage; landlords, the latter). But how much less, nobody seemed able to say. Of course, rent increases are nowhere popular with the victims; but there is perhaps a particular emotional passion about the reaction to a rent increase, as there is to an eviction, which in Ireland (north and south) exceeds the indignation shown in England or Scotland. As Professor Donnison has remarked, the Scottish Congested Districts Board never had the powers of its Irish counterpart, and there was never a Scottish Land Commission — although the problems in both countries were the same — because Scottish tenants never went so far as to shoot their landlords.

Until 1971, the Northern Ireland Housing Trust, and the other housing authorities, were required to balance their rent accounts, albeit with the help of subsidies on new building; so that rents, though lower, were not very much lower than historical costs required — especially for the Trust which had no pre-war stock over which to spread the burden. In its formative years, the Executive was expected to pursue the same course, though with considerably more handsome assistance from the taxpayer; which became increasingly necessary as inflation gathered pace. Indeed, during the Labour years the Executive was actually refused permission for a very modest rent increase, since it would have run counter to Government strategy for holding down costs and prices. The result was that, by 1979, average rents had fallen from 8% to 6.5% of average earnings. The burden on the tenant was lower, but the burden on the taxpayer was higher. I have little doubt that the return of Mrs Thatcher's first Government in 1979 owed much to a widespread feeling, from which I could not then, and do not now, altogether dissent, that the balance between benefits to the needy, and contributions from the sometimes only slightly better off, had gone badly amiss. The predictable result was that government ordained a sharp increase in rent levels: in 1981/82, though the Board of the Executive opposed it, it was formally directed by government to increase its rental income by 40%; in the following year, the Board reluctantly accepted a further 19% increase as the unavoidable condition for an enhanced new-build programme; increases of 6% and of 5% were to follow in the two ensuing years, but since they roughly reflected the then current rates of inflation these were not, like their predecessors, increases in real money terms.

The public has, I think, now come to realise that the sharp rent increases to which it has been subjected in the last few years are the result of government policy rather than of the malice or ineptitude of the Executive. But it is the Executive which must issue the notices of rent increase, and which is the front-line target for the fury of tenants and their representatives. And, now that it is the Executive which administers the new housing benefit system, it will no doubt be the Executive and its staff which will be the front-line targets for its imperfections, or for its inadequacy, or for cuts in benefit level. But at least the introduction of the new benefit was carried through far more smoothly than had been the case in Great Britain; serious complaints were astonishingly few; and for this, thorough and careful preparatory work, and an anxious willingness to learn from the experience of others, may be held responsible.

The whole subject of rents and rent levels is bedevilled by the fact that public announcements, and debate, are always expressed in terms of averages. It is hard, if not impossible, to find any other workable currency; but much acrimony springs from the fact that, inevitably, many people are faced with rent increases of more than the *average* amount, and are not slow to make their voices heard. And equally, average rent expressed as a percentage of average earnings invites forceful comments from those whose individual rents are very much more than 8% of their individual earnings. Nor are local politicians slow to make the most of these discrepancies.

The Board of the Executive has consistently argued for a lower level of increase in Northern Ireland, compared with the rest of the United Kingdom, to take account of lower incomes, higher prices, the sharp differential in the cost of living, and greater dependence on housing benefits and social security. It has also argued forcefully, and with somewhat more success, that rent increases should be treated as a separate issue from decisions on its capital programme. More recently, it pressed the case for at least a year's rent freeze to ease the introduction of a new system of distributing the total rent burden between the tenants of different kinds of houses: but without success.

One of the most difficult tasks facing the Executive in 1972 had been the rationalisation of the widely differing rents charged for similar dwellings by its predecessors. Such a scheme was in fact introduced in 1973; it was the brainchild of the then Director of Finance, Jack Brown; it was ingenious; it was accepted as fair, and for a number of years it worked very well, though it was in some respects a bit rough and ready; and it took a full decade to come near completing its introduction, due to the need to phase in increases in amounts manageable for the tenants, a particularly difficult task in the light of government anti-inflation policies. By 1981, however, a disquieting number of complaints was being received about the scheme, along the lines of 'Mrs Mulligan has a far better house than mine, why is my rent £2 a week higher than hers?' In 1982, the Board set up a Review Committee to engage in consultation, and to frame a new rents points scheme similar to those lately introduced by a number of English housing authorities.

The committee started by commissioning the Housing Research Group of Glasgow University to carry out a preliminary report. This confirmed that the existing scheme had become seriously distorted by the passage of time and the effects of inflation; that it took too little account of house types and far too much of age; that the characteristics on which rent assessment was based were too restricted; and that, unlike the English schemes, no account was taken of the quality of the environment. A rough outline of a new scheme was therefore prepared and very widely distributed for public comment and debate.

It is probable that this was the most extensive exercise in consultation yet undertaken by a housing authority in the British Isles: its results were in some respects startling. In the first place, unaccustomed to being consulted on such a scale, the public suspected a cosmetic exercise or plot, and treated the whole process with much distrust and suspicion. Despite the issue of pre-paid reply cards to every tenant, the response by post was only 3.5%, a disappointing figure; but tenants' groups and politicians made up for this by the vehemence of their comments. Second, many people either misunderstood, or understood but disapproved of, the comparatively limited scope of the review. There was a widespread view that *any* further increase in the rent payable for *any* dwelling would be intolerable, even if others were to benefit in equity from lower rents. Third, violent opposition was expressed to the use of the environment as a factor in assessing rents. Many Protestants saw it as a deliberate conspiracy, based on sectarian considerations, to require the tenants of 'good' (i.e. Protestant) estates to subsidise the tenants of 'bad' (i.e. Catholic) estates such as Divis. Other criticisms were, that the inclusion of the environment factor would drive low-income tenants out of the better estates; that there would be no incentive for tenants to take care of their estates, on the contrary, an actual incentive towards vandalism; that it would tend to create better and worse estates; and that rural tenants would end up subsidising city tenants.

The last comment was indeed wide of the mark: when the Commissioner of Valuation was asked to carry out sample gradings, he awarded the highest environmental points to inner-city urban areas, because of their proximity to all facilities, and the lowest gradings to provincial and rural areas. The results so produced were almost exactly the opposite of the general perception of the comparative attractions of inner-city high-rise blocks and settled seaside villages. And this too demonstrated the difficulty of finding universally acceptable objective criteria for measuring the quality of the environment.

Accordingly, although the use of the environment factor in rent schemes seemed to have worked perfectly well in England, the committee felt constrained to drop it completely on the grounds that 'in the circumstances of Northern Ireland, so large a subjective element in the calculation of rents would be widely unacceptable and would undermine support for the scheme as a whole.' The final report of the Review Committee was endorsed by the Board in February 1983; its amended scheme eventually received the general support, albeit somewhat guarded, of the Housing Council and the Assembly; but its introduction had to be deferred because of the workload involved in the prior introduction of housing benefit. The new rents points scheme was finally introduced in December 1984, though unhappily without the accompaniment of the rent freeze which the Board of the Executive so strongly urged on Government: and on the whole went remarkably smoothly, apart from an unhappy controversy over the definition of 'shared-access' flats resulting from the over-summary wording of an explanatory leaflet.

It remains to say a word on the subject of rent arrears: which, in Northern Ireland as in Great Britain, have risen astronomically in recent years. Unfortunately, the question of rent arrears, like so many others, has assumed sectarian significance. Ever since the anti-internment rent strike of 1972, it has been widely believed in the Protestant community that Republicans deliberately withheld their rent, and yet received favoured treatment. It is certainly true that, for a period of between two and three years, the rent arrears owed in Republican areas greatly exceeded those in Protestant areas, and for political reasons. It is certainly no longer true that this is the case — indeed, threats of rent strike, or of individual rent withholding, are now as common amongst Protestants as amongst Catholics. It is true, however, that the rent arrears figures tend to be higher in the most deprived areas of the province, which are mostly Catholic; though there are high arrears figures also in the least advantaged Protestant areas. All the evidence is to the effect that, in Northern Ireland as in Great Britain, high arrears bear a very close correlation with poverty and deprivation, and there is in the vast majority of cases neither a political nor a sectarian reason for the existence of the arrears. Nor is there any distinction to be drawn between the Executive's policies towards rent debtors within the two communities: great efforts are made, with varying success, to recover the arrears due from both factions, and the same penalties (restriction on transfer or exchange, for example) are imposed on both. Nevertheless, the archetypal Ulster Protestant holds to his folk-belief in the difference between the honest thrifty Prod who pays his debts as they fall due; and the feckless through-other Catholic who fails to do so. In truth, there has been a change of culture in both communities since the inception of the welfare state; in the old days, the housewife, Protestant or Catholic, would put the money for the rentman in the tea-pot on the mantlepiece, as a very first charge on the family finances, rather than risk eviction; today, while a large majority in both communities pays the rent punctually and conscientiously, there is a minority in each which, in the absence of the frightening sanctions of the past, takes a more relaxed view. But, even of that minority, only a few are genuinely reckless or culpable: the greater number are poor managers, or caught in the toils of poverty. A recent joint working party of officers of the Executive and the Department of the Environment expressly concluded that 'rent arrears are seldom due to extravagance on the part of tenants'. It is much to be hoped that the direct payment of rent under the housing benefit scheme, despite its incursion into their individual liberties, will nonetheless help many such individuals by saving them from ever-accumulating rent debt.

Apart from repairs and rents (and leaving aside allocations, transfers, exchanges, and questions of design and layout, dealt with in earlier chapters) the main concerns of public authority tenants are with security of tenure; heating systems; and the issues of tenant consultation and, possibly, participation. Since its inception, the Executive has *de facto* accorded full security of tenure; save for serious breaches of the tenancy agreement: and save, of course, for squatters. But even here, the Executive, as the sole provider of housing in Northern Ireland, finds

**Plate 37**

House or home? The occupant of No. 81, Lord Street, in East Belfast, was in no doubt. Unhappily but perhaps unsurprisingly, this unusual work of art was dismantled after his death.

**Plate 38** (above) **Plate 39** (below)

**Plate 38** (above) **Plate 39** (below)

**Plate 40**

Housing layout. *Left, above*, Lough Lea, in the Short Strand area of East Belfast, a 'defensible space' with all living-rooms looking inward onto the shared-surface courtyard: a design reflecting not only the problems of a Catholic enclave within predominantly Protestant East Belfast, but also the constraints of adjacent heavy industry, bus station, and main traffic routes. *Below left*, a triangular housing site at York Street in North Belfast sited between the Westlink road joining two motorways; Gallahers' enormous tobacco factory; and the tower blocks of the 'Artillery Flats' (built on a former barrack square).

*This page: above*, Rossville Flats, Derry, scene of some of the worst rioting from 1969 onwards, and of Bloody Sunday, 1972; photographed in 1982. *Below*, part of the rambling West Belfast Divis complex – Divis tower above the eight-storey deck-access flats – with new traditional housing tucked into the vacant ground adjoining the Westlink road.

**Plate 41**

**Plate 42**

City housing and overspill. *Above*, terrace in Derry incorporating local design ingredients. *Below*, new housing at Gortnamonagh, on the outskirts of West Belfast, to rehouse the former residents of the Turf Lodge flats. *Below right*, part of the controversial but, in the event, to date highly successful Poleglass estate. *Above right*, a curving row of semi-detached houses at Vernon Street, Belfast, an unusual design solution to an unusual set of constraints. The houses back onto a railway line to the south; the former terrace on the site was both noisy and sunless; by turning the houses sideways, each obtains either morning or evening sunlight, whilst no living-room faces the railway.

**Plate 43**

**Plate 44** (above) **Plate 45** (below)

**Plate 46**

*This page*, village housing. *Above*, new houses fitted into former long back gardens close to the heart of Glenarm, Co. Antrim. *Below*, respect for the traditional character and streetscape of Killyleagh, Co. Down; the stone houses were substantially rebuilt though their facades were retained.

*Right*, the Irish tradition of Georgian architecture: *above*, reproduction facades in the main street of Tandragee, Co. Armagh, a little stagey but not wholly unsuccessful. *Below*, the real thing; two houses at Joy Street, Belfast, painstakingly and expensively restored by the Housing Executive: the rest of the terrace now taken in hand.

**Plate 47**

**Plate 48** (above) **Plate 49** (below)

**Plate 50**

The author handing over the keys of the Executive's 50,000th new house at 7, Molyneaux Street, Belfast on 9th July 1981 to Miss Anne Ryan, the first tenant, and her mother.

itself under a legal obligation to rehouse even those few unsatisfactory tenants or squatters whom it is constrained to evict, if they have nowhere else to go. Security of tenure is not an issue in Northern Ireland, except occasionally in cases of broken marriage where husband and wife dispute which is to be entitled to the tenancy: and in such cases, subject always to the rulings of the courts, it is the general policy of the Executive to accord the tenancy to whichever party has custody of the children.

Heating systems are, and are likely to remain, a nightmare: especially in Northern Ireland, which has so far no indigenous source of fuel, except peat and, perhaps, lignite. Maybe there will be an oil or gas find in or around the coasts of Ulster; until then, the province must depend on imported coal, imported oil, perhaps piped Kinsale gas, or electricity generated from imported fuels. The district heating systems by which the engineers of the Housing Trust set such store have proved, by and large, a disastrous failure: inefficient, expensive, unreliable, hard to meter, and productive of heating arrears: much more acceptable to cockroaches than to humans. Most or all are soon to be removed and laboriously, and at great cost, replaced by closed fires and chimneys where fuel storage and ash disposal facilities can be provided: otherwise, presumably, by electricity. Town gas has been priced out of the market; the piping over the border of the Kinsale gas ('green gas' to those Unionists who object to any degree of reliance on the Republic) has been rejected by the Government, despite protests, as uneconomic. But for a special subsidy, electricity would be 30% dearer than in Great Britain. There is no obvious equivalent for cheap North Sea gas. There are deposits of lignite near Lough Neagh, but whether they are capable of providing heating in any convenient and economic form has yet to be proven. Proposals for combined heat-and-power on the continental model, using the surplus heat generated by power stations, are doomed to failure if their economic viability is dependent upon the efficiency of the existing district heating networks.

Heating costs in Northern Ireland are very high; so is heating debt; there is no easy answer. At present, central heating run off a closed coal-burning fire seems the best buy — for those who can afford it. Others court condensation on the one hand, hypothermia on the other hand, by striving to economise on their heating costs. An unheated house is, at any rate in the winter months, an uninhabitable house. No wonder that, as the comparative costs of different fuels change, so there follows pressure from tenants to change their heating systems, even though the existing installations may have many years of useful life before they are due for replacement. No country in the world could afford to rip out all its heating systems every few years and replace them: so the demands of tenants, not unreasonable in themselves, must often go unheeded. I see no way out of this difficulty; every housing authority must do its best to reconcile the conflicting arguments of economics and of humanity; and make sensible use of modern insulation methods to cushion the unavoidable hardship so far as possible. Unless and until some major new energy source is discovered and applied in the northern counties of Ireland, the heating problems afflicting housing will continue to be more severe in Northern Ireland than in Great Britain, and arguably, require some special social benefit entitlements.

The remaining current preoccupation of tenants and their representative groups is with the processes of consultation, now mandatory by statute, though it must be said that the Executive's record was better than that of most of its competitors. A difficulty here arises because the word 'consult' means different things to different people. When one 'consults' a doctor or a lawyer, one does not necessarily (perhaps usually) act on the advice received: give up smoking, or refrain from slandering the neighbours. When a housing authority 'consults' its tenants, it does not undertake in every case to act in accordance with the views they express: if it were to do so, it might well be in breach of statutory duty, and would certainly often be disregarding the views of others with a legitimate interest — those on the waiting-list, or the next generation of tenants, for example. What it does do, is to commit itself to considering carefully the views of its tenants, and to giving them due weight in the process of reaching the decision which is its responsibility alone. This has led to much misunderstanding and indignation. A new phrase has recently crept into currency — 'meaningful consultation' — by which those concerned mean 'consultation leading to the outcome we desire'. Any consultation which does not lead to that result is dismissed as cosmetic and 'meaningless'.

Housing authorities do not exist for the purpose of spiting or deliberately annoying their tenants; it stands to reason that any sensible and sensitive authority will try to give its tenants, so far as it can, what they want — *provided* there are not countervailing reasons and *provided* it can be shown that those who claim to speak for the tenants genuinely do so. But these two provisos are all-important. It is frequently the case that, in any given district, there exists a real conflict between the interests of the older and the younger generation; or between owner-occupiers and tenants; or between tenants of long standing, and those on the waiting-lists. What is more, there may well be differences of interest, and desire, between tenants of different factions — one party wanting a peace wall, for example, the other opposing it.

It is even more frequently the case that different spokesmen press for different decisions: there is a need to ensure that those who shout loudest do not drown the voices of the silent majority. And acute difficulties can arise where several different competing political, sectarian or even para-military groupings are jockeying for advantage amongst themselves. There can also be acute difficulties, where, for example, the locally elected representatives can speak only for those who voted for them but do not speak for a significant minority within their constituency: a situation which often arises in practice where there is a small Catholic pocket within a predominantly Protestant ward, or vice versa. It is this factor which makes it impossible, in Northern Ireland, for the Executive to take the comparatively easy way out of paying attention only to elected representatives. The processes of consultation in a deeply divided community are themselves, of necessity, tortuous, difficult, and often controversial.

If this is true of consultation, it must be even more true of tenant par-ticipation — though that is now the currently fashionable recipe for dealing with problem estates in Great Britain. Let me make it plain that I am much in favour of tenant participation in any reasonably demo-cratic, united and homogeneous society. But in a community which is deeply divided , it poses extreme dangers. There is the recurrent fear that paramilitary organisations may, through unassailable spokesmen, gain control of the tenant committees: far from improbable, it has happened on several occasions and in several places in Northern Ireland over the past decade.

On this score, Hywel Griffiths, first director of the Northern Ireland Community Relations Commission, has written tellingly: in 1971 and again at the time of the Ulster Workers' Council strike in 1974,

> the movement of population had become so great that the authorities were unable to check it or to prevent the usurpation of management responsibilities by local groups who declared their rights to say who should and who should not join them as neighbours. To some extent these newly-declared rights were taken over by the paramilitary organisations which on occasions used their powers of allocation in a manner not dissimilar from the much criticised Local Authority councillors whose control of housing had been taken away from them ... This loss of control lasted for a long period of time in some areas although the Executive never ceased to try to meet its responsibilities. Generally, the Housing Executive did win back control over most of its housing, but the exercise of management responsibility by local groups ... has left a residual and positive effect upon the relationship between the Executive and its tenants.

Is it any wonder that the Executive has ever since been chary of tenant participation as elsewhere understood?

So far, the Board of the Executive has been, rightly in my view, extremely cautious in its approach to tenant participation; and, while very willing to engage in consultation, careful always to reserve to itself the ultimate right and duty of decision-taking. I believe this to be the only sensible and defensible course in a community lacking almost entirely in consensus between majority and minority. But it can be represented as being undemocratic, paternalistic, and bureaucratic; a subject to which I return in the concluding chapter of this book.

Nobody loves a landlord. If tenants have their rights, and their wrongs too, it can be truthfully said that the lot of a landlord is no bed of roses.

# The Executive
## and the Private Sector

I have been able to discover no statistics showing the percentage of houses in owner-occupation, and the percentage rented from private landlords, in 1885; at that date, renting from public authorities could only have applied to labourers' cottages which constituted a tiny fraction of the total. In the Republic of Ireland, with the highest proportion of owner-occupation in Western Europe, a survey of 1979 estimated that of the total stock, 76% were owner-occupied, 12% rented from private landlords, and 12% public authority rented. Incredible though it may seem, questions on tenure were not included in the British census figures until 1961. Certainly, until at least 1945, the privately-rented sector constituted the largest proportion of the housing stock. But since then a dramatic change in tenure patterns has occurred: and the process is continuing at an accelerating rate. The following table, though some of the figures are estimates and all are subject to a certain margin of error, speaks for itself.

| Year | Owner Occupied % | | | Privately Rented % | | | Public Authority Rented % | | |
|------|------|------|------|------|------|------|------|------|------|
| | GB | NI | Eire | GB | NI | Eire | GB | NI | Eire |
| 1961 | 51 | 42 | 60 | 18 | 36 | 22 | 31 | 21 | 18 |
| 1971 | 50 | 47 | 69 | 19 | 19 | 15 | 31 | 34 | 16 |
| 1981 | 56 | 54 | 74 | 13 | 9 | 14 | 31 | 37 | 12 |

In 1956, in 'Rents and Houses' I wrote:

> The ultimate solution to our housing problem lies . . . in the public
> ownership of all houses let at a rent. There would then be only two
> ways of house-holding: one, ownership, which would be
> encouraged and assisted; the other, tenancy from a statutory body,
> responsible to parliament . . . . If present trends continue, this will
> in any case come almost true within the next century.

Not a bad piece of prophecy, I think.

The decline in the private rented sector followed inevitably from the
effects of the Rent Restriction Acts: and almost all attempts to revive the
building of new houses for private letting have so far failed. The sharp
decline in the privately-rented stock has come about in three ways: first,
the fact that many of these houses were the oldest and most dilapidated,
and so were the first candidates for clearance; second, the natural
tendency for hard-up private landlords to cut their losses and sell to
sitting tenants at discounted prices, or on the open market at higher
prices when vacancies arose; third, and (contrary to some political
folklore) the least significant factor, the process of deliberate so-called
municipalisation. In fact, this last process has come about in Northern
Ireland (apart from acquisition for demolition in redevelopment areas)
almost entirely as a result of the Executive's willingness to buy houses in
the market for those intimidated or forced from their houses as a result of
the Troubles.

The striking growth in home ownership in Northern Ireland is not,
contrary to appearances, directly related to the simultaneous decrease
in the private rented sector. Indeed, it has been largely a recent
phenomenon, due in part to much increased building society activity in
Northern Ireland, especially at the lower end of the market, and in part to
government policy since 1979. Perhaps these two factors have accen-
tuated what was already a spontaneous trend; there are other elements
too which at any given moment may affect the process — movements in
house prices, the inflation rate, interest rates, the availability of building
society funds, rent levels, the output of the construction industry.

Certainly, the most significant factor has been government policy on
home sales. Although the subject has been, in Great Britain, politically a
very controversial one, there has been since 1969 a rather larger element
of common ground in Northern Ireland as to the inherent desirability of
home ownership as a stabilising factor in the community. This argument
can be taken too far; there are plenty of bigots and paramilitaries who
are home-owners; and the owner-occupier suffered at least as much as —
indeed, arguably even more than — tenants, in the enforced population
movements of 1969-72. Nevertheless, both Labour and Conservative

ministers in Northern Ireland, and a majority of members of the Executive's Board, were prepared to look with some sympathy on sales of public authority houses to sitting tenants, so long as this could be done without detriment to the claims of those on the waiting-lists in areas of high need. As recounted on page 52, the Executive announced a scheme in 1978 for sales to its tenants in areas where housing need had been largely met (roughly two-thirds of the province) at moderate discounts, with its own home loans fund available to finance mortgages. This scheme had not really got off the ground however when the change of government of May 1979 heralded a much more drastic sales policy; to which the Board, after some hesitation, concluded it had no alternative but to conform.

Accordingly, tenants in Northern Ireland now enjoy exactly the same rights of purchase, and the same discount rates, as their counterparts in Great Britain. Surprisingly in so economically disadvantaged a community, the take-up rate has been running at around 4 per cent of the dwellings on offer, or about the same rate as in Great Britain: the demand until mid-1985 showed little sign of significant tailing off, though it must be finite. Nor has this been just the result of vigorous marketing; it seems to arise in part at least from the traditional land-hunger of the Irish countryside; it is noticeable that the take-up rate is particularly high in some of the border areas, and, so far as evidence is available, there is little sign that more prosperous Protestant areas have a significantly higher house-sales rate than even disadvantaged Catholic ones.

It is too soon to tell whether the scheme will have the ill effects so graphically foretold by its opponents. It is true that there are, in some districts, signs that the best houses in the stock are being sold, the worst remaining in the hands of tenants; a process (christened by academics, 'residualisation') which over a long period could come to have damaging consequences both socially and financially. The total stock of rented dwellings has not fallen sharply, since the rate of new building to date has nearly kept pace with the rate of sales. Contrary to expectations, the number of relets has risen rather than fallen, and the waiting lists have fallen rather than risen. It is true that, in some instances, the new owners have made startling, occasionally bizarre, alterations in the appearances of their homes; publicly blazoning their new status by, for example, cladding the front of a brick-built terrace house with multi-coloured artificial stone blockwork. When first I joined the Board of the Executive, I would have found this monstrously unacceptable; but I have come round to the view that the gain in the personal liberties of the individual outweighs the loss to the aesthetics of the environment, substantial as the latter certainly is.

The scheme as it stands can be criticised on a number of grounds. It is, to say the least, arguable that the discount rate, now raised to a maximum of 60 per cent of market value for those with thirty years occupancy, is much too high: and that the historic cost barrier, which provides that discounts cannot be used to bring the price of a dwelling built since 1973 below its actual cost, is unreasonably restrictive. These very artificial rules not only give rise to startling inequities as between one case and another, they also magnify the effects of inflation; those lucky enough to occupy houses built comparatively cheaply in past years can buy them even more cheaply now; those who occupy more recent and expensive houses may find the price prohibitive. The benefits of pooling of historic costs have been lost: and the desirability of purchase is conditional upon the continuation of high inflation rates.

It is certainly disconcerting that it requires the proceeds of sale of at least three older houses to finance the construction of one new one. Nevertheless, this source of capital receipts has, in Northern Ireland, provided a vastly welcome recourse for the funding of the newbuild programme: especially since the cost of financing tenants' purchases has been, to a great extent, taken up by the building societies, so relieving the Executive's home loans scheme of an overwhelming burden on the overall annual budget. But this source of funds is plainly not inexhaustible; and there is a sense in which the sale of so many publicly-provided assets at knock-down prices can be attacked as an eating of the seed-corn, a reckless realisation of the long-term capital of the community without reinvestment at a corresponding level.

My considered personal conclusion is that, though it errs on the side of generosity to the tenant at the expense of the community, the present house-sales policy is acceptable *provided* that houses sold from the public stock are replaced by new building; and *provided* that the needs of those who cannot for one reason or another afford to buy, or whose circumstances dictate renting rather than ownership, continue to be adequately catered for. I do not, however, extend that conclusion to cover the sales of homes purpose-built for the elderly; or specially constructed or adapted for the handicapped; or those constructed by the special-interest housing associations. In these cases, it seems to me that the long-term loss to the community will outweigh the undoubted benefits to be gained by the individuals concerned.

One remarkable ingredient in the growth of home ownership in Northern Ireland over a comparatively short period has been a complete reversal in the attitudes of the building societies movement. During all the post-war years there was a fairly considerable net outflow of funds from the province — by which I mean that the amount of local investors' money invested considerably exceeded the amount of the loans made on the security of property in Northern Ireland. This situation was greatly aggravated by the onset of the Troubles in 1969; there were a number of cases where building societies suffered losses as a result of the destruction or unsaleability of houses on which they had granted mortgages; their surveyors became understandably nervous, and there were many districts — for the most part, but not always, troubled areas — where the building societies flatly declined to lend: with disastrous consequences for sellers and buyers alike. It was largely to meet this crisis that the Executive's home loans service was established. But great damage had been done to the reputation of the British building societies, which were seen as having 'red-lined', in a discriminatory way, the most deprived areas of Northern Ireland: which of course included, though they were not confined to, the Catholic 'no-go' areas.

This unhappy situation led to much friction and recrimination; even within the Executive, the view was held that the building societies were acting oppressively and unreasonably; though it must in fairness be acknowledged that their duty to safeguard the resources of their investors could not have been ignored. This unhappy state of affairs was rectified in 1980 and the ensuing years, largely as a result of the persuasiveness and salesmanship of John Gorman, the chief executive, who took the initiative in arranging a series of meeting with the chairmen and general managers of the building societies' movement both in London and Belfast. The first objective was to persuade them to reverse their policies on down-market lending; the second to persuade them to act as financiers to the new generation of tenant purchasers, so setting free for new building funds which would otherwise have been tied up for many years in the Executive's home loans fund; the third, which developed from the first two, to persuade them to play a more active part in the regeneration of run-down areas, home improvements, and rehabilitation. The outcome was a striking success: in a mere four years a net outflow of funds of £7 million in 1978 was converted to a net inflow of funds of £82 million in 1982, and has remained in substantial surplus since then. Indeed, in a report of August 1983, the Support Scheme working party of the Building Societies' Association reported —

> the Executive is considered to be a model of a housing authority, partly because there is no party politics involved .... It is considered that the stage has been reached where the formal quotas can be ended, because trust, understanding and co-operation have developed to enable this to be done without adverse consequences.

This was one of a series of expedients, all pursued with much energy and in a pioneering spirit, designed to moderate the ill-effects of the cutbacks and moratoria of 1979-81. Some of them indeed had their origins in earlier years. But a sustained programme for the promotion of self-build schemes; equity sharing and co-ownership; and homesteading; took place during this period, largely as a result of John Gorman's initiative and innovative spirit. It cannot be said that any one of these schemes has had any very significant impact, taken alone. Up to the end of 1983, a total of 3,872 purchases through the Co-ownership Housing Association, though they had increased from 55 in 1978 to 1,507 in 1983, had still not included a single transaction under the home sales scheme; the total number of houses completed in self-build schemes was only 41; and the total number of satisfactorily completed homesteading ventures had reached only 243. Nevertheless, taken together these innovations had made a worthwhile contribution to the total effort.

At the same time, the housing association movement, first seriously promoted in Northern Ireland in 1976, was beginning to make a really substantial contribution to the total stock. In the early days, many of us had serious reservations about the suitability of housing associations to the circumstances of the province. There was a straightforward housing management argument: trained housing managers, whose skills could be ill spared from the public sector, were tempted away from the Executive in order to manage much smaller stocks; a considerable waste of scarce resources was involved and indeed it must still be questionable whether the smaller housing associations are genuinely economical entities, though the larger ones have now reached the point where they can be so. But a far larger question mark hung over the question whether associations, especially those which were either based in local communities or promoted by individual religious denominations, could establish and maintain standards of non-sectarianism comparable to those established by the Executive. Personally, I had very deep misgivings on this score, and they have not yet been wholly overcome, although I must acknowledge that so far the movement has been pretty free from the sectarian tarbrush. Nonetheless, it is not easy to believe that *no* preferential treatment for their own members will ever be displayed by bodies such as the Church of Ireland, the Baptist Union of Ireland, the Masonic, the Presbyterian, or the North Belfast Mission, Housing Associations; or by the community-based associations such as St Matthew's (a Catholic parish in the Short Strand area of Belfast) or Grove (in a hotly Protestant area near Tiger Bay in Belfast). And, indeed, there has been at least one case where an unmarried mother has been black-balled by the existing tenants of a community-based association, possibly for sectarian as much as moral reasons, despite the high points to which she was entitled. The specialist associations catering for students, nurses, battered wives, mentally handicapped, and the protégés of the Simon Community, seem at less risk. I have heard it alleged, though I do not believe it, that one of the housing associations catering for the elderly gives preference in its allocations to those who can play bridge. If that is the worst form that discrimination takes, it will not be too intolerable; but I still think that there are insufficient safeguards in the system, which is supposed to be policed by the Housing Associations branch of the Department of the Environment. It seems to me very much to be regretted that government refused to bring housing association allocations within the scope of the Ombudsman, as are the Executive's allocations, despite the fact that the dwellings of both are provided entirely out of public funds.

Notwithstanding these reservations, it would be churlish to deny that the positive achievements of the housing associations over quite a short period, under the energetic leadership of Erskine Holmes, the Federations's director, have been formidable. The number of recognised associations has risen in eight years from two to 44; in 1984, 733 new dwellings and 424 rehabilitation contracts were completed by the movement; and it seems likely that the numbers will continue to increase steadily. The contribution of the associations has been particularly notable in the field of provision for the frail elderly through sheltered dwelling complexes, an activity from which the Executive has now withdrawn in their favour: though there are those who have misgivings that some of the more institutional sheltered dwelling complexes will one day come to be seen in the same light as the old workhouses.

Another area of phenomenal growth, in Northern Ireland as elsewhere in the United Kingdom, has been that of grants. Expenditure under this head rocketed from a total of £1.8 million in 1976 to over £58 million in 1984-5. Part of this increase, but a comparatively small part, may be discounted for inflation. Both the numbers, and the amounts, of grants have increased: in 1984-5, approvals were granted for 24,367 repair grants; 5,657 improvement grants; 298 intermediate grants; and 273 conversion grants.

Until quite recently, it has been widely assumed that these generous grants to private owners have constituted excellent value for money; and so no doubt they often have; but the scheme has been somewhat un- selective, and doubts have begun to arise on two scores — and at two levels: for it is evident that Treasury, at the top, as well as housing management at the operative end, have been beginning to wonder how well-directed this vast investment really is. On the one hand, there is a growing belief that a proportion of it is going to people who would have carried out the work anyhow, and did not really require the stimulus of this extra, and no doubt delightful, hand-out. Moreover, there have certainly been instances where unscrupulous speculators have taken advantage of the grants available in order to extort unconscionable rents from students, nurses, and perhaps other vulnerable groups. On the other hand — and this relates more to improvement than to repair grants — there is a feeling that an undue amount is being spent, wastefully, on improvements to houses which really, on a value-for-money basis, are not worth improving at all; and which in any event will quite soon require to be demolished and replaced. Nor is this just the result of difficulties being experienced in proposed new redevelopment areas, where those owner-occupiers who have spent their own money, as well as the grant, on acquiring and improving a home, are understandably indignant when it is proposed a few years later to vest and demolish their investment. It stems from the much larger question whether a new bathroom glued on the back of a little old slum can ever provide an acceptable and economical investment.

The whole subject requires, and is in the process of receiving, analysis and research; until the outcome is known, it would be premature to jump to conclusions. But my own hunch is that quite a sizeable proportion of the money now spent on grants is ill-directed, and that a very much more selective and cost-beneficial system will have to be found if overall grants expenditure is to continue at anything like its present level.

Finally, I turn to the contributions made to the overall housing stock by private sector new building. This has been subject, over the years, to great fluctuations; and any discussion of the subject is made difficult by the notorious unreliability of the only available statistics. The numbers of starts and the numbers of completions never seem to add up; there are difficulties and discrepancies in the definition of each: a start may sometimes mean no more than the digging of a preliminary hole in a field: many completions seem to go unrecorded: for example, the officially compiled Digest of Northern Ireland Housing Statistics shows on the one hand 3,345 building society loans for new houses in 1982, on the other hand a total figure for private completions of only 2,762! Something is badly amiss; and if the private sector is to make a greatly increased contribution to housing need, then more reliable facts and figures will be urgently required both by the planners and by those concerned in the preparation of district housing plans.

It seems possible, on the figures currently available, to do little more than discern and project general trends. It seems clear that, from about 1948 until about 1961, private sector completions averaged around 2,000 a year for Northern Ireland as a whole; from about 1962 until about 1967, around 3,000 a year; from 1968 to 1974, between 4,000 and 5,000 a year; falling between 1975 and 1982 from a maximum of 3,750 to a low figure, in the last-named year, of 2,672. It also seems clear that starts began to rise again in 1981 and have been rising steadily ever since; so that a projected overall annual contribution from the private sector of 5,000 may not be wholly unrealistic.

If the performance of the private builders in terms of quantity has fluctuated greatly, so it has also in terms of quality. There has been a notable improvement in quality in recent years as a result of the establishment of the National House Builders' Council registratiom scheme in 1969, though there are still a considerable number of cowboys at large. In England, there has been a great improvement in the standards of design, layout and landscaping — a genuine and quite speedy response to a change in the character of the demand. That improvement has been slow in reaching Northern Ireland, probably in large part because of a failure on the part of potential customers to raise the levels of their own expectations as has happened in Britain.

There has been an outbreak, all over the province, of mock-Tudor and plastic-Georgian bungalows (and even, still more incongruous, ranches) in a style which has now, fortunately, passed out of fashion in England.

On the other hand, Northern Ireland has so far been spared the rash of so-called 'starter homes' which were briefly fashionable in many parts of Great Britain. These very cramped small units of accommodation may do well enough for a single person, or at a pinch, a young couple: but they are far too small to accommodate children without gross overcrowding. There is a real danger, especially in an area of high unemployment, that when the first child arrives, the owners will neither be able to afford to trade up-market, nor to add on an extension (experience in England shows that even where provision for an extension is an inherent part of the design, it is seldom built in practice). Moreover, dwellings of this kind sometimes fail to hold their value, and can only be resold at a heavy loss, especially in areas where similar new building is still going on nearby, and the builder is offering attractive inducements (free furnishings, free legal costs, and so on) to the purchasers of identical new, not second-hand, dwellings. This problem is all too likely to be increased by the appearance on the market of second-hand former public-sector houses as a result of the house-sales policy: expecially if the spiral of house-price inflation falls off. These will then directly compete in price with the 'starter homes', which could thus become the over-crowded and under-maintained poverty-traps of the next generation.

Most private builders in Northern Ireland would concede that the dwellings now being built by the Housing Executive are built to better standards all round — space, design, layout, detailing, materials — than those put up for sale by the average speculative builder. But, in defence, they would plead, first, that they are supplying the market with what it wants, at the price it can afford; and second that, unlike the Executive,

they are in business to make a profit. And indeed, it is one of the disquieting features of the construction scene in Northern Ireland that
some builders succeed in making enormous (excessive?) profits —
millionaires are not that scarce in the industry — whilst others end up
in bankruptcy, receivership, or liquidation, sometimes on a spectacular
scale. I have long held the private opinion that some kind of compulsory
registration of builders is required; there are too many chancers
operating with too little capital in the industry. The principal argument
against this proposal, and it is not totally without force though research
into the economics of the building industry fails to confirm it, is that
registration would prevent the enterprising small man with a wheel-
barrow from building up his business — and it is perhaps true that some
of the largest construction firms in Britain started in this way. But, at a
time when qualifications and training are more and more in demand in
practically every other walk of life, it may be questioned whether
builders alone should be treated differently.

The Executive's experience with builders (and with their federation,
of which by no means all practitioners are members) has been mixed. It
has been necessary to construct and refine a highly complex code of
contract procedure, designed to ensure fairness as between one tenderer
and another; the most efficient execution of building work; the preven-
tion, so far as humanly possible, of collusion, fraud, and mid-contract
insolvency; and the protection of enormous sums of taxpayers' money.
The system is on the whole pretty successful, but in the constant war of
attrition between sharply competitive rival contractors on the one hand,
and a large and somewhat cumbersome near-monopoly customer on the
other, the victories do not always go to the most virtuous. Having said
this, there has been a general and noticeable improvement in the
quality, and also the speed, of contracts for the public sector, unaccom-
panied by any excessive increase in prices. No doubt this results in part
from the sharpening of competition at a time of acute recession: but it
may promise greater efficiency and higher quality in new building for
the private market too. And if so, that will be welcome.

One of the sharpest disappointments suffered by the Board of the
Executive was the rejection by government in January 1984, after
prolonged debate, of its proposals for partnership schemes with private
builders on the model of those successfully evolved in the preceding
years by many English housing authorities, both Labour- and Con-
servative-controlled. The principle of such schemes was, that the
housing authority should negotiate with a selected builder or builders
for the construction, on land in public ownership, of new houses for sale
tailored to meet the needs of the local community, and to fit in with the
overall strategy and design policies of the authority concerned. It is

widely acknowledged that the Executive has succeeded in raising markedly the standards of new housing in the public sector; the Board had hoped to have an opportunity of giving a similar lead to the private sector through a kind of working partnership with a panel of some of the better builders, not dissimilar from that so successfully built up with the building societies. The government could very easily, without deviating from Tory principles, have followed the English precedents. Instead, it chose in this instance to take a very much stiffer line, and stand out for the free play of market forces, and the primacy of the highest bid for the land. This was the more disappointing, and rendered the Executive the more vulnerable to public and political criticism, since it had been envisaged that such schemes should be promoted on land in the ownership of the Executive, *not* surplus to the requirements of its programme; so that the Board considered that it had a legitimate claim to ensure that the dwelling types were suited to the potential purchasers — priority was to be given, through the co-ownership scheme, to existing tenants and those on the waiting lists — and to the surroundings, often an existing larger public-sector scheme. This (fortunately, comparatively rare) example of a major disagreement between the Board and government on the way in which overall policy should be gievn effect raises the sensitive question of the degree of independence which the Executive has, or ought to have; which is the subject-matter of the next chapter.

# Clients, Customers, Critics and Colleagues

It is plain that one of the principal reasons for the setting up of the Housing Executive was the desire to distance questions of housing policy and administration from questions of party politics, and especially, sectarian politics. And in this, it may be thought, the venture has been largely successful. But housing problems come at the very top of the list of constituency matters with which public representatives have to deal; and housing policies and conditions have so much to do with the overall standard of living, that housing matters lie inexorably close to the heart of politics: which in Northern Ireland means not just party politics but sectarian politics. So the conduct of a non-political course through a political minefield is a matter of extreme difficulty, requiring much dexterity and finesse. Also, a thick skin.

Within a week after I took up my appointment as chairman, I happened to meet a certain MP at an official function. His amiable greeting to me was this: 'You know, you exist only to be kicked. And it is our privilege, as members of Parliament, to choose whether to kick you in the teeth, the arse, or the balls.'

In their more cynical moments, members of the Executive's Board often feel that they exist only to provide a safety barrier between government (or civil service) and the public, so designed that the government of the day and its own bureaucrats may take the credit for every popular decision or successful achievement, while the Board exists only to carry the can for every shortcoming, every failure, and every unpopular decision. But there is another way of looking at this; Board members tend to see themselves not as agents of Government, but as trustees — trustees for the tenants, for the owner-occupiers entitled to grants, above all for those on the waiting lists.

The question of the degree of independence which the Executive enjoys, or ought to enjoy, is an extremely difficult one. There are those who assert that it should enjoy complete, or almost complete, independence; but that is an unrealistic argument, given the constitutional and financial framework within which it must work, which requires both parliamentary and financial accountability. Yet some degree of independence the Board must have, if it is to serve any useful function at all: for otherwise, it would be more sensible to conduct all housing business directly through the government department involved. Moreover, there is, in Northern Ireland, a very strong political argument for maintaining the non-political status of the housing authority.

Between 1971 and 1984, there were nine ministers with responsibility for housing: Roy Bradford, Unionist; Lord Windlesham and David Howell, Conservative; Austin Currie, Social Democratic and Labour Party; Don Concannon and Ray Carter, Labour; Philip Goodhart, David Mitchell and Chris Patten, Conservative. (During this same period, there were four permanent secretaries with departmental responsibility for housing: John Oliver, Ken Bloomfield, John Irvine, and, for the last few months of my chairmanship, Dan Barry. Their comparative durability undoubtedly increased their influence.) Each minister, whatever his party, to a greater or lesser degree, naturally wished to impose his own views on housing questions: after all, what ambitious junior minister of any party could ever conceive of standing aside altogether from housing questions, saying as he washes his hands in carbolic soap, 'No concern of mine, housing is entirely the business of a non-political quango . . .?' Yet it has been of great importance that the Board should distance itself to some extent from each; that is should not give the appearance of having swallowed holus-bolus the policies of Unionism or SDLP, Conservative or Labour; still more so, that it should not appear to reel blindly from one to another. And this degree of independence will become more important still if and when any kind of devolved government returns to the province; for if a separate housing authority is to remain in existence at all, it will have to demonstrate its ability to stand up to the pressures exerted by Unionist, DUP, Alliance, SDLP, or whatever other sectional party may then be concerned. For independence is the only guarantee of the impartiality and integrity required of a housing body in a deeply divided community.

The legal and constitutional position is, of course, quite different. After all, the government of the day has the statutory right to appoint seven of the ten members of the Board, including its chairman.

Moreover, it is built into the legislation that the government may, at any time, issue a formal direction to the Executive: with which the latter is then bound at law to comply. That power — to date used sparingly, but not altogether unused — constitutes the explicit sanction. There is also an implicit one: since the Executive derives less than one-quarter of its expenditure from rents, has no power to levy rates, and cannot even borrow without government approval, it is directly dependent on government for practically all its funds; so that a gentle twitch on the purse-strings can usually bring a recalcitrant Board to heel. There is no doubt who has the last word: and plainly, that is how it should be — it would be monstrous if, in a democracy, any quango (any more than the civil service, or the police, or the armed services) could, with impunity, defy the policies of an elected government.

Nevertheless, the Executive is not the poodle of minister or department, so long as it suits their interests to keep the Executive in being. In practice, both parties are to some extent in a bargaining position: and the positions of the parties are not quite so unequal as might, from the summary above, appear. For the arbiter in any dispute between government and Executive is likely to be public opinion. The government, if it has public opinion on its side, can plainly make mince-meat of the Board: that goes without saying. But the Executive, with public opinion on its side, can considerably embarrass, can indeed exert strong (though never irresistible) pressures on, government. So that a tough chairman and Board in practice enjoy a lot more power, if they exercise it with skill, than could be deduced from their legal con-stitution: especially since the legislation abstains from conferring upon the government of the day any express power to dismiss or remove chairman or Board members.

Dismissal is one thing; resignation is quite another. It is from time to time suggested that, when Board members are faced with a policy decision by government with which they disagree, they should 'have the courage of their convictions, and resign.' I personally believe that resignation is the ultimate weapon in one's armoury, to be used only as a very last resort on a matter of the very highest principle. It is also a very double-edged weapon, which usually hurts the user most. When Mrs May Robinson, a tenants' representative on the Board, impulsively ten-dered her resignation, at a meeting with Mr Goodhart in April 1980, in protest at that year's rent increase of 40 per cent, she gave a public demonstration of her personal integrity and honesty: but she thereby demonstrated nothing that was not already known. Her resignation did not help the Board; nor the Executive as a whole; nor the tenants; nor herself. I accept, of course, that there are some issues upon which resig-nation is the only honourable response. Not many, I think. I myself should certainly have resigned if any government, whatever its political complexion, had exerted pressure upon me to adopt a course of action which appeared to me to involve discrimination on religious or political grounds for or against any section of the community. I cannot easily imagine many other issues which could have impelled me to resign. One is appointed to do a job, and one must get on with it, to the best of one's ability, within the various constraints imposed by the democratic system.

So, broadly speaking, it seems to me, there are three zones within which a quango such as the Executive may exercise differing degrees of liberty: none at all, where major questions of national policy, especially those for which government has a clear electoral mandate, are concerned. So much only as it can secure for itself by persuasion of those in authority, and recourse to the support of public opinion, in matters of finance. But a much larger degree of freedom in that somewhat indefinite zone of lesser policy, and of administration, in which (as it seems to me) both ministers and civil servants have from time to time trespassed considerably farther than they should have done.

So far I have bracketed ministers and civil servants together; but there are material differences in the Executive's relationships with the two. So far as ministers are concerned the matter is one of parliamentary accountability: although technically MPs have no right to enquire into the day-to-day workings of the Executive, in practice the Board has always thought it right to accord in full whatever information is sought, however barbed the Parliamentary Question; and a suitable formula has been found, under which the minister replies in each instance, 'This is not a matter within my responsibility, but I am informed by the chairman of the Executive that....' This, after some teething troubles, worked well in practice. But so far as the civil service is concerned, the relationship hinges on the fact that the permanent secretary of the Department of the Environment (N.I.) is the accounting officer formally answerable for every item of expenditure within his vote, including the expenditure of the Executive. This responsibility he owes to Parliament through the Auditor-General and the Public Accounts Committee; a heavy burden indeed, as anyone who has ever had the terrifying experience of appearing before the PAC (as I have done) will testify. (I was lucky; I got off lightly; the Labour government fell that very night, and the members' minds were perhaps wandering elsewhere a little.) But this relationship poses difficulties of its own: for the ultimate power of decision-making rests with the departmental head, not with the Board of the Executive, except insofar as he feels confidence enough to delegate it. This can, at times, lead to duplication of controls, undesirable delays, and occasionally downright conflict; though on the other hand it has the advantage that the permanent secretary acts as spokesman and advocate for the Executive in the constant unchivalrous war of attrition that goes on with the knights of the Treasury; and at those private meeting between permanent secretaries of all the departments which probably do more to shape the course of events in Northern Ireland than all the activities of all the ministers and all the politicians put together. Not surprisingly, the concept and workings of financial accountability, the advantages and disadvantages of the existing system, have come under frequent and anxious scrutiny.

Before turning to other relationships, one word I must in fairness add: I count myself very fortunate that, during just over five years as chairman of the Executive, I found all four of the ministers at the Environment Department with whom I served courteous, competent, and friendly; even if we had our differences, both in public and in private. And my opinion of their senior civil servants with whom I had close dealings rose steadily, almost without faltering, throughout the same period. Some of them, indeed, were of quite outstanding calibre.

It is a fascinating question how far personalities, and their interplay, in reality influence the course of public affairs. The quadrilateral relationship between minister, chairman, permanent secretary, and chief executive (one of very considerable delicacy be it said) was throughout my time of the utmost significance for the success or failure of the Executive in carrying out the functions entrusted to it. I have no doubt that, whatever the political or philosophical gulfs which may divide the incumbents of such positions, a relationship of mutual trust and confidence between them makes an invaluable contribution to practical achievement: conversely, any area of mutual mistrust may undermine and vitiate the work of all concerned. I was lucky.

Not that we lived in each other's pockets. The minister formally met the full Board once or twice a year. Protocol laid it down that chairman should normally deal with minister, permanent secretary with chief executive, though all four would meet from time to time to sort out specific issues. I normally expected to meet 'my' minister once every six to eight weeks, not counting casual social meetings at opening ceremonies and suchlike. Yet I remember once travelling from London on the same early-morning shuttle flight with David Mitchell, not expecting to see him again for a month: only to meet him, an hour or so after landing and parting, at the scene of a devastating bomb which had exploded prematurely in the Springfield Road, wrecking many homes — an occasion when 'normal' security precautions and conventions alike went by the board.

As for other government departments, relationships with the

Executive were, during my time, fairly distant. One might, on rare occasions, have dealings on some specific issue with officials of the Department of Finance, or of the Northern Ireland Office; on very rare occasions indeed, with the Secretary of State himself. But nothing could be farther from the truth than the conspiracy theories — indulged in for the most part by the extreme parties, Sinn Féin and the DUP — to the effect that the Executive was constantly engaged in elaborate plotting with the Northern Ireland Office and the security forces to manipulate the political or sectarian configurations of different areas of the province. Except during the most violent troubles of 1969 to 1971, when all agencies did their best to work together in each of the most disturbed areas, relationships with the police were mostly distant and indirect; still more so with the army; though occasionally a battalion commander with a social conscience made well-intentioned but amateurish attempts to influence housing conditions in his bailiwick. Consultation has from time to time taken place regarding the security implications of building new houses close to a disputed sectarian interface; or the desirability of building a new peace wall; or the consequences of evicting a squatter from a house in one of the paramilitary strongholds. But I know of no instance where the security forces have intervened directly in any housing decision. Such consultations have taken place, if at all, through the intermediary of the department's planning service which, reasonably enough, has authority wide enough to allow it to seek the comments of any interested party, including both the Executive and the security forces, before coming to a decision.

So far as specialist housing planning has been concerned, the Executive — which after all is large enough to employ its own staff of corporate planners, both centrally and regionally — has been allowed a considerable amount of latitude. For some reason, most of the disputes between the Executive and the non-housing branches of the department of the Environment seem to have centred round the place in society of the motor car. There has been continuous debate with the planning service regarding the ratios of parking space to be provided in new scheme designs; just as there has been continuous debate with the roads service regarding layouts, shared surfaces, and maintenance responsibilities; not always, though usually, free of acrimony. Since in Northern Ireland, unlike Great Britain, planning, roads, water, sewage, and conservation are all centralised services controlled by the same government department, it has not proved unduly difficult to find reasonably effective means of co-ordination of effort with the housing authority. The same holds true of other centralised departments. The successful introduction of housing benefit resulted from close and harmonious working with the Department of Health and Social Services;

the Executive's relationships with medical officers, public health inspectors, social security offices, social workers, the fire service, and other public bodies, tend to be satisfactorily close and effective, and happily free (for the most part) from the kinds of interdepartmental jealousies which can be so harmful to the interests of the public.

If the relationship with other agencies and branches of central government is in general comparatively easy, the relationship with local authorities can be rather more complex. This exists at three levels: with individual councillors; with the 26 District Councils and their clerks; and with the Housing Council, comprising one of its own members elected by each of the District Councils.

Contrary to the gloomy forebodings expressed in the debates at Stormont when the Housing Executive and the Housing Council were established — as to which see pages 10 to 15 — the two bodies have not been at constant loggerheads with each other. This has been in large part due to the careful tact of successive chairmen of the Housing Council, which meets monthly, with press entitled to be present, receives regular reports on the issues coming before the Executive's Board, considers complaints from all over the province, tenders advice both to minister and to Board, and generally acts as a vehicle for the expression of local opinion. It is a very party-political body, and has not lacked extremist firebrands, mostly from the Protestant end of the spectrum since it has a permanent built-in Unionist/DUP majority. Nevertheless, it has mostly conducted its business responsibly and with moderation, probably in large part because it has the privilege of nominating three of its own members to the Board: though this can give rise to its own difficulties and conflicts, discussed below.

Relations with the District Councils themselves vary widely. Some have established effective liaison committees with the regional officers of the Executive; these have proved invariably useful. The Executive is bound by statute to consult each Council formally at least once a year — in practice, usually more often — particularly with regard to the programme of work to be carried out in the District concerned. The gradual development and refinement of District Housing Plans on the English model provides Councils with the opportunity to make practical contributions to the proposals for their respective areas. There is a tendency in some areas, particularly in Belfast, for the councillors to concentrate on the claims of their own wards, rather than on the needs of the community as a whole, but that is not a characteristic unique to Northern Ireland. Indeed, the Executive has to cope as best it can with the pressures exerted by no less than 526 individual aldermen and councillors, each with his own particular geographical and political special interests — and not least, his own interest in getting re-elected.

This can give rise to real difficulties for the Executive, an important part of whose function it is to balance fairly the conflicting claims of all parts of the province. Sometimes the councillor for the peaceful rural townland of Ballyboghilbo finds it impossible to accept that his constituents' needs are less pressing than those of people living in overcrowded and substandard conditions in the priority estates of West Belfast. Indeed, I have been accused to my face of gross discrimination against his constituents by a dissatisfied councillor for an area where a small group of isolated rural cottages still lacked internal lavatories; at a time when almost 25% of the housing stock of Belfast suffered exactly the same lack. There is nothing peculiar to Northern Ireland, however, about the permanent conflict between town and country, except the opportunity it affords for innuendos of sectarian malice. The problems of overspill from Belfast to the surrounding council areas differ only from the conflict between the inner and outer London boroughs by reason of the added factor of the sectarian divide.

The election in 1982 of 78 members to the Northern Ireland Assembly, brainchild of James Prior, added to the numbers of bodies by which, or by whose members, the Executive may be called to account. (In the past it was sometimes criticised for being insufficiently accountable; it seems to me that it has far too broad a spread of accountability, in the loose sense.) The Assembly's Environment Committee has frequently addressed itself to the consideration of housing questions; and its functions in consequence began to overlap uncomfortably with those of the Housing Council, a development which could give rise to serious conflicts in the future, the more so as, at the time of writing, the Assembly is notably less representative than the Council. Although ministers, civil servants, Board members and officers of the Executive, may all be called before the Assembly's committee, neither government nor Executive has any spokesman there, or right of audience. With some frequency, individual Assembly members air constituency housing grievances for the benefit of their local newspapers and electors in the course of adjournment debates; but there is no mechanism by which those attacked (and sometimes irresponsibly and unreasonably attacked) can exercise any right of reply. Naturally enough, relations between the Executive and the Assembly could be described as cool. How permanent the Assembly will prove to be, and if it is to be permanent how this coolness can best be tackled, must be questions for the future.

Relations with members of parliament have, on the whole, much improved over the years. The arrangements which have been developed for dealing with Parliamentary Questions, and for dealing with individual constituency letters and inquiries, appear to be working more smoothly than in the past. The attitudes of the fifteen individual Northern Ireland MPs who have taken their seats vary from extreme courtesy to, in one or two cases, extreme discourtesy; with Sinn Féin abstaining both from taking its seats and from involving itself in policy, as opposed to purely constituency, issues. It has become the practice in recent years for the Executive's Board to invite representatives of all the major political parties — including those, such as the Workers' Party, which have no seats in either Parliament or Assembly — to attend regular meetings to discuss housing matters generally; these meetings have proved extremely valuable, and have certainly served to increase understanding amongst politicians of the Executive' problems, and to reduce the level of hostile criticism (except from those pledged to the dismemberment of the Executive in any event).

The three Northern Ireland members of the European Parliament have been helpful and supportive to the Executive in its dealings with Brussels. Between 1980 and 1983, overtures were made to the EEC to provide special funds for Belfast housing, somewhat on the model of the special provision already voted for Naples. I myself travelled to Brussels three times to state the case. In the event, political objections from West Germany to any precedent for spending community funds directly on housing prevailed; but handsome funds were voted for the improvement of the urban infrastructure of Belfast, with an understanding that, on obtaining these additional funds, the British Government would set free additional funds of a corresponding amount for housing purposes. The arrangements were quite Byzantine in their intricacy — indeed Brussels has strong claims to being the new Byzantium — and probably incapable of definitive elucidation. It *seems* to be the case, however, that the Executive's housing budget benefited by an amount roughly corresponding to the amount of the EEC's infrastructure aid; it is impossible to point to any particular streets of new houses built or to be built with common market gold, as some over-zealous marketeers would wish to do; but the final outcome *appears* not unsatisfactory, and as I have no wish to bite the hands that fed me, and as in any case I doubt the adequacy of my own grasp of the subject, I will pursue it no further except to say that, as a lifelong European, I am deeply grateful to somebody for something, even if I am not quite certain to whom for what.

The Executive has dealings, like any other large public body, with a wide range of pressure groups and special-interest bodies. They include a fluctuating gamut of tenants' and residents' associations and federations; Shelter; Belfast Housing Aid; the N.I. Federation of Housing Associations; and national bodies such as the Institute of Housing, the Housing Centre Trust, and the National Mobility

Council. On the other hand, English housing and environment ministers, and D. of E. (Marsham Street), are anxious to disclaim any relationship whatever with the Executive; lest they tread on the sensitive corns of Northern Ireland ministers and departments. Although this attitude is defensible, it goes beyond reason when it deprives the Executive, as it does, of access to the housing circulars issued by the same government to which the Executive, too, is accountable. On a different plane, the Executive has close working relationships with the Building Societies' Association, the Builders' Federation, the estate agents (for whom many of its decisions will have far reaching consequences), and the professional organisations of architects, engineers, surveyors, solicitors, and so on. On a different plane again, it has regular dealings with the Northern Ireland Committee of the Irish Congress of Trade Unions; the Public Service Alliance; and the craft and manual unions whose members it employs. I will not dwell on its relationship with these groups, for every public body must deal with some such, except to draw attention to the large number and wide span of those with which the Executive is concerned; and to remark that it manages somehow to stay on good terms with most of them for most of the time.

The Board has dealings also, of course, with many voluntary bodies, and even from time to time with the churches. I was on one occasion prevailed upon by my colleagues to invite to lunch, for a general review of housing issues, the Cardinal Archbishop of Armagh, the Church of Ireland Archbishop of Armagh, the Moderator of the Presbyterian General Assembly, and the President of the Methodist Church in Ireland — together. It was an event which I viewed with apprehension; nonetheless, I devised a special housing grace — 'Lord, in thy Father's house are many mansions; pray see to it that in the next world, as in this, they are fairly allocated' — but at the last minute, was too cowardly to deliver it.

Last but far from least, the tenants, and the public: in one sense, the Executive's customers: in a still more significant sense, those whom it exists to serve. It is no easy matter to create, and maintain, any kind of human and personal relationship with a total of 180,600 tenants: especially when Government policy requires the Executive to send out that number of formal notices of rent increase in most years. There is intermittent pressure for the resumption of regular weekly or fortnightly visits from the rent collector to every household. Certainly, this would be in itself highly desirable, but it is hard to think of it as practical politics: not only because of the need for manpower economies, and the ever-increasing use of computer systems: but also because it seems inconceivable that, in the disturbed state of Northern Ireland, it can possibly, in the foreseeable future, be reasonable to ask members of staff to walk

through the streets carrying about on their persons cash to a total value of
£125 million a year.

It seems certain that in the future, as in the recent past, other means of
communication must be found. It is true that computerisation of rent
accounting has set free more housing assistants to be out and about
around the estates; but the main emphasis must now be on communication through the printed word, or through visual means.
Advertising campaigns and a steady flow of information through
features and news items, on television and sound broadcasting; the
positive use of the press; the dissemination of local news-sheets and
leaflets designed to inform particular estates or areas of the Executive's
plans and intentions; these are necessary ingredients of an active policy
of conveying information outwards from the Executive. The return flow
is more difficult to organise: in part it can be achieved by the use of
regular opinion polls and surveys, organised to professional standards,
and by the use of consumer satisfaction kits; in part it must rely on
letters, telephone calls, and personal visits from tenants and others.
Perhaps fortunately, Ulster people are not slow about letting those in
authority know of their grievances: the combined daily post-bag of
chairman, chief executive, and the six regional controllers, is enormous:
also informative: also, sometimes, heart-rending. But one other
initiative proved invaluable; the establishment in 1980 of a fully-
staffed Advice Centre in Belfast, aided by two travelling mobile Housing
Advice units (commonly known as Gormobiles, after their originator,
the Executive's John Gorman). These have proved to be of inestimable
value. They came into existence in Northern Ireland just when similar
pioneering ventures in England were being forced to close down, or at
the least cut back, for reasons of economy; in the exceptionally stressful
circumstances of Northern Ireland, it has been worth its weight in gold
to have three such regular points of contact with the public, where
trained advisers can dispense information that is universally acknowledged to be impartial and unbiased.

Indeed, one of the principal positive achievements of the Executive
has been the quality and professionalism of its staff. It has succeeded in
recruiting the committed and the idealistic, especially amongst the
younger people, from both Catholic and Protestant communities. It is
inevitable of course that out of some 3,500 white-collar, and 1,700 blue-
collar, workers, there are those who are less than perfect. Bigotry and
sectarianism have not completely disappeared; nor is courtesy at the
counter always what it should be; nor are telephone calls always
returned, or letters always replied to, with appropriate alacrity. But by
and large, Protestant and Catholic work together more happily and less
self-consciously than in any other organisation I have ever known in

Northern Ireland: there is a general enthusiasm for the work in hand, and its worth-while-ness, rarely to be found in branches of the public service: and a widespread willingness to work hard, when necessary outside usual hours, to achieve shared objectives and to provide a service, not just to deal in the commodity of housing. Despite all the grumbles from politicians and dissatisfied tenants, the community is more fortunate than perhaps it realises in the dedication and competence of the great majority of those who work for the Executive.

Finally, this seems the place to make some observations about the composition and workings of the Board itself. In my time, its nine members met, with about an equal number of senior officers, for a full day every three weeks. The amount of business transacted was formidable: the agenda and supporting papers generally constituted the best part of another day's reading-matter. Much work was delegated to officers, subject to ratification, but the Board was always slow to delegate any subjects of political or sectarian sensitivity. The Board was jealous of its prerogatives, and firmly committed to the view that the commonsense approach of amateurs when applied to the specialist advice of professionals provides a valuable safeguard for the public, in the democratic tradition of checks and balances. Between one and two hours were usually spent on the detailed consideration of scheme designs, presented by the architects responsible with the help both of slides and of drawings. Additional special meetings were held when required to deal with particular topics. Committees were appointed to deal only with ad hoc in-depth studies of particularly complicated problems. The Board periodically held its meetings outside Belfast. On one occasion, Board members and senior officers paid a three-day working visit to Dublin to compare housing problems and solutions there with those in Belfast. Neither press nor public were admitted to its meetings: this has been a periodic source of complaint and criticism. However, given the executive and management functions which the Board performs, the commercial confidentiality of much of is business, and above all the desirability of seeking consensus between persons of very different political background, it seemed better to leave public debate of housing issues to the monthly meetings of the Housing Council.

The number of Board members was increased in 1983 from nine to ten, in order to take account of the dual role of the chief executive, who, between 1980 and 1985, combined the post with the office of vice-chairman. Any further increase in numbers has been, and in ny view should be, stoutly resisted: the efficient conduct of so much business requires a very tightly-knit body whose members know each other well and trust each other. The balance between professional full-time

officers, and the amateur part-time Board which bears ultimate responsibility for all decisions, is a delicate one; but it has worked pretty well in
practice, with neither group steam-rolling the other. Any attempt to
remodel the Board by enlarging its numbers to correspond with those of
the Health, Education and Library Boards would, in my view, greatly
reduce the degree of commitment of the individual members, and their
executive efficiency, as well as destroying the close partnership which
has hitherto existed between officers and Board.

Of the ten members, three are nominated from amongst its own
number by the Housing Council. The part-time chairman, who may be
expected to spend up to half his working week on the post and is
remunerated accordingly, is appointed by the minister. The full-time
chief executive is appointed jointly by minister and Board. The
remaining members, who, with those nominated by the Housing
Council, receive a modest honorarium, are appointed, for variable
terms of office, by the minister: one of them at the least must be a
woman: by convention, one of them is appointed from the trade union
movement. In practice, the minister has therefore only four or five other
nominations with which to try to achieve an appropriate balance —
geographical, social, political, and religious. His task is made somewhat
easier by the fact that no member sits on the Board as, in any sense, a
delegate from any outside body, or a spokesperson for the claims of any
special interest group or geographical area. But it is a difficult one
nonetheless.

The difficulty is much enhanced by the practice of the Housing
Council, since 1981, of selecting all three of its members from the
Unionist parties. Moreover, the individuals elected tend to change from
year to year, which is bad for continuity of decision-making; and in any
case, it takes the best part of a year for a new member to obtain a
thorough grasp of the Executive's structure and business. Also, the
Housing Council nominees can, from time to time, find themselves in
real difficulties when, on some controversial issue, their own District
Council adopts one attitude; the Housing Council a different one; and
the Board a third. Fortunately, in almost every case members in this
position have accepted the view that their duties as Board members
over-ride their responsibilities to the two tiers below, by each of which
they were elected: but the conflict can be one of real embarrassment.

It was certainly the intention of the Stormont Parliament, of Brian
Faulkner, and of James Callaghan, when the Executive was set up, that
only one-third of its members should be practising local politicians and
that two-thirds should be non-political individuals with appropriate
financial, business, architectural, legal or other skills and experience.
Unhappily, the insistence of the majority on the Housing Council that

all their nominees must come from the Unionist and Protestant section of the community has required successive Ministers to appoint members of the SDLP and Alliance parties, usually Catholic, so as to redress the balance. But this has had the regrettable consequence of reducing the number of vacancies available for non-political independent figures who could have brought to the Board specialised skills. In my view, it would be highly desirable to reverse this process if means could be found. Of course, the problem would cease to exist if the Housing Council could be persuaded to exercise its powers in such a way as to accord representation to the Catholic minority in the province. But, given the sectarianism of party politics in Northern Ireland, that is perhaps too much to hope.

Although in my view the Board has become more party-political in composition than is desirable, there have been some corresponding advantages. First, the criticism that the Board is unelected, undemocratic and unaccountable is largely met when half of its members, and sometimes more, have been duly elected to District Councils. Second, since its membership includes individuals belonging to each of the main parties, it can fairly claim to be representative of each of the main strands of political opinion in the province. Third, largely owing to the fact that meetings are not held in public, the members of all the parties have worked surprisingly harmoniously together. Political loyalties are mostly left in the hatstand outside the boardroom door; some of those who have been most extreme and intransigent in public have proved amongst the most constructive and co-operative Board members in private. To an encouraging extent, individuals of all parties, of all religious beliefs, from all social backgrounds, have demonstrated a willingness to sit down together and hammer out agreed policies in the sensitive field of housing. If others elsewhere were only prepared to do likewise, the future for the divided community of Northern Ireland would look more hopeful.

# *Postcript*

In 1885, housing conditions in Belfast, Londonderry, and the six counties which now constitute Northern Ireland, were as good as any in the British Isles. By 1971 they had deteriorated to the point where they were among the worst. By 1985, a century after the report of the Royal Commission on Housing, and 60,000-odd new houses after the inception of the Executive, we had reached a curious position where Northern Ireland now has some of the best, but still has much of the worst, housing in the British Isles. We have aroused aspirations and expectations which cannot now be dowsed. When the inhabitants of the Turf Lodge T-block in Belfast (probably the worst in Ulster) saw it demolished, and were rehoused in the new Gortnamonagh estate nearby (among the best in the British Isles), their good fortune attracted the envy of many thousands of ill-housed families. We now have two separate nations — the well-housed, and the badly-housed. To some extent, of course, this is true of every country at every time. But it has serious consequences where the disparities between the best and the worst are so very marked: especially in a community which is so deeply divided along quite different religious, political, social and geographical fault-lines.

If inequalities of housing provision, as well as unfair discrimination in its allocation, played a part in the seismic disturbances which erupted along that fault-line in 1969, then it cannot be right or wise to stop when the righting of them is only half-done. Accordingly, housing policies over the next twenty years have a very material bearing on the possibilities of finding any peaceful solution to the larger Northern Ireland problem.

How far has the experiment of establishing a large-scale, regional, multi-purpose housing authority been a success? Of course my opinion is, of necessity, a partisan one; on the other hand, I can perhaps speak on the subject with more authority than most people. In my view, it has enjoyed a large measure of success within the constraints to which it is subject. First and foremost, it has restored a generally high level of confidence in the fairness, impartiality and integrity of the housing service provided. Second, it has made a major contribution to the overall stock, and as much in terms of quality as in terms of quantity. Third, it has been able to bring to bear in the housing field a combination of research, analysis, professionalism, and dedication which could have been commanded by no smaller organisation. And it has enjoyed three enormous advantages over any purely local housing authority; the ability to marshall the available resources geographically, in accordance with differing needs, without being hampered by administrative boundaries; the ability to marshall and redeploy resources as between different kinds of activity; and the ability, subject always to the vagaries of government, to take the longer rather than the shorter view. If all three of these are important, the last is the most important of all. Housing is a very long-lead business; an estate takes as long to plan and build as a battleship. Treasury restrictions on carry-over of funds are unhelpful and obstructive: so is its strictly annual system of budgeting and accounting. Ministers, politicians, councillors, all live from election to election; it is only the exceptional elected representative whose horizon stretches more than, at the very most, five years ahead. Just as the Board of the Executive sees itself as a trustee for those currently in need of new or better housing, so also it sees itself as a trustee for the future generations who will live in the houses built now.

There are, of course, disadvantages as well as advantages inherent in the concept of a single comprehensive authority. In particular, the Executive suffers from its total dependence on government for funding; from its consequently restricted degree of independence; from the weaknesses as well as the strengths derived from its monopoly position within the public sector; and from the difficulties of bureaucracy and remoteness which beset every large public body. On balance, it is my view that the advantages have greatly outweighed the disadvantages. I think this view is widely shared in Northern Ireland. Although there are periodic calls for the Executive's dismemberment, and the return of housing powers to local authorities or some other directly elected body, I believe that most of these are rhetorical rather than real. And, they tend to emanate from those politicians who are most intent on imposing their own views on those who disagree with them. I believe that, for the foreseeable future, any return of housing powers to an elected body of any kind in Northern Ireland should not be contemplated: for I see no evidence to convince me that the majority would not, once again, abuse its powers to the detriment of the minority; and I doubt if the minority would be any better. If and when any form of institutionalised power-sharing gains general acceptance in both sections of the community, then it may be worth weighing the advantages of increased democratic control against the advantages of a single comprehensive authority to which I have referred above. Until then, I hold firmly to the view that it is far better that the administration of housing should be in the hands of those who are *representative* of all sections of the community, than in the hands of those who have been *democratically elected* but represent only one section of the community. If this implies a kind of power-sharing at a practical rather than a party-political level, then I can only say that it seems to me that it has worked, on the whole, very well.

Has the Northern Ireland experiment any lessons for other parts of the British Isles? From an administrative point of view, this may seem an untimely question at a period when government is breaking up the Greater London Council and other Metropolitan Councils. Of course, I have no direct experience, though I have acquired some knowledge, of the structure and administration of housing by the English and Scottish local authorities. There have been occasional suggestions that a national housing service, on the same lines as the national health service, might have considerable advantages over the present system. I should be dubious about that; it seems to me that the Housing Executive is about as large as a single organisation can well be if it is to remain responsive and sensitive in so delicate a field; but I would guess that a network of regional housing authorities constructed on the model of the Executive, controlled by small boards partly nominated and partly elected like those of the New Town Commissions, would have much to commend it. But then, the prospects for such bodies would be questionable at a time when government is seeking to minimise public involvement in the provision of housing overall; and in any event evidently prefers smaller to larger units of administration.

So far as the Republic of Ireland is concerned, again, I have no direct experience; but I should have thought regional housing authorities on the Northern Ireland model for each of Munster, Leinster, Connaught — perhaps taking in Donegal, Cavan and Monaghan also — and Greater Dublin, would have had much to commend them. They would have the further advantage (in many, though not in all, eyes) of rendering some eventual harmonisation of structures between North and South very much simpler in the housing field.

This is perhaps the appropriate place to note that, if the pattern of housing legislation and administration in Northern Ireland has diverged very considerably over the years from that in Great Britain, the divergence between Northern Ireland and the Republic of Ireland has grown wider still in the sixty-five years since partition. This is no matter for surprise; just as it was in no way surprising that the successive Unionist governments of the North should have failed, or chosen not, to follow England at important turning-points in housing policy such as the Addison Act of 1919, the Wheatly Act of 1924, or the Greenwood Act of 1930. In fact, since the Irish Housing Act of 1932 and Labourers' Act of 1936, far more houses have been built for sale to their occupants at subsidised prices than for letting. The state provides the capital for local authority house-building, and bears the loan charges; in the private sector too, generous new-build subsidies for first-time purchasers or providers of new houses exist, though (confusingly to anyone accustomed to British terminology) these are known as 'grants', whilst repair or improvement grants are minimal. Instead of housing benefits or rent rebate scheme, there is a complex but effective differential rents system: in general, rents contribute only half the cost of maintenance and management, and make no contribution at all to the capital cost of the house. Despite the differences, there are common problems: Ballymun, on the outskirts of Dublin, suffers from many of the same problems as Rossville in Derry or Divis in Belfast; squatting is not unknown; itinerants and tinkers have caused severe housing difficulties and, sometimes, disturbances; to some extent, the Troubles in the north have caused housing headaches for county managers, particularly in those counties contiguous to the border. But the divergences are by now much greater than the similarities: and it would be a matter of very great complexity to integrate, or even to harmonise, the housing systems of north and south, if the occasion were ever to arise, unless a regional structure were to be introduced in the Republic.

An even larger question: has the Northern Ireland experiment any lessons for other divided communities? This is no idle question: there are many parts of the world which face problems not dissimilar to those of Ulster. And indeed, a Great Britain where, as we have recently learned, there are now two million Muslims as against one million Methodists; and where there plainly exist (at the least) pockets of disadvantaged members of racial or religious groups from many other parts of the world, may yet find the Northern Ireland experience relevant and useful. Indeed, public representatives and public servants alike may have found food for thought in this book. I do not think I can summarise the lessons: except to say, that the rigorous establishment, and maintenance, of an unassailable reputation for fairness, impartiality, and integrity, lies at the root of the matter. If this involves, as it may, a rigidity which excludes the flexible exercise of discretion on a humane and individual basis; or if it involves, as it may, conflicts between considerations of impartiality and of efficiency; then impartiality must come first. It is indispensable that there should be clearly agreed and understood rules especially for allocation, and in the authority's own employment policies; and that those rules be at all times strictly adhered to, and never broken or bent to meet the individual hard case which may provide the occasion for allegations of favouritism or discrimination.

Finally, the largest question of all: is there a future for a public-sector housing authority in the United Kingdom at all? My answer would be an emphatic 'yes'; but I suspect that the present Prime Minister would not give the same response. It is possible to interpret current events and policies as simply a temporary downward trend on the fluctuating graph of public-sector housing activity. It is, equally, possible to interpret them as meaning that the public sector has had its day, and will now inexorably wither away, just as the private rented sector has done over the past fifty years, leaving Britain to fall into line with the rest of Europe (including Ireland) where ownership is the dominant form of tenure; until in the end a greatly slimmed-down public-sector exists only as a provider of last resort for those incapable of providing themselves with a roof by any other means.

There are quite cogent arguments in favour of such a policy. It is certainly true that most people aspire towards home-ownership: why should they not have what they want, if means can be found of helping them to afford it? It is certainly true that public-sector housing costs have placed a heavy burden on the general body of taxpayers for many years past. It is certainly true that, in a time of recession, cuts in expenditure may have to be made by a nation which is spending more than it can earn; and housing cannot escape consideration as a candidate. It is certainly true that housing costs and rents diverged ever more widely in the years between, at any rate, 1918 and 1980. It is probably true that no other country in the western world has provided its citizens with subsidised housing to rent on the same scale as Britain. It is probably true that a fair proportion of those in public-sector rented housing could perfectly well afford to buy a home of their own.

There are equally cogent arguments to the contrary. Many of those who are tempted into home-ownership find they cannot afford to keep their houses in good repair — the 'hungry-white-elephant' syndrome. In areas of very high unemployment, and especially at a time of recession, the number of citizens needing help with housing is greater than ever before. The last place where cuts should be made, or bargain-basement sales indulged in, is in fixed assets of durable national value. The generous assistance which home-owners receive in the form of tax allowances on their mortgages should be redistributed in favour of the housing benefits of the most needy. Britain's housing system may be out of step with the rest of Europe, but it is widely admired and envied, and has in many ways proved far more successful than its continental alternatives. If the public regulation of housing came into existence in the first place in order to improve the standards of public health, and to eliminate the diseases associated with bad housing, may not its elimination lead both to new slums and to new epidemics? Above all, if the two nations of well-housed and ill-housed are to be perpetuated, may not social unrest and even violence result in Great Britain as well as in Northern Ireland?

And so on.

A century has passed since the last Royal Commission on Housing; a constructive white paper would be welcome, but would it be enough? It seems to me that the time has come for a complete and fundamental reappraisal of housing policies, economics, structures and policies, on the widest possible front, and above all on the longest possible time-scale. In the meanwhile, we must stagger on from crisis to crisis, from policy to policy, from government to government, as best we may, without any clear or certain or consistent sense of direction. And the fundamental division between the two schools of thought will remain unresolved: should the provision of housing be a service; or is housing a mere commodity? I hope it will be very plain indeed from this book that I belong to the former school.

# Principal Sources
# and Select Bibliography

I wish to record my gratitude to those authors and copyright-holders who have kindly given me permission to quote from their work, whether published or unpublished.

## 1. PRINTED PUBLICATIONS

Bardon, J., *Belfast, An Illustrated History*, Belfast, 1982.

Bigger, F. J., *Labourers' Cottages for Ireland*, Dublin, 1907.

Boal, F. W. and Douglas, J.N.H.., ed., *Integration and Division*, London, 1982.

Boyd, A., *Holy War in Belfast*, Tralee, 1969.

Budge, I, and O'Leary, C., *Belfast, Approach to Crisis*, London, 1973.

Callaghan, J., *A House Divided*, London, 1973.

Coleman, A., *Utopia on Trial*, London, 1985.

Darby, J. and Williamson, A., ed., *Violence and the Social Services in Northern Ireland*, London, 1978.

Deutsch, R. and Magowan, V., *Northern Ireland 1968-1974, A Chronology of Events*, 3 vols, Belfast, 1973-5.

Donnison, D.V., *The Government of Housing*, London, 1967.

Donnison, D.V. and Ungerson, C., *Housing Policy*, London, 1982.

Esher, L., *A Broken Wave: the Rebuilding of England, 1940-1980*, London, 1981.

Gailey, A., *Rural Houses of the North of Ireland*, Edinburgh, 1984.

Greve, J., *The Housing Problem*, London, 1969.

Gribbon, S., *Edwardian Belfast*, Belfast, 1982.

Jones, E., *A Social Geography of Belfast*, London, 1960.

Lawrence, R.J., *The Government of Northern Ireland 1921-1964*, Oxford, 1965.

Mogey, J., *Rural Life in Northern Ireland*, Oxford, 1947.

*Nomad's Weekly*, Belfast, 1899-1907.

N.I. Labour Party, *Rents and Houses*, Belfast, 1956.

N.I. Labour Party, *Programme for Progress*, Belfast, 1964.

Rose, R., *Governing without Consensus,* London, 1971.

Spicker, P., *The Allocation of Council Housing,* London, 1983.

Stewart, A.T.Q., *The Narrow Ground,* London, 1977.


## 2. RESEARCH PAPERS, ARTICLES, UNPUBLISHED THESES

Birrell, W.D., Hillyard, P.A.R., Murie, A. and Roche, D.J.D., *Housing in Northern Ireland,* Centre for Environmental Studies, London, 1971.

Bryson, G.H., *Memories of a Long Life,* Belfast, 1982.

Carleton, S.T., *The Growth of South Belfast,* M.A. thesis, Q.U.B., 1967.

Cleary, P.G., *Spatial Expansion and Urban Ecological Change in Belfast,* Ph.D. thesis, Q.U.B., 1979.

Hendry, J., *Obsolescence in Housing in the Villages of Northern Ireland,* Ph.D. thesis, Q.U.B., 1980.

McLennan, D., Wood, G. and Fry, J., *Response Maintenance in Northern Ireland,* Housing Research Group, Glasgow University, 1983.

O'Brien, Sir Lucius, Ms of *talk* at the Housing Centre, London, 27 February 1951.

O'Brien, Sir Lucius, *article* in Journal of Statistical and Social Inquiry Society of Ireland, Vol XIX, 1952-3.

Synnott, N.J., *Housing of the Rural Population of Ireland,* in Journal of Statistical and Social Inquiry Society of Ireland, Vol LXXXIV, 1902; and part 86, 1906.


## 3. OFFICIAL PUBLICATIONS AND SOURCE MATERIALS

Third Report of the Royal Commission on the Housing of the Working Classes, 1885.

Minutes of Evidence of Special Committee of Belfast Town Council to consider the Death Rate and Public Health of the City, 1896.

Reports of Local Government Board for Ireland.

Interim Report of Planning Advisory Board, *Housing in Northern Ireland,* 1944.

Official Reports, Parliament of Northern Ireland.

Quarterly Housing Returns for Northern Ireland.

Annual Reports of N.I. Housing Trust, 1945-1971.

Report of Belfast Corporation Housing Allocations Inquiry, 1954.

City Surveyor's Report on Slum Clearance, 1959.

Report of Belfast Corporation Inquiry, 1962.

Report of Working Party on Belfast Corporation Housing, 1965.

Annual Reports of Craigavon, Antrim and Ballymena, and Londonderry Development Commissions, 1966-1972.

Report of Cameron Commission, *Disturbances in Northern Ireland,* 1969.

Report of N.I. Community Relations Commission, *Flight,* 1971.

Annual Reports of N.I. Housing Executive, 1972-1985.

Report of N.I.H.E. Review Committee on *Housing Selection,* 1976.

Report of Rowland Committee, *Housing Executive Contracts,* 1979.

Report of N.I.H.E. *Rent Review* Committee, 1983.

Report of the Fair Employment Agency for N.I. into *The Northern Ireland Housing Executive,* 1985.

# *Appendix*

**March 1973**
**Paper No. 36/3(b) (i)**

## WORKING PARTY NO. 4 (DEVELOPMENT)

## STRATEGY FOR NEW BUILDING

**GENERAL:** While this paper deals in the main with houses and housing areas the Executive sees its role not merely in terms of houses but also in community development, both in the establishment of new communities and, insofar as it may prove possible, in the retention and stabilization of existing communities.

1. Until a very much more accurate assessment of present and future distribution of housing need is available, it will not be possible to lay down long-term plans for each area of Northern Ireland.

   However, it is plain from the outset that the needs of industrial cities, country towns, villages, and rural areas differ substantially. And it is possible at least to lay down certain general guiding principles of policy applicable to each category; and certain overall principles of policy applicable to all categories.

2. **City**

   City development falls into three categories: (a) building of new estates on virgin sites on the periphery; (b) clearance and redevelopment of central areas; (c) improvement and rehabilitation of existing stock. Given the extreme restriction on availability of sites; the geo-graphical limitations and the stop-line, even if extended; the want of existing recreational open spaces; and the extremely high density of past development: it is inescapable that one of three courses must be adopted. The apparently unpalatable alternatives are: the retention of maximum population through the use of complex multi-storey structures with consequent high financial and environmental costs; medium to high density low-rise development, which may produce many of the characteristics of the development which is being replaced, but nevertheless still forces some overspill of population; or low-rise, low-density development, which, while being environ-mentally acceptable, is accompanied by massive population dis-placement.

It is clear that the majority of residents wish to remain in the city area, indeed, in most cases they wish to return to the same district. It is clear that high-rise buildings are disliked and rejected by most Ulster people. If the Executive is to make any genuine attempt to meet the present wishes of the people, it must therefore adopt the policy of low-rise building to high densities, making all possible provision for open space and recreation areas within any such scheme.

Given this overall strategy, a number of propositions may be stated:—

(i)    A limited number of high-rise point blocks may in execptional circumstances be incorporated in schemes of all types, but in no case whatever should families with children under 16 be allo-cated dwellings higher than the third storey.

(ii)   High densities demand the very highest standards of design, quality, workmanship and materials if they are not to deterior-ate rapidly into a new generation of urban slums; the pressures upon buildings at high density are greater than those upon dwellings which are more widely dispersed.

(iii)  It is essential to avoid the grim tedium of endless repetition. Layout must be imaginative, and should make the greatest possible use of topographical and geographical features; a proportion of existing buildings, groups and features should be retained and incorporated in new schemes, after renovation, wherever possible; ample play-areas and recreation areas for children of different age-groups must be provided; the use of materials and finishes should be varied within any one project, and much attention should be paid to visual considerations, to roof-lines and where possible vistas, and to practical and well-designed detailing.

(iv)　A large proportion of the Executive's efforts and resources should be directed to improvement, upgrading and rehabilitation of existing housing, both publicly-owned and privately rented or owner-occupied. However, a campaign on these lines cannot be mounted at full strength until dwellings capable of benefiting have been identified; the first step will be the preparation of a 5-year Belfast rehabilitation programme.

(v)　Wherever possible — and it will not always be possible — both new estates on virgin sites, and redevelopment areas, should be broken up into units of manageable size. The average size of a 'unit' should not much exceed 100 dwellings; the average size of an 'estate', comprising several units, should not much exceed 400 dwellings. Belfast and Londonderry have both grown up as aggregations of local areas, each with a strong sense of identity; everything possible should be done to retain the intimate scale of residential developments within the city.

## 3. Country Towns

This category is taken to include quite large urban manufacturing areas such as Portadown or Ballymena, and the smaller towns which serve as local centres for the surrounding agricultural countryside. Both types have in the past 25 years been smitten by the same disease; the decay of the residential areas of the town centre, and the growth of peripheral suburban housing estates unrelated to the original character, layout and function of the town. The practical problem has in fact arisen because people are no longer willing to live in the main street, whether over the shop or in a separate dwelling — they prefer to live in modern houses at some distance, where they will have more space and less traffic.

The greatest need is to put heart back into the towns as living communities; and to do this, the town centres must be revitalised and the residential areas surrounding them brought back into an organic relationship with the centres.

In most cases, there is no great difficulty in finding sites for new housing on the outskirts of these towns; but, though more expensive and more time-consuming, it would be much preferable to redevelop the grey areas in or near the town centres.

Town centre commercial and shopping redevelopment is not a function of the Executive, but a mixture of residential redevelopment is essential.

(i)　The Executive should seek early consultation with the Ministry of Development planners with a view to planning mixed commercial and residential redevelopment in town centres.

(ii)    Improvement schemes, and in some instances conservation schemes, for dwellings in the grey areas in or near town centres should be initiated as soon as possible. The rehabilitation of existing buildings, including those in mixed use, should be integrated with new building to suitable designs taking account of the scale and character of the towns concerned.

(iii)   New estates should not in future be built in a disconnected way around the outskirts; every possible step should be taken both to relate new residential developments, and those already in existence, into the community of which they form part. This may in some instances involve reconsideration of existing road and other proposals.

(iv)   At the same time, it is important to relate new estates on the edges of towns to the existing countryside; too many towns peter out into sprawl and untidiness; others end in an uncomfortably sharp edge. A natural and comfortable progression from town to country can often be achieved by the intelligent use of existing, or new, trees, hedgerows and walls, not always in straight lines.

(v)    Paragraph 2 (v) applies here also although even those figures may be too large for some of the smaller country towns.

## 4. **Villages**

The villages of Northern Ireland have in most cases a very distinctive character, built either around a cross-roads, a river crossing or on the axis of a single street. Much village housing is old, potentially attractive, but in poor order and lacking modern amenities. Where a demand for new housing exists, there has been a tendency to slap down a grid of new buildings in a rectangular field at a distance from the main street, and to allow the main street itself to crumble.

(i)    In villages, it is essential that new development be related to the existing organism of the community, and that street lines and layout be respected.

(ii)   Improvement schemes and in some instances conservation schemes should be initiated as soon as possible for those dwellings which have not deteriorated too far.

(iii)   Wherever possible, a policy of 'infilling' should be adopted for new building; where substantial developments are needed, they should be so laid out as to form an integral part of the community, and not an inconsequential addendum to it.

(iv)   In certain specific circumstances where existing housing is very scattered consideration may be given to the establishment of new villages in order to accommodate both public and private housing as a positive balance to the policy of discouraging isolated new development in rural areas being pursued by the Ministry of Development as planning authority.

5. **Rural Areas**

It appears unlikely that the Executive will be called upon to build any substantial number of houses, outside the villages, in rural areas. Due to the decreasing rural population, the trend is in the opposite direction; many of the 'labourers' cottages' built by local authorities before the last war have now been sold. There are many fewer farm labourers than there were a generation ago.

However, it remains the duty of the Executive to provide homes for those in need of them, even in remote country areas, and where a real need can be demonstrated to exist, the necessary building should be undertaken.

(i)    The Executive should encourage improvement and modernisation of isolated rural dwellings wherever a real need for accommodation exists, subject only to the possible restraints attached to the servicing of such dwellings with roads, power supply and sewerage.

(ii)   Where new dwellings are needed, they should be to a design suited to the countryside: urban designs should not be transplanted to surroundings to which they are inappropriate.

(iii)  The Executive should consult with the Ministry of Agriculture so as to ensure that the latter's farm modernisation programme is co-ordinated with the Executive's policies and standards.

6. **General Principles**

In theory, under existing legislation, the cost of a new dwelling is written off over a period of 60 years. In practice, there is no prospect that this or any other country will renew its entire housing stock every 60 years, and a much longer lifetime is both realistic and desirable. Some of the best-built (and most expensive to buy) houses in the British Isles are more than 250 years old. Some of the worst-built are some of the most recent. Current redevelopment schemes in Belfast largely involve the demolition and replacement of houses built between 60 and 90 years ago; but these were ill-built and ill-designed even by the standards of the day; many other houses of the same date, or earlier, have years of life left in them, and are well suited to modernisation or improvement.

The basic problem is that a balance must be found between the high initial cost of new dwellings built to the highest standards and of the best materials; and the high (and ever-increasing) maintenance costs, and short life, of new dwellings built to less expensive standards and of less expensive materials.

Comparisons are sometimes made between the apparently higher cost of publicly-built dwellings, and the apparently lower cost of dwellings built by private or speculative developers. Two factors distort any such comparisons; first, private developers, building for sale, cannot be expected to have the same interest in the durability of their product, nor in the maintenance costs. Second, private developers can pick and choose their sites, whereas it is plain that the Executive cannot; and the cost of site works accounts for a very large proportion of total building costs.

Ultimately, one gets what one is prepared to pay for. It would be possible for the Executive to restrict the size, quality and cost of its dwellings now; but this would be a short-sighted policy, and a very poor investment for the future. The Executive's policy should be to provide dwellings of at least the same standards of accommodation, services, space, materials and amenity as those regarded as minimal in the rest of the United Kingdom.

(i)   The Executive should adhere to its present policy of regarding Parker-Morris standards as the minimum acceptable; and on any review of Parker-Morris standards in Great Britain, should at once bring its own standards into line.

(ii)  The Executive should examine methods of achieving flexibility of use within houses to meet the changing requirements arising through the normal cycle of family life.

(iii) Until fuller information on housing need, waiting lists, and housing mix, is available, it will not be possible to lay down a detailed policy on house types. However, certain principles can be stated. The Executive should so far as possible provide a wide range of house types and sizes, and should encourage transfers and exchanges in order to make the best possible use of its stock, together with a balanced relationship to the private sector.

(iv)  High-rise flats, if built at all, should be confined to city and surrounding areas, and designed for the use of single persons, childless couples, and other small family units. No families including children under 16 should be allocated dwellings above the third storey.

(v)   Maisonettes and deck-access dwellings should form a small proportion only of the housing stock, and should be employed only as subsidiary components in high-density schemes.

(vi) A reasonable proportion of houses providing adequate accommodation for large families should be provided in every development. The proportion must be dictated by analysis, and not by any other yardstick. A revival of the use of three-storey terraced houses in high-density developments should be seriously considered.

(vii) The use of standardised dwelling-type designs is to be encouraged up to a certain point, but a measure of variety in both design and materials is indispensable if a feeling of drab and depressing uniformity is to be avoided in any given development.

(viii) The use of system, factory or pre-fabricated building should be continuously explored, and experimental developments should from time to time be undertaken by the Executive. Such ventures are particularly to be encouraged if increased local employment can be thereby generated. But in general, no system has yet emerged which is demonstrably superior to traditional or rationalised-traditional methods.

Proposals for system building should be kept under review, but at this stage the Executive should not, without prior small scale experimentation, embark on any major project to introduce system building on a large scale.

(ix) It is important that materials should be of good quality, giving rise to the lowest possible maintenance costs; that they should be varied as far as is compatible with economy in each development; and that they should be suited to the character and environment of the site. Bricks (whether concrete or traditional) are reasonably well suited to the city areas and the larger towns, but they look out of place in most smaller towns and villages where roughcast, wet-dash, dry-dash, whitewash or colour-wash are more suitable. Red tiles are foreign to Ireland, and should be used very sparingly; slate is the traditionally acceptable roofing material, though now too expensive for normal use, but substitutes of similar tone and colouring are to be preferred.

(x) The highest possible standards of landscaping and planting should be maintained in all developments and great efforts should be made to see that landscaping does not lag behind the completion of dwellings, leaving incoming tenants to swim through acres of mud. If trees and plants are reasonably well established before tenants move in they have an appreciably better chance of survival. Landscaped areas and associated play and recreation facilities must be conceived and executed as part of an organic whole and not left as the treatment of space left over in a plan.

(xi) While the provision of communal buildings is primarily a function for the local authority, the Executive should co-operate closely with district councils to see that community halls are available early in the life of each new development. Indeed it may well be entirely logical that, where community buildings are of a local character, the Executive should construct these facilities on an agency basis. Should excessive delays occur, then the Executive should seek approval from the Ministry of Development for direct execution of the work. Costs would be subsequently recovered from the appropriate authority. Wherever appropriate the Executive should be prepared to provide residents' club-rooms as soon as the first families move in.

## 7. Private Residential Development

The Executive will in carrying out its general functions also promote where necessary areas of private residential development. This may take the form of (a) Plots of land leased to a developer who will undertake all normal site development cost, but subject to controls laid down by the Executive to ensure satisfactory standards and a satisfactory programme of completion; or (b) the main roads, services, footpaths etc., will be provided by the Executive and the housing plots leased to a developer either with or without controls; or (c) the Executive may provide the totally developed site and lease individual plots to those who wish to build their own homes; or finally (d) the Executive may itself in certain circumstances build houses for sale.

## 8. Definitions

For the purposes of this paper, the following definitions have been adopted:—

| | |
|---|---|
| Low Rise | — one to three storeys |
| Medium Rise | — Three to five storeys |
| High Rise | — six storeys and over |
| Low Density | — 10 to 20 dwellings per acre |
| | 35 to 70 bedspaces per acre |
| Medium Density | — 20 to 35 dwellings per acre |
| | 70 to 125 bedspaces per acre |
| High Density | — 35 to 45+ dwellings per acre |
| | 125 to 160+ bedspaces per acre |

**NOTE:** All figures are net.

**Net Density**        —Net density is an expression of the number of
                        bedspaces within a housing development divided
                        by the net area of the site.

**Gross Density**      — Gross density is an expression of the number of
                        people living within a neighbourhood (including
                        **local** shops, schools, recreation areas etc.)
                        divided by the gross area of the neighbourhood.

## RECOMMENDATION:

That the general principles be adopted as a basis for discussion with
the Ministry of Development.

# Index

Addison Act, 1919 149
Advice Centre, Belfast 142
Agriculture, Ministry of 27
Ainsworth Avenue 66
Alliance Party 78, 133, 145
allocation 8, 33, 41
   by housing associations 126-7
   need for rules 150
   *see also* points system
Amsterdam 69
Andersonstown 65, 73
Andersonstown Co-operative Society 76-7
Antrim 22, 68, 103
Antrim Road 75
Antrim and Ballymena Development
   Commission 34-5
architects 29, 31, 45, 93, 100-1
Ardglass 68
Ardoyne 21, 62-3, 75
Ardoyne Housing Committee 71
Ardrey, Robert 61
Armagh 64, 66, 100
Armagh, Cardinal Archbishop of 141
Armagh, Church of Ireland Archbishop of
   141
Artillery Flats 92 *plate 39*
Atkins, (Sir) Humphrey 52, 53, 90
Aughton Terrace *plate 25*

'back-to-backs' 18
backyards 18, 96, *plates 34, 35*

Ballycastle 32
Ballymacarrett 20, 63
Ballymagroarty 95
Ballymena 14
Ballymun 149
Ballynagard 67
Ballysillan 75
Banbridge 101
Bangor Provident Trust 36
Baptist Union of Ireland Housing
   Association 126
Bardon, Jonathan 25, 63-4
Barrack Street, Derry *plate 42*
Barry, Dan 133
bathrooms 96, 97, 128 *plate 35*
Bawnmore 75
Beattie, Emily 6-7
Beatty's Entry *plate 4*
Beechmount estate 66
Belfast
   building record 21-2, 31, 32-4, 54, 89-
      94, 96
   Catholic areas 48-9, 72, 75, 78-80
   councillors 138-9
   corruption 21, 33
   death rate 19
   disparities in housing 80
   East Belfast 65, 66, 75, 96
   high-rise flats 92-4, 149
   historical background 16-22, 146

North Belfast 65, 71
points scheme 10
Protestant areas 48, 49-50, 63-5, 66, 71-2, 75, 78, 80
riots 10, 63-6, 71, 75-6
segregation 63-6, 74
squatting 68-70
West Belfast 48, 63, 58, 72, 75, 79-80, 92, 139
Belfast Corporation 20-2, 39, 40, 45, 66, 68, 73
amnesty for squatters 69
Belfast Housing Aid Society 140
Belfast Improvement Order, 1910 *plates 3, 4, 5*
*Belfast Telegraph* 7-8, 89
Belmont 75
Belvoir estate 29
Benefits Allocation Branch 47
Bigger, Francis Joseph 23 *plates 6, 7, 8, 9*
Birrell, W. D. 24-5, 32
Bloomfield, Ken 51, 133
Bogside, battle of 8
Bombay Street 40, 64 *plates 20, 21*
bombs 38, 40, 45, 49-50, 136 *plate 29*
Boundaries Commission 88
Bowman, Alexander 17
Bradford, Rev Robert MP *plate 15*
*Bradford, Roy 14, 133*
*Brady, Mr 7*
*Bretland, Josiah 17-18, 19 plate 12*
Brett, C. E. B. 2-3, 50, 54, 76, 104, 136 *plates 1, 26, 50*
chairman of Executive 52
chairman of points scheme sub-committee 81-2
experience of segregation 62-3
experience of troubles 66, 76
housing article by 89-90
on 'need versus desire' 60
on newbuild schemes 96-7
on resignations 134-5
bricklayers 50
British Army 10, 64, 69, 73-4, 137
Brooke, Sir Basil 25
Brown, Hugh 14
Brown, Jack 39, 114
Bryson, Herbert 27, 31
Budge, I and O'Leary, C 21
Builders' Federation 53, 141

building materials 18-19, 160 *see also* concrete; timber
building programmes 48-9, 53, 94-7
need for 104-5, 124
building societies 20, 46, 53, 124-6
Building Societies' Association 125, 141
Burntollet march 8
Cairncross, James 29
Cairncross, Neil 74
Caledon 66
squat at 7-8, 10, 37
Callaghan, James 10, 31, 144
Calvert, John G 25, 27
Cameron Commission 8-9, 10
Camlough Road, Newry 68
Campaign for Social Justice 8,9
car-parking 101, 137
Carter, Ray 51, 133
Castlereagh 75
Catholic Citizens' Defence Committee 73
Catholics
in Belfast 48-9, 72, 75, 78-80
in Derry 32
discrimination against 9, 37, 87
on executive staff 142-3
family size 83
and Housing Trust 27-8, 30-1
rent arrears 115-16
Central Housing Authority 11, 67
centralisation 10-11, 44, 51
Chichester-Clark, James 10
Church of Ireland Housing Association 126
churches 68, 141
land ownership and redevelopment 33
civics education 93
Civil Defence Authority 27
Civil Rights Association 8
civil rights movement 27, 37
civil service 132, 135-8
Cleary, P. G. 18
Cluan Place 77-8 *plate 2*
Coalisland 8, 66
cold-bridge effect 92
Coleman, Alice 92
Commissioner for Complaints 10, 85, 127
Commissioner of Valuation 115
Community Relations Commission 65, 119
Concannon, Don 133 *plate 27*

concrete systems 29, 92, 160
conservation 99-100
Conservative Party 88, 133
    housing policy 52, 97, 104, 111, 113, 130
contractors 50, 67
contracts system 44, 130
Co-Ownership Housing Association 53, 126
Cork 17
corruption 21, 33
costs, pooling of 111-2, 124
cottages, rural 22-3, 56, 91 *plates 6, 7, 8, 9*
councillors 10, 138-9 *see also* local authorities
Craig, William 12
Craigavon 33, 68, 103 *plate 36*
Craigavon Development Commission 34, 43
Cranbrook Gardens 21, 71
Cregagh estate 29, 92
Creggan estate 32, 67
Crossmaglen 14
Crozier's Row *plate 3*
Crumlin Road 21, 64
Cullingtree Road 30, 33
Culmore Road 67
Cupar Street 77
Currie, Austin 7-8, 133

death-rate 19
'defensible space' 102 *plate 38*
Democratic Unionist Party 78, 133, 137, 138
density policy 43
Derry *see* Londonderry
Derrybeg 68
design 43, 54, 101, 129, 143
Deutsch, R and Magowan, V 73-4
Development, Ministry of 38
Development Commissions 34-5, 39, 105
differential rents system 149
*Digest of Northern Ireland Housing Statistics* 128
Dilke, Sir Charles 16
    alleged discrimination 7-10, 37, 69, 87
    and housing associations 126-7
    and Housing Executive 44-5, 51, 78-80, 85
    and Housing Trust 30-1
District Councils 138-9
district heating 29, 92, 97-8, 117

District Housing Plans 138
divided communities 149-50
Divis Demolition Committee 93
Divis Flats 29, 33, 92, 93, 115, 149 *plate 41*
Dixon, (Sir) Daniel 20, 21 *plate 10*
DOCS reports 51
Donaghadee 58, 96
Donegall Pass 75
Donegall Road 65, 75
Donnelly, James 14
Donnison, D. V. 112
    and Ungerson, C 56, 106
Down 22
Downpatrick 22-4, 32, 68, 97, 100
drainage *plate 12*
dry closets 19
Dublin 17, 18, 20, 143, 149
Dunbar Street Link *plate 13*
Dundonald 75, 92
Dungannon 7, 8, 26, 30, 64, 66, 88
Dunmurry 72, 75, 79

Edward, Prince of Wales 16
electoral boundaries 9, 32, 87-8, 109
electricity 31, 91, 99, 117
elephants, white, hungry 94, 150
Elliott, Eddie 14
emergency lists 41, 45
emergency repairs 45
Enforcement of Judgements Office 70
England *see* Great Britain
Enniskillen 26, 30, 32, 66, 100
Environment, Department of (NI) 100, 116, 135-6
Environment, Department of (GB) 141
equity sharing 53, 54, 83, 126
Essex Street *plate 33*
estates
    hard-to-let *plate 36*
    integrated 38, 70-2
    problem 59-60, 85-6
European Economic Community 53, 140
European Parliament 140
evacuated dwellings purchase scheme (SPED) 45-6
Evans, Rae 39, 43, 48, 71
eviction 69-70
exchanges 58, 70, 85

Fair Employment Agency 45
Fairy Knowe 75

Falls Road 30, 63, 65, 66, 75, 80
family size 9, 57, 83
Famine, the Great 22
farmhouses 27
Farringdon Gardens 21, 40, 71 *plates 22, 23, 24*
Faulkner, Brian 11, 12, 14, 144
Fermanagh 11, 14, 23, 88
Finance, Department of 137
fireplaces 98, 99, 117
Fitt, Gerry 13
flats *see* high-rise flats
*Flight* 65, 78, 80

gable paintings, *plates 14, 15, 16, 17, 18, 19*
Galway 16
garden cities 36
gardens 102
gas 19, 117
Gildernew, Mrs 6-7
Gilford 97
Glasgow 20
Glen Road 72
Glenalpin Street *plate 16*
Glenard estate 21, 71-2 *plate 22*
Glenarm 97 *plate 46*
Glengormley 23 *plates 8, 9*
glossary 4-5
Gobnascale 67
Goodhart, (Sir) Philip 52-4, 133, 134
Gorman, John 53, 125-6, 142
Gormobiles 142
Gortnamonagh estate 146 *plate 43*
*Governing without Consensus* (Rose) 9
Government of Ireland Act 33
Grant, William 25, 26 57-8
grants 24, 35-6, 47, 94-6
   rent subsidies 112
   in the Republic 149
   value of 127-8
Great Britain
   housing benefit 54
   housing design 129
   housing policy 20, 22, 25, 33, 46, 88, 107, 130-1, 141, 150-1
      compared with Northern Ireland 148-9
   housing surveys 43, 90, 91
   problem estates, 59, 60, 86
   rehabilitation 33, 49
   rents 110-11, 113

tenants 110, 119
tenant sales 122-3
Great Patrick Street *plate 13*
Green, Ronald 27, 28
Greencastle 75
greenfield building 94-7, 103
Greenwood, Anthony 106
Greenwood Act 1930 149
Greve, John 94
Griffiths, Hywel 119
ground rents 20, 33
Grove area 126

Hamill Street *plate 5*
Health and Social Services, Department of 137
heating 117-18 *see also* district heating; fireplaces
high-rise flats 29, 39, 43, 67, 92-4, 97, 155, 159 *plates 30, 31, 39, 40, 41*
Holmes, Erskine 127
Holy Land (Belfast) 20, 75
Home Loans Fund 53, 123
home loans scheme 46, 125
homesteading 53, 126
Horn Drive 72-4
House Condition Surveys 42-3, 89
'house or home' 58, 60 *plate 37*
house sales *see under* tenants
housing (Northern Ireland)
   background (history) 16-37
      Belfast 16-22
      local authorities 22-4
      post-war 25-7
      rural 22-3
   centralisation of 10-11, 44, 51, 147-8, 150
   as a civil right 55-7
   comparisons with Great Britain and Republic 148-9
   crisis in 36-7
   demand patterns 57-8, 102-3
   disparities in 23-4, 146-7
   finances 53, 105, 147
   policy reappraisal 151
   as a political issue 8-13
   as a social service 25, 151
   and the Troubles 40, 45, 49-50
   *see also* integration; sectarianism; segregation; squatting
Housing Act 1956 33

Housing Advice units 142
housing associations 53, 54, 126-7
housing benefit 42, 58, 106, 112, 113
    direct payment of 116
    introduction of 54, 115, 137
Housing Bill 1944 25-6, 58
Housing Centre Trust 140
Housing, Committee on 25
Housing Council 82, 84, 115, 138, 139,
    143-4
Housing Executive *see* Northern Ireland
    Housing Executive
Housing Executive Bill 11-14
Housing, Ministry of (GB) 10
Housing Research Group (Glasgow) 110,
    114-15
housing stock 89, 107
Housing of the Working Classes Acts 24
Howard, Ebenezer 36
Howell, David 133
Hume, John 13

inflation 47, 124
inner-city redevelopment 33-4, 48
Institute of Housing 140
insulation 118
integrated communities 31, 38, 48, 62
    Belfast 31, 33, 48, 63, 75
    failures of 48, 63, 65, 70-1
intimidation 40, 46, 50, 67
*Irish Builder* 20
Irish Congress of Trade Unions 141
Irish Housing Act 1932 149
Irish Republican Army (IRA) 67-8, 71-6
    *passim*, 79-80
Irvine, John 133
itinerants 85, 149

'jawbox' 5
Jenkins, Joe 38
Jones, Mildred 14
Joy Street 100 *plate 49*

Keir, (Sir) Lindsay 25
Killyleagh 96 *plate 47*
Kinghan, Frank 14
Kingstown 16
'kitchen houses' 5, 24, 90, 95-6

Labour Party (GB) 47, 51, 52, 88, 130, 133
Labour Party (NI) *see* Northern Ireland
    Labour Party

Labourers' Act 1936 149
Labourers (Ireland) Acts 22-4
Land League 70
landscaping 29, 34, 160-1

Larne 92
Lawrence, R. J. 24
layout 54, 101-2, 137 *plates 38, 39*
Lazenbatt, John 39, 72
Le Corbusier 60
Lecky Road 67
Legahory Green, Craigavon *plate 36*
Lenadoon 72-3
Leningrad 57
lignite 117
Ligoniel 48, 75
Limerick 16
Lisburn 75, 79, 80, 100
Little Ship Street *plate 14*
Liverpool 20
Livingstone, Ken 79
local authorities
    and Housing Executive 138-9
    housing record 22-5, 31-2, 48, 67-8, 105
    sectarianism 9, 81, 87-8
Local Government Board 22, 24
local preference 41, 84
London 20, 69
Londonderry 8, 54, 67, 70, 82, 95 *plate 52*
    high-rise flats 92, 149 *plate 40*
    housing record 16, 17, 31, 66-7, 146
    Housing Trust 26, 30
    sectarianism 50, 64, 88
Londonderry Development Commission
    35, 40, 67
Lord Street *plate 37*
Lorimer, (Sir) Desmond 14, 39, 42-3, 47,
    49, 51, 68, 72 *plate 26*
Lough Rea estate, *plate 38*
Loughran, Seamus 73
Lowry, Robert, QC 33
Lurgan 64, 68

McArdle, Pat 14
McCall, Bradley, QC 33
McClure Street *plate 32*
McConnell, Bertie 14
McConnell, (Sir) Robert 20, 21
McGrattan, Annie *plate 13*
McKees 21
McKibbins 21

McMahon, S. J. 34
Macmillan, Harold 106
Macrory Review Committee 14
McSheffrey, Gerry 48-9
McVicker, Robert 17
maintenance 109-10, 137
Malone Road 66
managers 30, 41, 85, 126
Manning, Cardinal 16
Markets area 63, 75
Marsh, James 38
Masonic Housing Association 126
Matthew Report 33
Mawson, E. P. 36
means tests 86, 111
Megaw Commission 21
Merville Garden Village 36
Methodist Church, President of 141
metrication 43
Millfield 63
Mitchell, David 53, 105, 133, 136
Mitchell, Moyra 98
mixed communities *see* integrated com-
  munities
mixed marriages 63
Mogey, John 23
Molyneaux Street *plate 50*
Morrison, John 8
mortgage relief 150-1
Morton, (Sir) Brian 66
Moyard estate 65, 92
Munce, James 19-20
municipalisation 122
murals *plates 14, 15, 16, 17, 18, 19*
Murray, John 52

National Building Agency 43
National Consumer Council 110
National House Builders' Council 129
National Mobility Scheme 58, 141
New Barnsley estate 65
New Homes Marketing Board 53
New Lodge 75
New Mossley 48
New Ross 16
New Town Development Commissions 15
New Towns 32, 33, 34
New Towns Act, 1965 12, 35
Newry 32, 64, 67-8, 97
Newtownabbey 32, 34, 36, 48
no-go areas 66, 67

North Belfast Mission Housing Association 126
Northern Ireland, map of ix
Northern Ireland Assembly 109, 115, 139
Northern Ireland Committee of the ICTU
  141
Northern Ireland Federation of Housing
  Associations 127, 140
Northern Ireland Housing Executive
  aims of 2 3-4, 15, 38, 104
  Board of 39-40, 42, 44-5, 52-3, 143-5,
    *plate 28*
  building programme 48-9, 54, 104
  and churches 141
  and civil service 132, 135-8
  consultants' reports on 51
  evaluation of 54, 147-8
  finance 47, 53-4, 135-6, 147
  foundation 7-15
  housing stock 34-5, 42-3, 89
  and Housing Trust 34-5, 39-40, 42, 47
  impartiality of 50-1, 54, 78-80, 88, 133
  independence of 131, 132-45, 147-8
  and local authorities 138-9
  offices of 99-100 *plate 29*
  and politics 87-8, 109, 132-6, 139-40
  and private sector 120-31
  public relations, 40, 42, 114, 142
  regionalisation 51-2
  rehabilitation policy 49-51
  rents system 111-15 *passim*
  Rowland Commission on 50-1
  staff of 44-5, 48, 142-3 *and see caption to*
    *plate 29*
  *see also* design; layout; points system;
    rents; tenants
Northern Ireland Housing Trust 10, 13,
  26-31, 33, 38, 42, 99
  composition of 27-8, 30-1
  emergency housing 68
  and the Executive 39, 40
  finance 28
  heating 117
  housing managers 30
  housing standards 28-9
  numbers built 105
  rents 112
Northern Ireland Labour Party 2, 9-10,
  11, 12, 122
Northern Ireland Office 137

Northern Ireland Parliament (Stormont) 9, 10-11, 24, 28, 139-40
'numbers game' 49, 104

O'Brien, (Sir) Lucius 27, 28-9
O'Hara, James 14, 30, 39-40, 50-1 *plate 27*
O'Hara, Peter 39
O'Hare, Gerry 73
Octavia Hill system 30
Official Unionist Party 78
old people's accommodation 99
Oliver, John 133
Omagh 97
ombudsman 10, 85, 127
Ormeau Road 75
overholding 70
owner-occupiers 27, 94, 120-8 *passim*
    grants to 127-8
    tenant sales 122-4

Paisley, Rev Ian 13
paramilitaries 40, 65, 68, 76-7, 119
    control of housing 50, 51, 66, 69, 71-2, 92
Paris *caption to plates 17, 18, 19*
Parker, Dame Dehra 31
Parker-Morris standards 33, 34, 43, 54, 95, 97, 106, 159
Parliamentary Questions 50, 78, 135, 139
'parlour houses' 5, 24, 90, 95-6
partnership schemes 130-1
Patten, Chris 133
'peace walls' 64-5, 69, 75-8, 118, 137 *plate 2*
place, attachment to 57
Planning Advisory Board 25
plumbing 19, 92
points system 8, 10, 33, 40-1, 66
    and Housing Executive 81-5
    for rents 114-15
    review committee 81-2, 84
Poleglass 45, 48, 75, 78-9 *plate 45*
politics and housing 87-8, 109, 132-6, 139-40 *see also* electoral boundaries
Poor Law Guardians 22, 24
population movements 48, 50, 63-6, 79, 119
Portadown 68
Portaferry 68, 101
Portballintrae 58
Pound area 63
power-sharing 148

pre-fabs 32
Presbyterian General Assembly, Moderator of 141
Presbyterian Housing Association 126
Prior, James 53, 105, 139
private developers 19-20, 35-6, 54, 95, 128-31
private owners *see* owner-occupiers
private renting 122
problem estates 59-60, 85-6 *plate 36*
problem families 85-6
Protestants 67-8
    in Belfast 48-50, 63-5, 66, 71-2, 75, 78, 80
    in the Executive 142-3
    family size 83
    rent arrears 115-16
Public Service Alliance 141
quality versus quantity 49, 54, 105-6, 155, 158-9

Quakers 27

'rack-rent' 112
Radburn principle 101
Rankin, Brian 70
rate fund 110
rates strikes 40, 46-7
Rathcoole 29, 31, 75
Rea, James 20
recession 103, 105
redevelopment 33, 48, 94-7, 102, 122, 128
Reform Bill, 1832 63
regionalisation 51-2, 148
rehabilitation 38, 49, 94-9, 125
    problems 95-6 *plates 33, 35*
Reid, Roy 100
'rent direct' 47
rent collectors 40, 41, 66, 141-2
rent freeze 114, 115
Rent Restriction Acts 112, 122
rent strikes 21, 40, 46-7, 66-8, 115-16
rents
    alternatives 110-14
    arrears 115-16
    computerisation 142
    and Housing Trust 26, 28, 30
    increases in 47, 53, 141
    points scheme 114-15
    rationalisation of 38, 42, 114-15
    rebates scheme 42, 54, 112

Rents and Houses (Brett) 2, 122
repairs 94, 108-10
Republic of Ireland 111, 121, 149
  compared with GB, NI 148-9
'residualisation' 123
resignation 32, 134-5
Rippingham, T. F. O. 29
Robinson, May 134
roofs 29, 100
Rose, Prof Richard 9
Rossville Flats 29, 32, 67, 92, 149 *plate 40*
Rowland Commission 44, 50
Royal Commission on Housing 16-18, 19,
  146, 151
Royal Ulster Constabulary (RUC) 69, 70,
  74, 87
rubbish disposal 92
rural housing 22-3, 49, 91-2 *plates 6, 7, 8, 9*
Ryan, Anne *plate 50*

St Matthew's Housing Association 126
Salisbury, Lord 16
Sandy Row 63, 75
sanitation, internal 19, 89-92
Scarman, Lord 38
Scotland 112, 148
Scottish Special Housing Association 26,
  28
sectarianism 8, 25, 32-3, 48
  Belfast 63-4, 80
  housing divisions 62-80
  public enquiry 63-4
security of tenure 116-17
segregation 9, 41, 62, 64, 70-6 *see also*
  population movements
self-build schemes 53
sewage systems 19, 31, 91 *plate 12*
Seymour Hill estate 29, 31, 92
Shankill Road 49, 63-4, 75, 80, 92 *plate 31*
Shantallow 67
shared surfaces 101, 137
Shaw, Ken 100
Shearman, Hugh 8
Sheffield 94
Shelter 104, 140
Shore Road 75
Short Strand 63, 65, 75, 126 *plates 2, 38*
Simon Community 127
Simpson, Harry 39, 42-3, 49, 58, 68, 71-2
  *plate 26*
Sinclair, Maynard 26

Sinn Féin 76, 78-9, 137, 140
slaters 50, 66
sleech 5
slob 5
small households 57, 83, 99
Smithfield 63
Social Democratic and Labour Party
  (SDLP) 78, 133, 145
Soldiers' and Sailors' Land Trust 27
Spamount Street 66
SPED 45-6
Spence, Bob 49, 53 *plate 27*
Spicker, Dr 86
Springfield Road 136
Springhill 38
Springmartin 65
squatting 21, 40, 46, 65, 137, 149
  organised 66, 67, 69-70
  precautions against 79
  rehousing 116-17
  *see also* Caledon
'starter homes' 129
Steadfast Tenants' Association 71
Stephens, James 56
Stewart, A. T. Q. 61, 74
Strabane 32, 67
Strang, Bob 100
Stranmillis 75
'Strategy for New Building' 43, 97, 154-62
subsidies *see* grants
subsistence, definition of 106-7
Suffolk estate 31, 72-4, 75
sunlight 98
surveys 42-3, 89
Synnott, Nicholas 24

Taggart, Edith 13
Tandragee 101 *plate 48*
Taughmonagh 75
tenants 108-20
  consultation with 42, 93-4, 118-20,
    141-2
  and repairs 108-10
  sales to 52-3, 86-7, 107, 122-4
tendering system 44, 77, 98, 130
tenements 17, 18
tenure, security of 116-17
terraced houses 97
territorial imperative 61, 74, 80
Thatcher, Margaret 86, 106, 113, 150
Tiger Bay 75, 126

tilers 50
timber-frame systems 29, 68, 98-9, 160
Tomlinson, Lt-Col 73-4
Torrens 75
townscape 100-1
transfers *see* exchanges
Trevelyan, Denis 74
Tughan, Fred 36
Turf Lodge estate 92, 93, 146 *plates 30, 48*
Twinbrook estate 31, 48, 71, 75
Twomey, Seamus 73-4
typhoid 19

'Ulster Cottage' 31-2
Ulster Defence Association (UDA) 72, 76
Ulster Defence Regiment (UDR) 87
Ulster Garden Villages Ltd 36
Ulster Workers' Council 119
Unionists 8-9, 12-14, 26, 133
  on Executive Board 144-5
  and Housing Council 138, 144-5
UN Declaration of Human Rights 55
Unity Flats 64, 75
Unity Walk 92
University area, Belfast 75
USSR 57, 110-11

Velsheda Gardens 21, 71
Vernon Street *plate 44*
Victoria Housing Estates 36

waiting lists 54, 67, 82-4, 103
Walker, William *caption to plate 10*
water supplies 19, 23, 31, 91
Waterford 16
'Weetabix' flats *plate 31*
West, Harry 12, 88
West Germany 53, 140
Westland Road estate 66
Westlink Road *plates 39, 41*
Wheatley Act, 1924 22, 149
Whitelaw, William 68-9
Whitewell 75
Wilson, Harold 10
Wimpeys 36
Windlesham, Lord 133
Workers' Party 78, 140
World War I 21
World War II 25

York Street *plate 39*

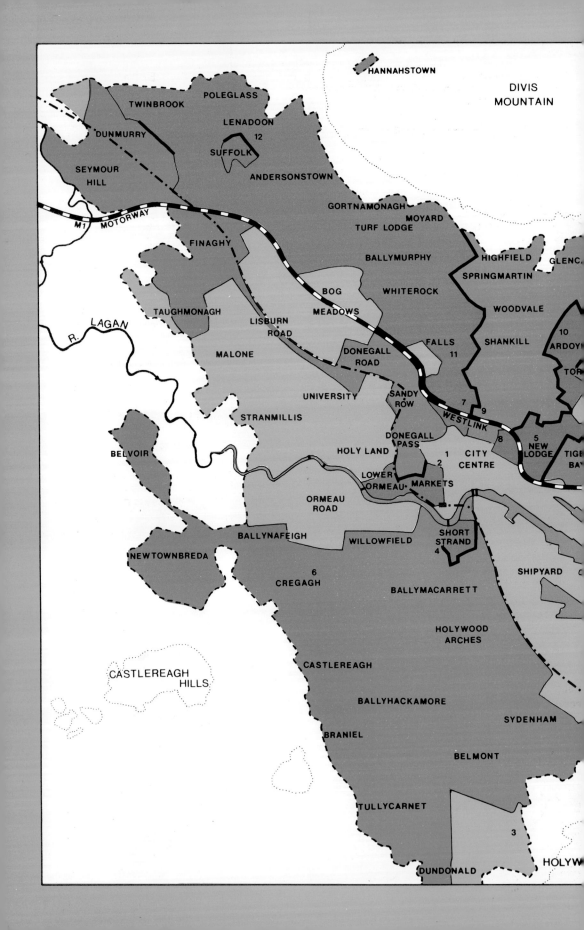